MULTIPLE INTELLIGENCES

IN THE CLASSROOM

4th Edition

ASCD MEMBER BOOK

Many ASCD members received this book as a
member benefit upon its initial release.

Learn more at: **www.ascd.org/memberbooks**

MULTIPLE INTELLIGENCES IN THE CLASSROOM

4th Edition

THOMAS ARMSTRONG

Alexandria | Virgina USA

ASCD®

1703 N. Beauregard St. • Alexandria, VA 22311-1714 USA
Phone: 800-933-2723 or 703-578-9600 • Fax: 703-575-5400
Website: www.ascd.org • E-mail: member@ascd.org
Author guidelines: www.ascd.org/write

Deborah S. Delisle, *Executive Director;* Robert D. Clouse, *Managing Director, Digital Content & Publications;* Stefani Roth, *Publisher;* Genny Ostertag, *Director, Content Acquisitions;* Julie Houtz, *Director, Book Editing & Production;* Liz Wegner, *Editor;* Jodie Custodio, *Graphic Designer;* Mike Kalyan, *Director, Production Services;* Keith Demmons, *Production Designer;* Andrea Hoffman, *Senior Production Specialist*

All web links in this book are correct as of the publication date below but may have become inactive or otherwise modified since that time. If you notice a deactivated or changed link, please e-mail books@ascd.org with the words "Link Update" in the subject line. In your message, please specify the web link, the book title, and the page number on which the link appears.

PAPERBACK ISBN: 978-1-4166-2509-4   ASCD product #118035
PDF E-BOOK ISBN: 978-1-4166-2511-7; see Books in Print for other formats.
Quantity discounts are available: e-mail programteam@ascd.org or call 800-933-2723, ext. 5773, or 703-575-5773. For desk copies, go to www.ascd.org/deskcopy.

ASCD Member Book No. F18-2 (Nov. 2017 PSI+). ASCD Member Books mail to Premium (P), Select (S), and Institutional Plus (I+) members on this schedule: Jan, PSI+; Feb, P; Apr, PSI+; May, P; Jul, PSI+; Aug, P; Sep, PSI+; Nov, PSI+; Dec, P. For current details on membership, see www.ascd.org/membership.

Library of Congress Cataloging-in-Publication Data
Names: Armstrong, Thomas, author. | Association for Supervision and
    Curriculum Development.
Title: Multiple intelligences in the classroom / Thomas Armstrong.
Description: Fourth Edition. | Alexandria, Virginia, USA : ASCD, [2018] |
    Includes bibliographical references and index.
Identifiers: LCCN 2017034788 (print) | LCCN 2017038899 (ebook) | ISBN
    9781416625117 (PDF) | ISBN 9781416625094 (paperback)
Subjects: LCSH: Teaching. | Cognitive styles. | Learning. | Multiple
    intelligences.
Classification: LCC LB1025.3 (ebook) | LCC LB1025.3 .A76 2018 (print) | DDC
    371.102—dc23
LC record available at https://lccn.loc.gov/2017034788

27 26 25 24 23 22 21 20 19 18   1 2 3 4 5 6 7 8 9 10

MULTIPLE INTELLIGENCES IN THE CLASSROOM

4th Edition

Preface

Over 30 years ago, a friend lent me a copy of *Frames of Mind: The Theory of Multiple Intelligences* (1983) by Howard Gardner. I held on to it for a couple of months and then handed it back to my friend, unread. The next year, during a course in cognitive psychology at the California Institute for Integral Studies in San Francisco, our professor used a couple of the visual thinking exercises in *Frames of Mind* to demonstrate the practicality of Gardner's multiple intelligences (MI) theory. Suddenly, I was hooked. Shortly thereafter, I began research on my doctoral dissertation, which focused on assessing the strengths of children diagnosed with learning disabilities using MI theory as an organizing framework (Armstrong, 1987a). In 1987, I wrote my first book on multiple intelligences, *In Their Own Way* (Armstrong, 1987b), and began giving workshops to teachers on using MI theory to understand and help students who learn in different ways. Today, over 30 years and hundreds of presentations later, the theory of multiple intelligences retains for me the freshness of vision that it had so many years ago.

I wrote the first edition of this book in 1994. Ron Brandt, the director of publishing at ASCD at the time, was excited about the possibilities of the book being read by many teachers. I hesitated for a time, but then agreed with him, and was delighted when ASCD sent more than 100,000 copies of the book to educators around the world as a membership benefit. Throughout the 1990s and 2000s, I crisscrossed the world in a whirlwind of travel—MI theory had become one of the hottest educational theories around. Though the travel sometimes exhausted me, I felt blessed to reach so many educators with this marvelous learning model.

As I write these words in 2017, more than 400,000 copies of prior editions of this book are in print. In this 4th edition, I've made several important changes to make the material of greater value to new teachers, veteran teachers, administrators, and professors of education in colleges and universities. First, I've completely revised Chapter 11, on special education, to incorporate the work I've been doing over the past decade in the rapidly expanding field of neurodiversity. Second, I've added two new chapters: Chapter 12 focuses on the emerging movement toward greater personalization and deeper learning in the classroom, and Chapter 13 provides a survey of some of the many new learning technologies available to educators in the form of software, tablet and smartphone apps, websites, social media channels, and virtual reality tools. Third, I've completely rewritten the lesson plans in Appendix A so that they align with the standards movement, including lessons based on the Common Core State Standards, the Next Generation Science Standards, and the National Art Standards. Fourth, I've changed the names of the eight intelligences in much of the book to more user-friendly terms (e.g., "body smart" instead of "bodily-kinesthetic intelligence"). Finally, I've incorporated information related to Carol Dweck's (2007) concept of the *growth mindset,* which seems to me to be an important adjunct to MI theory.

This is a difficult time for our culture and for education. For almost three decades, there has been a growing climate of rigid accountability, cookie-cutter standardization, and pseudo-scientific quantification in education that threatens to stifle the pluralism and qualitative values inherent in MI theory. In addition, our public schools are becoming captive to a movement that favors the development of for-profit schools that may leave students behind in pursuit of a fat financial bottom line. Now more than ever, we need to embrace a philosophy of education that recognizes the diversity of our students. There's never been a time in U.S. education when we were so in need of a differentiated and personalized approach to learning that gives voice to all students and engages them with the curriculum. I believe it's time for a resurgence in MI theory to counterbalance the pedagogical narrowness threatening to overwhelm our culture. I hope that this 4th edition of *Multiple Intelligences in the Classroom* makes a small but significant step in the right direction.

Thomas Armstrong
Sonoma County, California
August 7, 2017

1

The Foundations of MI Theory

It is of the utmost importance that we recognize and nurture all of the varied human intelligences, and all of the combinations of intelligences. We are all so different largely because we all have different combinations of intelligences. If we recognize this, I think we will have at least a better chance of dealing appropriately with the many problems that we face in the world.

—*Howard Gardner*

In 1904, the minister of public instruction in Paris asked the French psychologist Alfred Binet and a group of colleagues to develop a means of determining which primary grade students were "at risk" for failure so these students could receive remedial attention. Out of their efforts came the first intelligence tests. Imported to the United States several years later, intelligence testing became widespread, as did the notion that there was something called "intelligence" that could be objectively measured and reduced to a single number or "IQ" score.

Almost 80 years after the first intelligence tests were developed, Harvard psychologist Howard Gardner challenged this commonly held belief. Saying that our culture had defined intelligence too narrowly, he proposed in the book *Frames of Mind* (Gardner, 1983) the existence of at least seven basic

1

intelligences. More recently, he has added an eighth and discussed the possibility of a ninth (Gardner, 1999). In his theory of multiple intelligences (MI theory), Gardner sought to broaden the scope of human potential beyond the confines of the IQ score. He seriously questioned the validity of determining intelligence through the practice of taking individuals out of their natural learning environment and asking them to do isolated tasks they'd never done before—and probably would never choose to do again. Instead, Gardner suggested that intelligence has more to do with the capacity for (1) solving problems and (2) fashioning products in culturally supported, context-rich, and naturalistic settings.

The Eight Intelligences

Once this broader and more pragmatic perspective was taken, the concept of intelligence began to lose its mystique as people began to see it working in people's lives in a variety of ways. Gardner provided a means of mapping the broad range of abilities that humans possess by grouping their capabilities into the following eight comprehensive "intelligences":

Linguistic intelligence: The capacity to use words effectively, whether orally (e.g., as a storyteller, orator, or politician) or in writing (e.g., as a poet, playwright, editor, or journalist). This intelligence includes the ability to manipulate the syntax or structure of language, the phonology or sounds of language, the semantics or meanings of language, and the pragmatic dimensions or practical uses of language. Some of these uses include rhetoric (using language to convince others to take a specific course of action), mnemonics (using language to remember information), explanation (using language to inform), and metalanguage (using language to discuss language).

Logical-mathematical intelligence: The capacity to use numbers effectively (e.g., as a mathematician, tax accountant, or statistician) and to reason well (e.g., as a scientist, computer programmer, or logician). This intelligence includes sensitivity to logical patterns and relationships, statements and propositions (if-then, cause-effect), functions, and other related abstractions. The kinds of processes used in the service of logical-mathematical intelligence include categorization, classification, inference, generalization, calculation, and hypothesis testing.

Spatial intelligence: The ability to perceive the visual-spatial world accurately (e.g., as a surveyor or cartographer) and to perform transformations upon those perceptions (e.g., as an interior decorator, architect, artist, or inventor). This intelligence involves sensitivity to color, line, shape, form, space, and the relationships that exist between these elements. It includes the capacity to visualize, to graphically represent visual or spatial ideas, and to orient oneself appropriately in a spatial matrix.

Bodily-kinesthetic intelligence: Expertise in using one's whole body to express ideas and feelings (e.g., as an actor, a mime, an athlete, or a dancer) and facility in using one's hands to produce or transform things (e.g., as a craftsperson, sculptor, mechanic, or surgeon). This intelligence includes specific physical skills such as coordination, balance, dexterity, strength, flexibility, and speed, as well as proprioceptive, tactile, and haptic capacities.

Musical intelligence: The capacity to perceive (e.g., as a music aficionado), transform (e.g., as a composer), express (e.g., as a performer), and discriminate among (e.g., as a music critic) musical forms. This intelligence includes sensitivity to the rhythm, pitch or melody, and timbre or tone color of a musical piece. One can have a figural or "top-down" understanding of music (global, intuitive), a formal or "bottom-up" understanding (analytic, technical), or both.

Interpersonal intelligence: The ability to perceive and distinguish among the moods, intentions, motivations, and feelings of other people. This can include sensitivity to facial expressions, voice, and gestures; the capacity for discriminating among many different kinds of interpersonal cues; and the ability to respond effectively to those cues in some pragmatic way (e.g., by influencing a group of people to follow a certain line of action).

Intrapersonal intelligence: Self-knowledge and the ability to act adaptively on the basis of that knowledge. This intelligence includes having an accurate picture of oneself (one's strengths and limitations); awareness of one's inner moods, intentions, motivations, temperaments, and desires; and the capacity for self-discipline, self-understanding, and self-esteem.

Naturalist intelligence: Expertise in the recognition and classification of the numerous species—the flora and fauna—of an individual's environment. This also includes sensitivity to other natural phenomena (e.g., cloud formations and mountains) and, in the case of those growing up in an urban environment, the capacity to discriminate among inanimate objects such as cars, sneakers, and smartphones.

Gardner's terms are useful within an academic context. However, because this book focuses on practical applications of MI theory, I'm choosing to use terminology that more clearly and directly reflects the essential nature of each intelligence, as follows:

- Linguistic Intelligence → Word Smart
- Logical-Mathematical Intelligence → Number/Logic Smart
- Spatial Intelligence → Picture Smart
- Bodily-Kinesthetic Intelligence → Body Smart
- Musical Intelligence → Music Smart
- Interpersonal Intelligence → People Smart
- Intrapersonal Intelligence → Self Smart
- Naturalist Intelligence → Nature Smart

I feel that these terms make MI theory more accessible to students, their families, and the community at large. They also make it easier for educators to envision practical applications of the theory in the classroom. Educators are free, of course, to continue using Gardner's nomenclature as they wish, and I myself will at times also be using those terms when they seem to add clarity to the text.

The Theoretical Basis for MI Theory

Many people wonder why Howard Gardner insisted on referring to the eight categories as *intelligences* rather than *talents* or *aptitudes*. Gardner realized that people are used to hearing expressions like "He's not very intelligent, but he has a wonderful aptitude for music"; thus, he was quite conscious of his use of the word *intelligence* to describe each category. "I'm deliberately being somewhat provocative," he once said. "If I'd said that there are seven kinds of competencies, people would yawn and say 'Yeah, yeah.' But by calling them 'intelligences,' I'm saying that we've tended to put on a pedestal one variety called intelligence, and there's actually a plurality of them, and some are things we've never thought about as being 'intelligence' at all" (quoted in Weinreich-Haste, 1985, p. 48).

To provide a sound theoretical foundation for his claims, Gardner set up the following eight basic criteria that each intelligence had to meet to be considered a full-fledged intelligence and not simply a talent, skill, or aptitude:

1. Potential isolation by brain damage
2. The existence of savants, prodigies, and other exceptional individuals
3. A distinctive developmental history and a definable set of expert "end state" performances
4. An evolutionary history and evolutionary plausibility
5. Support from psychometric findings
6. Support from experimental psychological tasks
7. An identifiable core operation or set of operations
8. Susceptibility to encoding in a symbol system

Potential Isolation by Brain Damage

At the Boston Veterans Administration, Gardner worked with individuals who had suffered accidents or illnesses that affected specific areas of the brain. In several cases, brain lesions appeared to have selectively impaired one intelligence while leaving all the other intelligences intact. For example, a person with a lesion in Broca's area (in the left frontal lobe) might have a substantial portion of his Word Smart damaged and thus experience great difficulty speaking, reading, or writing, but still be able to sing, do math, dance, reflect on feelings, and relate to others. A person with a lesion in the temporal lobe of the right hemisphere might have Music Smart capacities selectively impaired, while frontal lobe lesions might primarily affect the personal intelligences (Self Smart and People Smart).

Gardner, then, is arguing for the existence of eight relatively autonomous brain systems—a more sophisticated and updated version of the "right brain/left brain" model of learning that was popular in the 1970s. Column 5 in Figure 1.1 shows the primary affected neurological systems for each intelligence.

The Existence of Savants, Prodigies, and Other Exceptional Individuals

Gardner suggests that we can see single intelligences operating at especially high levels in certain individuals, much like huge mountains that rise up against the backdrop of a flat horizon. Savants are individuals who demonstrate superior abilities in one intelligence at the expense of full functioning of the others. Such individuals seem to exist for each of the eight

Figure 1.1
MI Theory Summary Chart

Intelligence	Core Components	Symbol Systems	High End-States	Neurological Systems (Primary Areas)	Developmental Factors	Ways That Cultures Value	Evolutionary Origins	Presence in Other Species	Historical Factors (Relative to Current U.S. Values)
Word Smart	Sensitivity to the sounds, structure, meanings, and functions of words and language	Phonetic languages (e.g., English)	Writer, orator (e.g., Virginia Woolf, Martin Luther King Jr.)	Left temporal and frontal lobes (e.g., Broca's/ Wernicke's areas)	"Explodes" in early childhood; remains robust until old age	Oral histories, storytelling, literature	Written notations found dating to 30,000 years ago	Apes' ability to name things by pointing	Oral transmission more important before printing press
Number/ Logic Smart	Sensitivity to, and capacity to discern, logical or numerical patterns; ability to handle long chains of reasoning	Computer languages (e.g., HTML)	Scientist, mathematician (e.g., Madame Curie, Blaise Pascal)	Left frontal and right parietal lobes	Peaks in adolescence and early adulthood; higher math insights decline after age 40	Scientific discoveries, mathematical theories, counting and classification systems	Early number systems and calendars found	Bees calculate distances through their dances	More important with advent of "coding" skills (computer programming)
Picture Smart	Capacity to perceive the visual-spatial world accurately and to perform transformations on one's initial perceptions	Use of line, shape, form, color, perspective, and so on.	Artist, architect (e.g., Frida Kahlo, I. M. Pei)	Posterior regions of right hemisphere	Topological thinking in early childhood gives way to Euclidean paradigm around age 9–10; artistic capacity stays robust into old age	Artistic works, navigational systems, architectural designs, inventions	Prehistorical cave drawings of Lascaux and other sites around the world	Territorial instinct of many species	More important with advent of mass media, video, the internet, and other image-based technologies
Body Smart	Ability to control one's body movements and to handle objects skillfully	Sports diagrams (e.g., football playbook)	Athlete, dancer, sculptor (e.g., Mohammed Ali, Martha Graham, Auguste Rodin)	Cerebellum, basal ganglia, motor cortex	Varies depending upon skill (strength, flexibility, endurance) or domain (gymnastics, baseball, mime)	Crafts, athletic performances, dramatic works, dance forms, sculpture	Evidence of early tool use in prehistoric times	Tool use of primates, anteaters, and other species	More important in agrarian pre-20th century culture

Music Smart	Ability to produce and appreciate rhythm, pitch, and timbre; appreciation of the forms of musical expressiveness	Musical notational systems (e.g., modern staff notation)	Composer, performer (e.g., Stevie Wonder, Midori)	Right temporal lobe (left temporal lobe in professional musicians)	Earliest intelligence to develop; prodigies often go through developmental crisis in adolescence	Musical compositions, performances, recordings	Evidence of musical instruments back to Stone Age	Bird song	Was more important during oral culture, when communication had a musical component
People Smart	Capacity to discern and respond appropriately to the moods, temperaments, motivations, and desires of other people	Social cues (e.g., gestures, body posture, and facial expressions)	Family counselor, political leader (e.g., Virginia Satir, Nelson Mandela)	Frontal lobes, temporal lobe (especially right hemisphere), limbic system	Attachment/bonding during first 3 years critical; gradually develops as we acquire social experience	Political documents, social institutions	Communal living groups required for hunting-and-gathering cultures	Maternal bonding observed in primates and other species	More important with the increase in service (as opposed to industrial) economies
Self Smart	Access to one's own "feeling" life and the ability to discriminate among one's emotions; knowledge of one's own strengths and weaknesses	Symbols of the personal self (e.g., in dreams and artwork)	Psychotherapist, entrepreneur (e.g., Sigmund Freud, Richard Branson)	Frontal lobes, parietal lobes, limbic system	Formation of boundary between "self" and "other" during first 3 years critical, gradually develops as we acquire life experience	Self development systems (e.g., psychotherapies), rites of passage	Prehistoric evidence of human burial sites	Chimpanzees can locate self in mirror, experience fear	Especially important in modern times with increasingly complex society requiring choice-making and self-promotion
Nature Smart	Expertise in distinguishing among members of a species; recognizing the existence of other neighboring species; and charting out the relations, formally or informally, among several species	Species classification systems (e.g., Linnaeus)	Naturalist, animal activist (e.g., Charles Darwin, Jane Goodall)	Areas of left parietal lobe important for discriminating "living" from "nonliving" things	Shows up dramatically in some young children; schooling or experience increases formal or informal expertise	Folk taxonomies, herbal lore, hunting rituals, animal spirit mythologies	Prehistoric hunting tools reveal understanding of other species	Hunting instinct in innumerable species to discriminate between prey and non-prey	Was more important during agrarian period; then fell out of favor during industrial expansion; now "earth smarts" are more important than ever to preserve endangered ecosystems

intelligences. For instance, in the movie *Rain Man*, which is based on the true story of Kim Peek, Dustin Hoffman plays the role of Raymond Babbitt, a Number/Logic Smart savant. Raymond rapidly calculates multidigit numbers in his head and does other amazing mathematical feats, yet he has poor peer relationships, low language functioning, and a lack of insight into his own life (low People Smart and Self Smart).

There are also savants who draw exceptionally well (e.g., Stephen Wiltshire), savants who have amazing Music Smart memories, who can play a composition after hearing it only once (e.g., Leslie Lemke or Gloria Lenhoff), savants who read complex material but don't comprehend what they're reading (hyperlexics), and savants who have exceptional sensitivity to nature or animals (see Grandin & Johnson, 2006, and Sacks, 1985, 1995).

A Distinctive Developmental History and a Definable Set of Expert "End-State" Performances

Gardner suggests that intelligences are galvanized by participation in some type of culturally valued activity and that an individual's growth in such an activity follows a developmental pattern. Each intelligence-based activity has its own developmental trajectory; that is, each activity has its own time of arising in early childhood, its own time of peaking during one's lifetime, and its own pattern of either rapidly or gradually declining as one gets older. Musical composition, for example, seems to be among the earliest culturally valued activities to develop to a high level of proficiency: Mozart was only 4 years old when he began to compose, 8 when he wrote his first symphony, and 11 when he wrote his first opera. Numerous composers and performers have been active well into their 80s and 90s, so expertise in musical composition also seems to remain relatively robust into old age.

Higher mathematical expertise appears to have a somewhat different trajectory. It doesn't emerge as early as music composition ability (4-year-olds do not create new logical principles), but it does *peak* relatively early in life. Many great mathematical and scientific ideas were developed by teenagers such as Blaise Pascal and Karl Friedrich Gauss, and both Albert Einstein and Isaac Newton made their major contributions to science by their mid-twenties. A review of the history of mathematical ideas suggests that few original mathematical insights come to people past the age of 40. Once people reach this age, they're considered over the hill as higher mathematicians! Most of us can breathe a sigh of relief, however, because this decline generally does not seem to affect more pragmatic skills such as balancing a checkbook.

One can become a successful novelist at age 40, 50, or even later. Nobel Prize–winner in literature Toni Morrison didn't publish her first novel until she was almost 40. One can even be over 75 and choose to become a painter: Grandma Moses did. Gardner points out that we need to use several different developmental maps in order to understand the eight intelligences. Piaget provides a comprehensive map for Number/Logic Smart, but we may need to go to Erik Erikson for a map of how personal intelligences develop, and to Noam Chomsky or Lev Vygotsky for developmental models of Word Smart. Column 6 of Figure 1.1 includes a summary of developmental trajectories for each intelligence.

Gardner (1993a) points out that we can best see the intelligences working at their zenith by studying the "end-states" of intelligences in the lives of truly exceptional individuals. For example, we can see Music Smart at work by studying Beethoven's Eroica Symphony, Nature Smart through Darwin's theory of evolution, or Picture Smart via Michelangelo's Sistine Chapel paintings. Column 4 in Figure 1.1 includes examples of high end-states for each intelligence.

An Evolutionary History and Evolutionary Plausibility

Gardner notes that each of the eight intelligences meets the test of having its roots deeply embedded in the evolution of human beings and, even earlier, in the evolution of other species. So, for example, Picture Smart can be studied in the cave drawings of Lascaux, as well as in the way certain insects orient themselves in space while tracking flowers. Similarly, Music Smart can be traced back to archaeological evidence of early musical instruments and be heard in the wide variety of bird songs. Column 8 in Figure 1.1 includes notes on the evolutionary origins of the intelligences.

MI theory also has a historical context. Certain intelligences seem to have been more important in earlier times than they are today. Nature Smart and Body Smart, for example, were probably valued more 150 years ago in the United States, when most of the population lived in rural settings and the ability to hunt, harvest grain, and build barns had strong social approval. Similarly, certain intelligences may become more important in the future. The computer revolution has certainly enlisted the Number/Logic Smart capabilities of many people who might otherwise have had few opportunities to use these gifts. As more and more people receive their information from films, television, the internet, and video games, the value placed on having a strong Picture Smart intelligence seems to be increasing. There is also now a growing need for individuals who have expertise in Nature Smart to help protect endangered ecosystems. Column 10 in Figure 1.1 notes some of the historical factors that have influenced the perceived value of each intelligence.

Support from Psychometric Findings

Most theories of intelligence (as well as many learning-style theories) rely on standardized measures of human ability to ascertain the validity of a model. Although Gardner is no champion of standardized tests, and in fact has been an ardent supporter of alternatives to formal testing (see Chapter 10), he suggests that many existing standardized tests support the validity of MI theory (although Gardner would point out that standardized tests assess multiple intelligences in a strikingly decontextualized fashion). For example, the Wechsler Intelligence Scale for Children includes subtests that require Word Smart (e.g., information, vocabulary), Number/Logic Smart (e.g., arithmetic), Picture Smart (e.g., picture arrangement), and to a lesser extent Body Smart (e.g., object assembly). Still other assessments tap personal intelligences (e.g., the Vineland Society Maturity Scale, the Coopersmith Self-Esteem Inventory). Chapter 3 includes a survey of the types of formal tests associated with each of the eight intelligences.

Support from Experimental Psychological Tasks

Gardner suggests that examining psychological studies can help us see intelligences working in isolation from one another. For example, in studies where subjects master a specific skill, such as reading, but fail to transfer that ability to another area, such as mathematics, we see the failure of Word Smart to transfer to Number/Logic Smart. Similarly, in studies of cognitive abilities such as memory, perception, or attention, we can see evidence that individuals possess selective abilities. Certain individuals, for instance, may have a superior memory for words but not for faces; others may have acute perception of musical sounds but not of verbal sounds. Each of these cognitive faculties, then, is intelligence-specific; that is, people can demonstrate different levels of proficiency across the eight intelligences in each cognitive area.

An Identifiable Core Operation or Set of Operations

According to Gardner, much as a computer program requires a set of operations to function, so too does each intelligence maintain a set of core operations to drive its various activities. Core operations of Music Smart, for example, may include sensitivity to pitch or the ability to discriminate among various rhythmic structures. In Body Smart, core operations may include the ability to imitate the physical movements of others or to master established fine-motor routines for building a structure. Gardner speculates that these core operations may someday be identified with such precision as to be simulated on a computer.

Susceptibility to Encoding in a Symbol System

Gardner notes that one of the best indicators of intelligent behavior is the ability to use symbols. The word *cat* as it appears in this sentence is simply a collection of marks printed in a specific way, yet it more than likely conjures up a range of associations, images, and memories. What has occurred is the bringing to the present (the "re-present-ation") of something that is not actually here. Gardner suggests that the ability to symbolize is one of the most important factors separating humans from most other species. He notes that each of the eight intelligences in his theory meets the criterion of being able to be symbolized. Each intelligence, in fact, has its own unique symbol or notational systems. For Word Smart, there is the great diversity of written languages such as English, Hebrew, and Russian; for Picture Smart, there are a number of graphic languages used by architects, engineers, and designers, as well as some of the ideographs used in Chinese and Japanese communication. Column 3 in Figure 1.1 includes examples of symbol systems for all eight intelligences.

Key Points in MI Theory

Beyond the descriptions of the eight intelligences and their theoretical underpinnings, it's important to keep in mind the following key ideas.

Each person possesses all eight intelligences. MI theory is not a "type theory" for determining the *one* intelligence that fits each person. It is a theory of cognitive functioning, and it proposes that each person has capacities in all eight intelligences. Of course, the eight intelligences function together in ways unique to each person. Some people appear to possess extremely high levels of functioning in all or most of the eight intelligences—for example, German poet-statesman-scientist-naturalist-philosopher Johann Wolfgang von Goethe. Other people, such as certain severely impaired individuals in institutions for the developmentally disabled, appear to lack all but the most rudimentary aspects of the intelligences. Most of us fall somewhere in between these two extremes—being more highly developed in some intelligences, modestly developed in others, and relatively under-developed in still others.

Most people can develop each intelligence to an adequate level of competency. Although individuals may bewail their deficiencies in a given area and consider their problems innate and intractable, Gardner suggests that most typically developing individuals have the capacity to develop all eight intelligences to a reasonably high level of performance if given the appropriate encouragement, enrichment, and instruction. He points to the Suzuki Talent Education Program as an example of how individuals of relatively modest biological musical endowment can achieve a sophisticated level of proficiency in playing the violin or piano through a combination of the right environmental influences (e.g., an involved parent, exposure from infancy to classical music, and early instruction). Such educational models can be found in other intelligences as well (see, e.g., Edwards, 2012, for a method that improves one's Picture Smart abilities through drawing). Gardner's emphasis on effort in the development of the intelligences is very much in line with Dweck's (2007) idea of maintaining a "growth mindset" in the classroom (see p. 43 for a discussion of this concept).

Intelligences usually work together in complex ways. Gardner points out that each intelligence is actually a "fiction"; that is, no single intelligence exists by itself in real life (except perhaps in very rare instances among savants and brain-injured individuals). Intelligences are always interacting with each other. To cook a meal, for example, one must read the recipe (Word Smart), perhaps double the recipe (Number/Logic Smart), develop a menu that satisfies all members of the family (People Smart), and placate one's own appetite (Self Smart). Similarly, when a child plays a game of kickball, she needs Body Smart (to run, kick, and catch), Picture Smart (to orient herself to the playing field and to anticipate the trajectories of flying balls), and Word Smart and People Smart (to successfully argue points during disputes in the game). The intelligences have been taken out of context in the formal articulation of MI theory only for the purpose of examining their essential features and learning how to use them effectively. We must always remember to put them back into their unique culturally valued contexts when we are finished with their formal study.

There are many ways to be intelligent within each category. There is no standard set of attributes that one must have to be considered intelligent in a specific area. A person may not be able to read, yet be highly Word Smart because he can tell a terrific story or has a large oral vocabulary. Similarly, a person may be quite awkward on the playing field, yet possess superior Body Smart ability when she weaves a carpet or creates an inlaid chess table. MI theory emphasizes the rich diversity of ways in which people show their gifts *within* intelligences as well as *between* them. (See Chapter 3 for more information on the varieties of attributes in each intelligence.)

The Existence of Other Intelligences

Gardner points out that his model is a tentative formulation; after further research and investigation, some of the intelligences on his list may not meet certain of his eight core criteria and therefore be struck from the list. Similarly, we may identify *new* intelligences that do meet the various tests. In fact, Gardner acted on this belief by adding a new intelligence—the naturalist—after deciding that it fit each of the eight criteria. His consideration of a ninth intelligence—the existential—is also based upon its meeting most of the criteria (see Chapter 14 for a detailed discussion of the existential intelligence). Other intelligences that have been proposed by individuals other than Gardner include spirituality, moral sensibility, humor, intuition, creativity, culinary (cooking) ability, olfactory perception (sense of smell), the ability to synthesize the other intelligences, high-tech competency, and mechanical ability. It remains to be seen whether these proposed intelligences can, in fact, meet each of Gardner's eight criteria.

The Relationship of MI Theory to Other Intelligence Theories

Gardner's theory of multiple intelligences is certainly not the first model to grapple with the notion of intelligence. There have been theories of intelligence since ancient times, when the mind was considered to reside somewhere in the heart, the liver, or the kidneys. In more recent times, theories of intelligence have emerged touting anywhere from 1 (Spearman's "g") to 150 (Guilford's Structure of the Intellect) types of intelligence.

Some educators have compared MI theory to different learning style models. Gardner, however, has sought to differentiate the theory of multiple intelligences from the concept of "learning style." He writes: "The concept of *style* designates a general approach that an individual can apply equally to every conceivable content. In contrast, an *intelligence* is a capacity, with its component processes, that is geared to a specific content in the world (such as musical sounds or spatial patterns)" (1995, pp. 202–203). There is no clear evidence yet, according to Gardner, that a person highly developed in Picture Smart, for example, will show that capacity in every aspect of his or her life (e.g., washing the car spatially, reflecting on ideas spatially, socializing spatially). He suggests that the existence of "intelligence styles" remains to be empirically investigated (for an example of a step in this direction, see Silver, Strong, & Perini, 1997).

For Further Study

1. Form a study group on MI theory using Gardner's *Frames of Mind* as a text. Each member can be responsible for reading and reporting on a specific chapter. For an example of how a multiple intelligences school arose from such a study group, see Hoerr (2000).
2. Use Gardner's comprehensive bibliography on MI theory, found in his books *Intelligence Reframed: Multiple Intelligences for the 21st Century* (1999) and *Multiple Intelligences: New Horizons in Theory and Practice* (2006a), as a basis for reading more widely about the model.
3. Propose the existence of a new intelligence and apply Gardner's eight criteria to see if it qualifies for inclusion in MI theory.
4. Collect examples of symbol systems in each intelligence. For example, one might look on the internet for symbols in Picture Smart used by

designers, architects, artists, or inventors or Music Smart symbols that are different from those used on the base and treble clef.

5. Read about savants in each intelligence. Some of the footnoted entries in Gardner's *Frames of Mind* identify sources of information on savants in Number/Logic Smart, Picture Smart, Music Smart, Word Smart, and Body Smart. In addition, the work of neurologist Oliver Sacks (1985, 1995) provides engagingly written case studies of savants and other individuals with specific brain damage that has affected their intelligences in intriguing ways.

6. Relate MI theory to a learning-style model (e.g., VAKT, Myers-Briggs, Dunn and Dunn) and note their similarities and differences.

2

MI Theory and Personal Development

What kind of school plan you make is neither here nor there; what matters is what sort of a person you are.

—*Rudolf Steiner*

Before applying any model of learning in a classroom environment, we should first apply it to ourselves as educators and adult learners, for unless we have an experiential understanding of the theory and have personalized its content, we are unlikely to be committed to using it with students and to using it effectively. Consequently, an important step in implementing the theory of multiple intelligences (after internalizing the basic theoretical foundations presented in Chapter 1) is to determine the nature and quality of our *own* multiple intelligences and seek ways to develop them in our lives. As we begin to do this, it may become apparent how our particular fluency (or lack of fluency) in each of the eight intelligences can affect our competence (or lack of competence) in the various roles we have as educators.

Identifying Your Multiple Intelligences

As you will see in the later chapters on student assessment (Chapters 3 and 10), developing a profile of a person's multiple intelligences is not a simple matter. No test can accurately determine the nature or quality of a person's intelligences. As Gardner has repeatedly pointed out, standardized tests measure only a small part of the total spectrum of abilities. The best way to assess your own multiple intelligences, therefore, is through a realistic appraisal of your performance in the many kinds of tasks, activities, and experiences associated with each intelligence. Rather than perform several artificial learning tasks, look back over the types of real-life experiences you've already had involving these eight intelligences. The MI inventory in Figure 2.1 can help you to do this.

Figure 2.1
MI Inventory for Adults

Check the statements that apply in each intelligence category. Space is provided at the end of each category for you to write additional information not specifically referred to in the inventory items.

Word Smart

_____Books are very important to me.

_____I can hear words in my head before I read, speak, or write them down.

_____I get more out of listening to the radio or an audio recording than I do from video sources.

_____I enjoy word games like Scrabble, Anagrams, and Password.

_____I enjoy entertaining myself or others with tongue twisters, nonsense rhymes, or puns.

_____I have a good vocabulary and am continually adding new words to my speaking and writing activities.

_____English, social studies, and history were easier for me in school than math and science.

_____Learning to speak or read another language (e.g., French, Spanish, German) has been relatively easy for me.

_____My conversation includes frequent references to things that I've read or heard.

_____I've written something recently that I was particularly proud of, that was published, or that earned me recognition from others.

Other Word Smart Abilities:

Continued

Figure 2.1 (*continued*)
MI Inventory for Adults

Number/Logic Smart

____I can easily compute numbers in my head.

____Math or science were among my favorite subjects in school.

____I enjoy playing games or solving brainteasers that require logical thinking.

____I like to do experiments that involve scientific thinking.

____My mind searches for patterns, regularities, or logical sequences in things.

____I'm interested in new developments in science and technology.

____I believe that most things have a rational explanation.

____I pay particular attention to statistics, graphs, and charts in the news.

____I like to troubleshoot the causes of objects that malfunction.

____I feel more comfortable when something has been measured, categorized, analyzed, or quantified in some way.

Other Number/Logic Smart Abilities:

Picture Smart

____I often see clear visual images when I close my eyes.

____I have strong opinions concerning colors.

____I like to take photos or video of what I see around me.

____I enjoy doing jigsaw puzzles, mazes, or other visual puzzles.

____I have vivid dreams at night.

____I can generally find my way around unfamiliar territory without a map.

____I like to draw or doodle.

____Geometry was easier for me than algebra in school.

____I can easily imagine how something might appear if it were looked down upon from directly above, in a bird's-eye view.

____I prefer reading material that is heavily illustrated.

Other Picture Smart Abilities:

Body Smart

_____I engage in at least one sport or physical activity on a regular basis.

_____I find it difficult to sit still for long periods of time.

_____I like working with my hands at activities like sewing, weaving, carving, carpentry, model building, or other hands-on crafts or hobbies.

_____My best ideas often come to me when I'm out for a long walk or a jog or when I'm engaging in some other kind of physical activity.

_____I often like to spend my free time doing something physical or hands-on.

_____I frequently use hand gestures or other forms of body language when conversing with others.

_____I need to manipulate objects physically to learn more about them.

_____I have a good sense of touch and enjoy tactile sensations.

_____I would describe myself as well coordinated.

_____I need to _practice_ a new skill rather than simply read about it or watch a video that describes it.

Other Body Smart Abilities:

Music Smart

_____I have a pleasant singing voice (at least I think it's pleasant!).

_____I can tell when a musical note is off-key.

_____I frequently listen to music in my spare time.

_____I play at least one musical instrument.

_____My life would be poorer if there were no music in it.

_____I sometimes catch myself walking down the street with a tune running through my mind.

_____I can easily keep time to a piece of music with a drum or other percussion instrument and/or have a good sense of rhythm.

_____I know the tunes to many different musical pieces.

_____If I hear a musical selection once or twice, I am usually able to hum or sing it back fairly accurately.

_____I often make tapping sounds or sing little melodies while working, studying, or learning something new.

Other Music Smart Abilities:

Continued

Figure 2.1 (*continued*)
MI Inventory for Adults

People Smart

_____I'm the sort of person others come to for advice and counsel at work or in my neighborhood.

_____I prefer group sports like football, volleyball, or softball to solo sports such as swimming and jogging.

_____When I have a problem, I'm more likely to seek out another person for help than try working it out on my own.

_____I have at least three close friends.

_____I favor social games such as Monopoly or bridge over individual recreations such as video games and solitaire.

_____I enjoy the challenge of teaching others what I know how to do.

_____I consider myself a leader (or others have called me that).

_____I feel comfortable in the middle of a crowd.

_____I like to get involved in social activities connected with my work, house of worship, or community.

_____I would rather spend my evenings at a lively party than stay at home alone reading or doing other solo activities.

Other People Smart Abilities:

Self Smart

_____I regularly spend time alone meditating, reflecting, or thinking.

_____I have attended psychotherapy, counseling sessions, or personal growth seminars to learn more about myself.

_____I am resilient in the face of setbacks.

_____I have a special hobby or interest I engage in that few people know about.

_____I have goals for my life that I think about on a regular basis.

_____I have a realistic view of my strengths and weaknesses (borne out by feedback from other sources).

_____I would prefer to spend a weekend alone in a cabin in the woods than at a fancy resort with lots of people around.

_____I consider myself to be strong-willed or independent-minded.

_____I keep a personal diary or journal to record the events of my inner life.

_____I am self-employed or have at least thought seriously about starting my own business.

Other Self Smart Abilities:

Nature Smart

_____I like to spend time backpacking, hiking, or just walking in nature.

_____I belong to a volunteer organization related to nature (e.g., Sierra Club) or I'm concerned about helping to save nature from environmental degradation.

_____I love having an animal or animals around the house.

_____I'm involved in a hobby that involves nature in some way (e.g., bird-watching).

_____I've enrolled in courses relating to nature (e.g., botany, zoology, ecology).

_____I'm quite good at telling the difference among types of trees, dogs, birds, and/or other plants or animals.

_____I like to read books and magazines or watch television shows or movies that feature nature in some way.

_____When on vacation, I prefer to go off to a natural setting (e.g., park, campground, hiking trail) than to a city or cultural location.

_____I love to visit zoos, aquariums, or other places where the natural world is celebrated.

_____I have a garden and enjoy working regularly in it.

Other Nature Smart Abilities:

It's important to keep in mind that this inventory is _not_ a test and that quantitative information (such as the number of checks for each intelligence) has no bearing on determining your intelligence or lack thereof in each category. The purpose of the inventory is to begin to connect you to your own life experiences with the eight intelligences. What sorts of memories, feelings, and ideas emerge from this process?

Tapping MI Resources

The theory of multiple intelligences is an especially good model for examining teaching strengths as well as areas needing improvement. Perhaps you avoid drawing pictures on the whiteboard or stay away from using visual materials in your presentations because Picture Smart is not particularly well developed in your life. Or possibly you gravitate toward learning strategies or ecological activities because you are a People Smart or Nature Smart sort of learner or teacher yourself. Use MI theory to survey your own teaching style and see how it matches up with the eight intelligences. Although you don't have to be a master in all eight intelligences, you should know how to tap resources in the intelligences you typically shy away from in the classroom. Here are some ways to do this.

Draw on colleagues' expertise. If you don't have ideas for bringing music into the classroom because your Music Smart is undeveloped, consider getting help from the school's music teacher or a musically inclined colleague. The theory of multiple intelligences has broad implications for team teaching. In a school committed to developing students' multiple intelligences, the ideal teaching team or curriculum planning committee will include people with expertise in each of the eight intelligences.

Ask students to help out. Students can often come up with strategies and demonstrate expertise in areas where your own knowledge may be deficient. For example, students may be able to draw pictures on the board, provide musical background for a learning activity, or share knowledge about lizards, insects, flowers, or other fauna or flora if you don't feel comfortable or competent doing these things yourself.

Use available technology. Tap your school's technical resources to convey information you might not be able to provide through your own efforts. For instance, you can use audio recordings of music if you're not Music Smart, video if you're not picture-oriented, calculators and spreadsheets to supplement your shortcomings in Number/Logic Smart areas, and so forth. See Chapter 13 for more information about the wealth of technological learning tools now available to teachers and learners.

Cultivate your intelligences. MI theory provides a model through which you can activate your neglected intelligences and create a sense of balance among all eight (see Armstrong, 1999 for a comprehensive self-help guide to cultivating your own multiple intelligences).

Developing Your Multiple Intelligences

I've been careful not to use the terms "strong intelligence" and "weak intelligence" in describing individual differences in people's intelligences, because someone's "weak" intelligence may actually turn out to be her strongest intelligence once it is given the chance to develop. As mentioned in Chapter 1, a key point in MI theory is that most people can develop all their intelligences to a relatively acceptable degree of mastery. The development of an intelligence depends upon three main factors:

1. **Biological endowment**—hereditary or genetic factors and damage to the brain before, during, or after birth
2. **Personal life history**—experiences with parents, teachers, peers, friends, and others that awaken intelligences, keep them from developing, or actively repress them; also epigenetic events that turn genes off or on in response to environmental stimuli
3. **Cultural and historical background**—the cultural values and intellectual and historical climate of the time and place in which you were born and raised

We can see the interaction of these three factors, for example, in the life of Wolfgang Amadeus Mozart. Mozart undoubtedly came into life possessing a strong biological endowment (a highly developed right temporal lobe, perhaps). And his home environment provided a great deal of support for his burgeoning musical interests: His father, Leopold, was a musician who sacrificed much of his own career to support his son's Music Smart development. Finally, Mozart was born at a time in Europe when musical expression was flourishing and wealthy patrons (counts, barons, princes, bishops, etc.) supported composers and performers. Mozart's genius, therefore, arose through a confluence of biological, personal, and cultural/historical factors. We have to ask ourselves what would have happened if Mozart had been born to tone-deaf parents in Puritan England, where music was generally considered to be associated with the devil's work. His Music Smart gifts likely would never have developed to a high level due to these other forces working against his biological endowment.

The interaction of the above factors is also evident in the Music Smart proficiency of many of the children who have been enrolled in the Suzuki Talent Education Program. Although some Suzuki students may be born with a modest genetic musical endowment, they are able to develop their Music Smart to a relatively high level through experiences in the program. MI theory is a model that values nurture as much as, and in many ways more than, nature in accounting for the development of each of the eight intelligences.

Activators and Deactivators of Intelligences

Crystallizing experiences and *paralyzing experiences* are two key processes in the development of intelligences. Crystallizing experiences, identified by David Feldman (1980) at Tufts University and further developed by Walters and Gardner (1986), are the sometimes trivial-seeming events that can activate the development of an intelligence. Often these events occur in early childhood, although they can occur any time during our lives. For instance, when Albert Einstein was 4 years old, his father showed him a magnetic compass. The adult Einstein later said this compass filled him with a desire to figure out the mysteries of the universe. Essentially, this experience activated his genius and started him on his journey toward discoveries that would make him one of the towering figures in 20th-century science. When Yehudi Menuhin was almost 4 years old, his parents took him to a concert by the San Francisco Symphony Orchestra. The experience so enthralled him that afterward he asked his parents for a violin as a birthday present and said he wanted the violin soloist they heard that evening to teach him to play it. Martha Graham had never danced before when her father took her to see the dancer Ruth Saint Denis perform. Martha was 16 at the time and decided then that she wanted to become a dancer. Crystallizing experiences are the sparks that light an intelligence and start it on its way toward mature development.

I've come up with the term *paralyzing experiences* to refer to experiences that essentially shut down an intelligence. Perhaps a teacher humiliated you in front of your classmates when you showed your favorite drawing during art period and the event marked the end of a good part of your artistic development. Possibly a parent yelled at you to "stop making a racket" on the piano, and you never went near a musical instrument again. Or maybe you were punished for bringing your "messy" leaf collection into the house, without any acknowledgment of the emerging naturalist within you. Paralyzing experiences are often characterized by feelings of shame, guilt, fear, anger, and other negative emotions that prevent intelligences from growing and thriving. (See Miller, 1996, for a further description of how parental shaming can influence one's intellectual and emotional development.)

The following environmental influences also promote or suppress the development of intelligences:

- **Access to resources or mentors:** If your family was unable to afford a violin, piano, or other instrument, your Music Smart might well have remained undeveloped.
- **Cultural factors:** If you were a female student who demonstrated "proclivities" in mathematics at a time when males ruled the world

of math and science, the development of your Number/Logic Smart would likely have been hindered.

- **Geographic factors:** If you grew up on a farm, you might well have had more opportunity to develop certain aspects of Nature Smart than if you were raised on the 62nd floor of a Manhattan apartment building.
- **Familial factors:** If you wanted to be an artist but your parents wanted you to be a lawyer, their influence might well have promoted the development of your Word Smart at the expense of your Picture Smart.
- **Situational factors:** If you had to help take care of a large family while you were growing up and you now have a large family yourself, you may have had little time to develop in areas of promise.

MI theory offers a model of personal development that can help educators understand how their own profile of intelligences affects their teaching approaches in the classroom. Further, it opens the gate to a broad range of activities that can help develop neglected intelligences, activate underdeveloped or paralyzed intelligences, and bring well-developed intelligences to even higher levels of proficiency.

For Further Study

1. Fill out the inventory in Figure 2.1. Talk with a friend or colleague about the results of the inventory. Make sure to share something about what you perceive as your most and least developed intelligences. Avoid talking in terms of quantitative information (e.g., "I had only three checks in Music Smart"). Speak instead in anecdotal terms (e.g., "I've never felt very musical in my life; my classmates used to laugh at me when I had to sing solo in music class"). Reflect on how your developed and undeveloped intelligences affect what you do in the classroom. What types of teaching methods or materials do you avoid because they involve using your underdeveloped intelligences? What sorts of things are you especially good at doing because of one or more highly developed intelligences?
2. Select an intelligence that you would like to nurture. Perhaps it is one you showed particular promise in as a child but never had the opportunity to develop (it may have gone "underground" as you grew up). Perhaps it's an intelligence you have had great difficulty with or

one that you would like to experience with greater competence and confidence. Or, possibly, it's a highly developed intelligence that you want to take to an even higher level of accomplishment. Create a time line showing the development of a selected intelligence from early childhood to the present (use a long sheet of mural paper to do this). Note significant events along the way, including crystallizing and paralyzing experiences, people who helped you develop the intelligence (or sought to suppress it), school influences, what happened to the intelligence as you became an adult, and so forth. Leave space on the time line to include information about the *future* development of the intelligence (see item 4 below).

3. Create a curriculum planning team or other school group that consists of individuals representing each of the eight intelligences. Before beginning the planning work, take time to share personal experiences of your most highly developed intelligence.

4. Select an intelligence that is not highly developed in your life and create a plan for cultivating it. Look over suggestions for developing the intelligences in *7 Kinds of Smart* (Armstrong, 1999), or create your own list of ways to nurture each intelligence. As you begin personally developing an intelligence, notice whether this process influences what you do in the classroom. Are you bringing more aspects of that intelligence into your professional work?

3

Describing Intelligences in Students

Hide not your talents
They for use were made.
What's a sundial in the shade!

—*Ben Franklin*

Although it's true that each child possesses all eight intelligences and most can develop all eight to a reasonable level of competence, children begin showing what Howard Gardner calls "proclivities" (or inclinations) toward specific intelligences from a very early age. By the time children begin school, they have probably established ways of learning that run more along the lines of some intelligences than others. In this chapter, we will examine how you can begin to describe students' most developed intelligences so that more of their learning in school can take place through their preferred or most highly developed intelligences.

Figure 3.1 provides brief descriptions of the capacities of children who display proclivities in specific intelligences. Keep in mind, however, that most students have strengths in *several* areas, so you should avoid pigeon-holing a child in only one intelligence. You will probably find each student fits two or more of these intelligence descriptions.

Figure 3.1
Eight Ways of Learning

Children who are highly . . .	Think . . .	Love . . .	Need . . .
Word Smart	in words	reading, writing, telling stories, playing word games	books, audio recordings, writing tools and paper, diaries, dialogue, discussion, debate, storytelling
Number/Logic Smart	by reasoning, measuring, and quantifying	experimenting, questioning, doing logical puzzles, calculating	science materials, math manipulatives, trips to science museums, measuring equipment, calculators, coding instructions
Picture Smart	in pictures and images	designing, drawing, visualizing, doodling	art materials, Legos, videos, cameras, movies, slides, imagination games, mazes, puzzles, illustrated books, trips to art museums
Body Smart	through somatic sensations and physical actions	dancing, running, jumping, building, touching, gesturing	role-play, drama, movement, building materials, sports and physical games, tactile experiences, hands-on learning
Music Smart	via rhythms and melodies	singing, whistling, humming, tapping, listening to music, playing a musical instrument	audio (musical) recordings, musical instruments, trips to concerts, musical composition apps
People Smart	by bouncing their ideas off other people	leading, organizing, relating, manipulating, mediating, partying	friends, group games, social gatherings, community events, clubs, mentors, apprenticeships
Self Smart	in relation to their personal needs, feelings, and goals	setting goals, meditating, dreaming, planning, reflecting	secret places, personal journaling, time alone, self-paced projects, choice-based activities
Nature Smart	through nature and natural forms	playing with pets, gardening, investigating nature, raising animals, caring for planet earth	access to and sufficient time in nature, opportunities for interacting with animals, tools for investigating nature (e.g., magnifying glasses, binoculars)

Assessing Students' Multiple Intelligences

There is no "mega-test" on the market that can provide a comprehensive survey of your students' multiple intelligences. If anyone should tell you they have a computer-scored test that in 15 minutes can provide a bar graph showing the eight "peaks" and "valleys" of each student in your class or school, I'd suggest that you be very skeptical. This isn't to say that formal testing can't provide some information about a student's intelligences; as I discuss later, it can provide clues to various intelligences (see, e.g., the Multiple Intelligences Diagnostic Assessment Scales developed by Branton Shearer [Shearer, 2013]). The single best tool for assessing students' multiple intelligences, however, is probably one readily available to all of us: simple observation.

I've often suggested to teachers (half jesting) that one good way to identify students' most highly developed intelligences is to observe how they *misbehave* in class. The strongly Word Smart student will be talking out of turn, the highly Picture Smart student will be doodling or daydreaming, the People Smart student will be socializing, the Body Smart student will be fidgeting, and the Nature Smart student might have smuggled an animal into class without permission! These students are essentially saying through their misbehaviors, "This is how I learn, teacher, and if you don't teach me in the way that I learn, guess what? I'm going to do it *anyway!*" These intelligence-specific misbehaviors, then, are diagnostic indicators of how students want to be taught.

Another good observational indicator of students' proclivities is how they spend their free time in school. In other words, what do they do when nobody is telling them what to do? If you have a "choice time" in class when students can choose from a number of activities, what activities do students pick? Highly Word Smart students might gravitate toward books, People Smart students toward group games and gossip, Picture Smart students toward drawing, Body Smart students toward hands-on building activities, and Nature Smart students toward the gerbil cage or the aquarium. Observing kids in these student-initiated activities can tell you a great deal about how they learn most effectively.

Every teacher should consider keeping a notebook, diary, or journal for recording observations of this kind. Of course, if you're working with 150 students a day at the middle- or high-school level, regularly recording observations for each student would be practically impossible. You might, however, single out two or three of the most troublesome or puzzling students in your class and focus your assessment of the eight intelligences on them. Even if you have a class of 25 to 35 students, writing a couple of lines about each student per week may pay off in the long run. Writing two lines a week for 40 weeks yields 80 lines, or three to four pages of solid observational data for each student.

To help organize your observations of a student's multiple intelligences, you can use a checklist like the one in Figure 3.2. Keep in mind that *this checklist is not a test*. It has not been subjected to any protocols necessary to establish reliability and validity and should be used only in conjunction with other sources of assessment information when describing students' multiple intelligences.

Figure 3.2
MI Inventory for Students

Name of Student: _____
Check items that apply.

Word Smart

____Writes better than average for age

____Enjoys telling stories, jokes, or other oral communications

____Has a good memory for facts and trivia

____Enjoys word games

____Enjoys reading books (or if in preK, gravitates toward books and engages in emergent literacy activities
      with them)

____Spells words accurately (or if in preK, does developmental spelling that is advanced for age)

____Appreciates nonsense rhymes, puns, tongue twisters

____Enjoys listening to the spoken word (stories, commentary on the radio or internet, audio books)

____Has a good vocabulary for age

____Communicates to others in a highly verbal way

Other Word Smart Abilities:

Number/Logic Smart

_____Asks a lot of questions about how things work

_____Enjoys working or playing around with numbers

_____Enjoys math class (or if in preK, enjoys counting, sorting, classifying, and doing other logical tasks)

_____Enjoys math or logic games on the computer (or if no exposure to computers, enjoys non-tech math or science games)

_____Enjoys playing chess, checkers, Go, or other strategy games

_____Enjoys working on logic puzzles or brainteasers (or if in preK, enjoys hearing logical nonsense such as is found in books by Lewis Carroll or Edward Lear)

_____Enjoys putting things in categories, logical patterns, or hierarchies (e.g., worst to best, highest to lowest)

_____Likes to do experiments in science class or during free play time

_____Shows interest in science-related subjects at home

_____Shows interest or aptitude in coding (e.g., computer programming)

Other Number/Logic Smart Abilities:

Picture Smart

_____Reports visualizing in clear visual images

_____Enjoys looking at drawings, photos, and other graphics more than text

_____Daydreams (visualizes) a lot during class time

_____Enjoys art activities

_____Is good at drawing or enjoys it a great deal

_____Likes to view movies, video on the internet, or other highly visual presentations

_____Enjoys doing puzzles, mazes, or similar visual activities

_____Is good at or greatly enjoys building three-dimensional structures (e.g., with wooden blocks, Legos)

_____Gets more information from pictures than words when reading books

_____Doodles in class workbooks, on worksheets, or on other materials

Other Picture Smart Abilities:

Continued

Figure 3.2 (*continued*)
MI Inventory for Students

Body Smart

_____Excels in one or more sports (or if in preK, shows physical abilities advanced for age)

_____Frequently moves, twitches, taps, or fidgets while seated

_____Cleverly mimics other people's gestures or mannerisms

_____Loves to take things apart and has a facility for putting them back together again

_____Likes to handle objects he or she has just seen or been introduced to in the classroom

_____Enjoys running, jumping, wrestling, or similar physical activities

_____Shows skill in a craft (e.g., woodworking, sewing, mechanics) or displays good fine-motor coordination in other ways

_____Has a dramatic way of expressing himself or herself

_____Reports having positive physical sensations that are linked to thinking or problem solving (e.g., "gut feelings")

_____Enjoys working with clay or having other tactile experiences (e.g., finger painting)

Other Body Smart Abilities:

Music Smart

_____Can tell when music is off-key or disturbing in some other way

_____Remembers melodies of songs

_____Has a good singing voice

_____Plays a musical instrument or sings in a choir or other group (or if in preK, enjoys playing percussion instruments or singing in a group)

_____Is particularly sensitive to sounds in the classroom (e.g., school bells)

_____Unconsciously hums to herself

_____Taps rhythmically on the table or desk as he or she works

_____Enjoys dancing to music

_____Responds emotionally to music

_____Sings songs that he or she has learned outside of the classroom

Other Music Smart Abilities:

People Smart

____Enjoys socializing with peers

____Seems to be a natural leader

____Gives advice to friends who have problems

____Seems to be street-smart

____Belongs to clubs, committees, organizations, or informal peer groups

____Enjoys informally teaching other kids new things

____Likes to play games with other kids

____Has two or more close friends

____Has a good sense of empathy or concern for others

____Is sought out by others for social activities

Other People Smart Abilities:

Self Smart

____Displays a sense of independence or a strong will

____Has a realistic sense of his or her abilities and weaknesses

____Does well when left alone to play or study

____Marches to the beat of a different drummer in his or her style of living and learning

____Has an interest or hobby that he or she doesn't talk much about

____Has a good sense of self-direction

____Prefers working alone to working with others

____Accurately expresses how he or she is feeling

____Is able to learn from his or her failures and successes in life

____Displays resilience in response to adverse experiences

Other Self Smart Abilities:

Continued

Figure 3.2 (*continued*)
MI Inventory for Students

Nature Smart

_____Talks a lot about favorite pets or preferred places in nature during class sharing

_____Enjoys field trips in nature, to the zoo, to a natural history museum, or to other places where nature is studied, celebrated, or appreciated

_____Shows sensitivity to natural formations (e.g., while walking outside with the class will notice and comment on mountains, clouds, plants, or animals)

_____Likes to tend to plants in the classroom or enjoys gardening at home

_____Likes to hang around and tend to the gerbil cage, the aquarium, the terrarium, or to spend time with other natural phenomena in class or outdoors

_____Gets excited when studying ecology, nature, plants, or animals

_____Speaks out in class for the rights of animals or the preservation of planet earth

_____Enjoys doing nature projects, such as bird-watching; collecting butterflies, rocks, or insects; studying trees; or raising animals

_____Brings bugs, flowers, leaves, or other natural things to school to share with classmates or teachers

_____Would rather learn outside than in an indoor classroom

Other Nature Smart Abilities:

In addition to observing and filling out checklists, here are some other excellent ways to get assessment information about students' multiple intelligences:

Collect documents. Anecdotal records are not the only way to document students' strongest intelligences. Teachers should consider using their smartphones to snap pictures of students displaying evidence of their multiple intelligences. Photos are particularly useful for documenting products or experiences that might be thrown away or disassembled, such as writing samples or Lego structures. If students show a particular capacity for telling stories or singing songs, use the audio recording feature of your smartphone to record them and save the audio file. If students have drawing or painting abilities, keep samples of their work or take photos of them. If students show their greatest assets playing football, fixing a machine, or planting a flower, capture their performances on video. Ultimately, MI assessment data will consist of several types of documents, including photos, sketches, samples of schoolwork, audio and video files, and more. Maintain an online folder (with students' permission and confidentiality protections) of all these documents available for review by teachers, administrators, parents, and the students themselves. (For more on assessment using the eight intelligences, see Chapter 10.)

Review school records. As two-dimensional and lifeless as they sometimes appear, cumulative records can sometimes provide important clues about a student's multiple intelligences. Look at a student's grades over the years. Are those in math and science consistently higher than those in reading and the social sciences? If so, this may be evidence of an inclination toward Number/Logic Smart rather than Word Smart. High grades in art and graphic design may indicate a well-developed Picture Smart ability, and As and Bs in physical education or shop class may point toward Body Smart capacities.

Similarly, standardized test scores sometimes provide differential information about a student's intelligences. The most commonly used intelligence tests include subtests related to Word Smart (vocabulary and "information" categories), Number/Logic Smart (analogies, arithmetic), and Picture Smart (picture arrangement, block design). A number of other tests may point toward specific intelligences. Here is a partial list of the types of tests that may relate to each intelligence:

- **Word Smart**—reading tests, language tests, the verbal sections of intelligence and achievement tests
- **Number/Logic Smart**—Piagetian assessments, math achievement tests, the reasoning sections of intelligence tests
- **Picture Smart**—visual memory and visual-motor tests, art aptitude tests, performance items on intelligence tests, mechanical reasoning tests
- **Body Smart**—manual dexterity tests, motor subtests in neuropsychological batteries, physical fitness tests
- **People Smart**—social maturity scales, sociograms, interpersonal projective tests (e.g., Family Kinetic Drawing)
- **Self Smart**—self-concept assessments, projective tests, tests of emotional intelligence
- **Nature Smart**—test items that include questions about animals, plants, or natural settings

School records may also contain valuable *anecdotal* information about a student's multiple intelligences. One of the most valuable sources I've discovered in a cumulative file is the kindergarten teacher's report. She is often, sadly the last educator to have seen the child regularly using all eight intelligences (this is becoming less common with the advent of the academic kindergarten). Consequently, comments like "loves finger painting," "moves gracefully during music and dance time," or "creates beautiful structures with blocks" can provide clues to a student's Picture Smart, Music Smart, or Body Smart proclivities.

When reviewing a student's cumulative records as a consultant to school districts years ago, I found it helpful to photocopy the complete contents of the folder (with permission from the school and parents, of course) and then take a yellow highlighter and highlight all the positive information about that student, including the highest grades and test scores and the positive observations of others. I would then type up the highlighted information so that all the positive information was together in one place. This practice provided me with solid information about a student's most developed intelligences that I could then communicate to parents, administrators, and the student's teachers during IEP meetings or other school conferences. This approach can also be used to begin parent-teacher conferences so that they start on a positive note, and is particularly useful with troubled and troublesome students to facilitate constructive solutions to their problems.

Talk with other teachers. If you have students only for English, math, or some other single subject class other than music or PE, then you're usually not in a position to observe them displaying Body Smart or Music Smart gifts (unless, of course, you are regularly teaching through the multiple intelligences). Even if you work with students through all subject areas, you can get additional information by contacting specialists who are working more specifically with one or two of the intelligences. Hence, the art teacher might be the best person to talk with about a student's Picture Smart capabilities, the physical education teacher about certain Body Smart abilities, and the school counselor about People Smart or Self Smart proclivities (although the counselor's ability to share information may be limited due to issues of confidentiality). Regard your colleagues as important sources of assessment information about students' multiple intelligences and meet with them periodically to compare notes. You may find that a child who appears quite "low functioning" in one class will be one of the stars in a class that highlights a different set of intelligences.

Talk with parents. I regard parents as truly significant experts on a child's multiple intelligences. They've had the opportunity to see the child learn and grow under a broad spectrum of circumstances encompassing all of the intelligences. Consequently, they ought to be enlisted in the effort to identify the child's most developed intelligences. During back-to-school night, parents should be introduced to the concept of multiple intelligences and be provided with specific ways through which they can observe and document their child's strengths at home (perhaps using a modified version of the inventory in Figure 3.2). Suggest that the next time you meet for parent-teacher conferences, they bring in information related to their child's multiple intelligences, including scrapbook photos, video clips, samples of their child's work, and any other artifacts related to the child's special hobby or other interests (with the child's permission, of course). This sharing process can get the parent-teacher relationship off on the right foot and also begin the process of seeing the student within a strengths-based context.

Many years ago, the phrase "the six-hour learning disabled child" was used to describe a student who showed little promise or potential in the classroom but was a real achiever outside of school, perhaps as the leader of a youth group, a jack-of-all-trades for neighbors who needed something repaired, or a fledgling entrepreneur with a flourishing small business. Obtaining assessment information from the home is critical in discovering ways to transplant such successes from the home to the school.

Ask students. Students are the ultimate experts on their multiple intelligences because they've lived with their eight intelligences 24/7 since birth. After they've been introduced to the idea of multiple intelligences (see Chapter 4 for ways of teaching MI theory to your students), you can sit down and interview them to discover what they consider to be their most highly developed intelligences. I've used the "MI Pizza" shown in Chapter 4 (Figure 4.1) as a record-keeping tool for making notes while I ask students individually about their abilities in each area. You can also have students draw pictures of themselves doing things in their most developed intelligences (a Picture Smart approach), rank their most to least developed intelligences from 1 to 8 on the MI Pizza (a Number/Logic Smart approach), or pantomime their most developed intelligences (a Body Smart approach). Some of the other activities in Chapter 4 can also help you glean assessment information about students' multiple intelligences.

Set up special activities. If you regularly teach through the multiple intelligences, then you also have frequent opportunities to assess them in your students. For example, if you teach a lesson on fractions eight different ways, note how different children respond to each activity. The child who is falling asleep during the Number/Logic Smart strategy may come alive when the Body Smart approach begins, only to tune out again when a Music Smart method is used. Seeing little lightbulbs go on and off during the course of a day is both an affirmation of the existence of these intelligences as well as a record of the individual differences in your class. Similarly, setting up activity centers for each intelligence (see Chapter 7) provides opportunities for seeing how students function in each area or which areas of the classroom students naturally gravitate toward when they are free to choose. Finally, many of the activities in Chapter 5 (MI Theory and Curriculum Development) and Chapter 6 (MI Theory and Teaching Strategies) can be used as diagnostic indicators as well as teaching activities.

For Further Study

1. Fill out the inventory in Figure 3.2 for each student in your classroom (or, for middle and high school teachers, choose students who are most in need of help). Notice which items can't be answered for lack of sufficient background information about the student and identify methods you can use to obtain information about these items (e.g., parent or child interview, experiential activities). Then use these information-gathering strategies to help complete the inventory. How does your view of individual children change as a result of framing their lives in terms of MI theory? What implications do the inventory results have for your teaching? Alternatively, use Branton Shearer's Multiple Intelligence Developmental Assessment Scales (MIDAS) to glean information (www.miresearch.org).

2. Keep a journal to record observations of students' multiple intelligences. If you observe students outside the classroom (e.g., as a recess or lunchroom monitor), notice if their behavior there differs from their behavior in the classroom. What evidence for each student's multiple intelligences emerges from the anecdotal data?

3. Select one form of documenting students' learning activities that you haven't yet tried, such as creating audio, video, or photo files to capture student learning. Experiment with an approach and notice how effective it may be in providing and communicating information about students' multiple intelligences.

4. Have students express to you their preferred intelligences through one or more of the following forms: writing, drawing, pantomime, group discussion, or personal interview. Make sure they have first been introduced to MI theory through some of the activities described in Chapter 4.

5. During parent-teacher conferences, devote time to gathering information about a student's use of multiple intelligences at home.

6. Review selected students' cumulative files, focusing on data that suggest the presence of special proclivities in one or more of the eight intelligences. If possible, obtain copies of the file material so you can highlight strengths and transcribe them onto separate sheets of paper. Distribute these "strength profiles" at the next meeting called to discuss students' learning.

7. Confer with other teachers about students' multiple intelligences. Set aside special time so that teachers who are responsible for different intelligences in school (e.g., math, shop, art, literature, biology, music) can reflect upon students' performances in each setting.

4

Teaching Students About MI Theory

Give me a fish and I eat for a day. Teach me to fish and I eat for a lifetime.

—*Proverb*

One of the most useful features of MI theory is that it can be explained to a group of children as young as 5 or 6 in as little as five minutes in such a way that they can then use the MI vocabulary to talk about how they learn. While many other theories of learning and personality contain terms and acronyms not easily understood by adults, let alone children (e.g., the INFJ, or "introverted, intuitive, feeling, judging person," of the Myers-Briggs Type Indicator), the eight intelligences of MI theory are linked to concrete things that both young and old alike have had experiences with: words, numbers, pictures, the body, music, people, the self, and nature.

Research in cognitive psychology applied to education supports the notion that children benefit from instructional approaches that help them reflect upon their own learning processes (Price-Mitchell, 2015). When children engage in this type of metacognitive activity, they can select appropriate strategies for problem solving. They can also serve as advocates for themselves when placed in new learning situations.

Five-Minute Introduction to MI Theory

How does a teacher present the theory of multiple intelligences to a group of students? Naturally, the answer to that question will depend in part on the size of the class, the developmental level and background of students, and the instructional resources available. The most direct way to introduce MI theory to students is simply to explain it to them.

When I used to do demonstration teaching of multiple intelligences strategies in school districts, I usually began with a five-minute explanation of the theory so that students would have a context for understanding what I was doing there. I usually began by asking, "How many of you think you're smart?" I discovered over the years that there seems to be an inverse relationship between the number of hands that go up and the grade level—the lower the grade level, the more hands go up, and the higher the grade level, the fewer hands go up. This reminds me of New York University professor Neil Postman's remark that "children go into school as question marks and leave school as periods" (Postman & Weingartner, 1971, p. 60). What do we do in the intervening years to convince children that they're not intelligent?

Regardless of the number of hands that went up, I usually said, "All of you are intelligent—and not just in one way. Each of you is intelligent in at least eight different ways." I would then draw an "MI Pizza" (a circle divided into eight slices) on the blackboard and begin to explain the model. "First, there is something called Word Smart." As shown in Figure 4.1, I accompany each term with a graphic symbol to spatially reinforce the intelligence. For each intelligence, I asked a related question, such as "How many people here can speak?" After hands go up, I'll respond, "In order to speak, you have to use words, so all of you are Word Smart!" Essentially, I asked questions that build inclusion. I steered clear of questions that might exclude lots of students, such as "How many of you have read 15 books in the past month?" This is a learning model not for deciding which exclusive group one is a member of, but for celebrating all of one's potential for learning. Otherwise, teachers might be preparing the way for students to say, "I just learned in school today that I'm not Word Smart." Here is a list of questions you might ask relating to the other intelligences:

- **Number/Logic Smart:** "How many of you can do math?" "How many of you have done a science experiment?"

- **Picture Smart:** "How many of you draw?" "How many of you can see pictures in your head when you close your eyes?" "How many of you enjoy watching television and films or playing video games?"
- **Body Smart:** "How many of you like sports?" "How many of you enjoy making things with your hands, like models or Lego structures?"
- **Music Smart:** "How many of you enjoy listening to music?" "How many of you have ever played a musical instrument or sung a song?"
- **People Smart:** "How many of you have at least one friend?" "How many of you enjoy working in groups at least part of the time in school?"
- **Self Smart:** "How many of you have a special place you go to when you want to get away from everybody and everything?" "How many of you like to spend at least part of the time working on your own here in class?"
- **Nature Smart:** "How many of you enjoy being out in nature?" "How many of you have pets or enjoy spending time with animals?"

Figure 4.1
MI Pizza

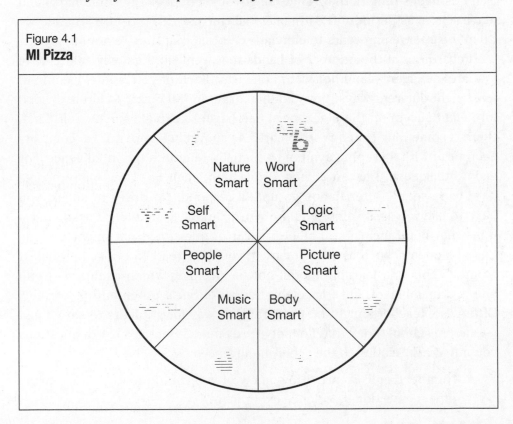

You can develop your own questions to illustrate each intelligence. Just make sure they build in inclusion and give children a chance to see themselves as intelligent. You can also give examples of what Howard Gardner calls the "end-states" of each intelligence—that is, examples of people who have developed one or more intelligence to a high level of competence. These examples provide students with inspirational models. Pick famous figures and heroes from the students' own cultural worlds (see Figure 4.2). Examples might include the following:

- Authors of children's literature that the class has been reading (Word Smart)
- Famous scientists students have studied in class (Number/Logic Smart)
- Illustrators of children's literature, famous cartoonists, and filmmakers (Picture Smart)
- Famous sports heroes and actors (Body Smart)
- Famous rock stars, rappers, and other musicians (Music Smart)
- Talk show hosts and politicians (People Smart)
- Famous entrepreneurs and other "self-made" individuals (Self Smart)
- Animal experts and nature explorers (Nature Smart)

Before you finish your brief introduction to MI to your class, take a few extra minutes to explain to your students that their success in school and in life depends upon how much time and effort they're willing to put into developing their eight intelligences. The work of Stanford social psychologist Carol Dweck (2007) is instructive here. She makes a distinction between two types of "mindset" regarding implicit views of intelligence. To Dweck, people with a *fixed mindset* believe that intelligence is innate; you're either born with it or you aren't. By contrast, those with a *growth mindset* believe that success and the intelligence that supports it depend more on hard work than anything. Here's how Dweck put it:

> In a fixed mindset students believe their basic abilities, their intelligence, their talents, are just fixed traits. They have a certain amount and that's that, and then their goal becomes to look smart all the time and never look dumb. In a growth mindset students understand that their talents and abilities can be developed through effort, good teaching and persistence. They don't

necessarily think everyone's the same or anyone can be Einstein, but they believe everyone can get smarter if they work at it." (quoted in Morehead, 2012)

Figure 4.2
Prominent Individuals from Minority Cultures

Intelligence	African American	Asian and Polynesian American	Hispanic American	Native American
Word Smart	Toni Morrison	Amy Tan	Isabel Allende	Vine Deloria Jr.
Number/ Logic Smart	Benjamin Banneker	Yuan Lee	Luis Alvarez	Robert Whitman
Picture Smart	Elizabeth Catlett Mora	I.M. Pei	Frida Kahlo	Oscar Howe
Body Smart	Jackie Joyner-Kersee	Kristi Yamaguchi	Juan Marichal	Jim Thorpe
Music Smart	Mahalia Jackson	Midori	Linda Ronstadt	Buffy Sainte-Marie
People Smart	Martin Luther King Jr.	Daniel K. Inouye	Xavier L. Suarez	Russell Means
Self Smart	Malcolm X	S.I. Hayakawa	Cesar Chavez	Black Elk
Nature Smart	George Washington Carver	Nainoa Thompson	Severo Ochoa	Wilfred Foster Denetclaw Jr.

According to Dweck's research, people with a growth mindset are more willing to work through failure and keep persisting until they succeed. Thus, they achieve better grades and higher test scores than their peers. Her research also indicates that those with a fixed mindset can be taught to embrace a growth mindset, leading to improved academic performance and increased resilience in the face of bullying or peer exclusion (Yeager &

Dweck, 2012). It may be helpful to explain to students Dweck's research and the importance of having a growth mindset.

Activities for Teaching MI Theory

As you teach your students about MI theory, you'll want to go beyond a simple verbal explanation of the model. Ultimately, you should strive to teach the model through all eight of the intelligences, so that you practice what you preach. There are a number of ways of following up your five-minute introduction with reinforcing activities and supplementary experiences. Here are some examples.

Career Day: If you regularly bring members of your community into the classroom to talk about their jobs, begin to situate this activity within a multiple intelligences framework. Bring in an editor to talk about the kinds of Word Smart activities he engages in, a financial planner to speak about how being Number/Logic Smart enables her to help people with their budgets, or an architect to explain the usefulness of being Picture Smart in her career. Other Career Day guests might include an athlete (Body Smart), a professional musician (Music Smart), a counselor (People Smart), a person who has started a business (Self Smart), or a veterinarian (Nature Smart). Keep in mind that each career usually requires several intelligences; you might want to discuss how each vocation brings together a combination of intelligences in a unique way. These presentations are very important in emphasizing to students that each of the intelligences plays a vital part in people's success in the world. You may want to speak beforehand with the guests about the model so they can work it into their presentations. Or you can simply follow up their appearances by relating what they said or did to one or more of the eight intelligences.

Field trips: Take students to places in the community where each of the intelligences is particularly valued and practiced. Destinations might include a library (Word Smart), a science lab (Number/Logic Smart), a crafts factory (Body Smart), a radio station that plays music (Music Smart), a graphic design studio (Picture Smart), a public relations firm (People Smart), a psychologist's office (Self Smart), or a zoo (Nature Smart). Again, seeing these intelligences in context gives students a more accurate and real-life picture of MI theory than they could ever get in a classroom setting.

Biographies: Have students study the lives of well-known people proficient in one or more of the intelligences (see Gardner, 1993b). Subjects for study might include Toni Morrison (Word Smart), Marie Curie (Number/Logic Smart), Vincent Van Gogh (Picture Smart), Roberto Clemente (Body Smart), Yo-Yo Ma (Music Smart), Martin Luther King Jr. (People Smart), Sigmund Freud (Self Smart), and Jane Goodall (Nature Smart). Make sure the people studied are representative of your students' cultural, racial, gender, and ethnic backgrounds (see Figure 4.2).

Lesson plans: Teach an eight-way lesson on a particular subject or in a specific skill area (see Chapter 5 for guidelines on creating MI lessons). Explain beforehand to students that you are going to teach this material using each of the eight intelligences and that they should pay attention to how each of the eight intelligences is covered. After the lesson, ask students to describe your use of each intelligence. This activity requires students to reflect upon the kinds of processes necessary for each intelligence and helps develop their metacognitive abilities. You may also want to ask them which particular method or methods they liked best. In this way, you can help students begin to appreciate which strategies they prefer to use when learning something new.

Quick experiential activities: Have students complete eight simple activities, each one of which draws primarily upon the use of one intelligence. Here are some examples:

- "Write down a few lines from a poem that you know." (Word Smart)
- "Tell me how long ago a million seconds ago was." (Number/Logic Smart)
- "Draw a picture of an animal." (Picture Smart)
- "Go outside and run to the end of the block and back." (Body Smart)
- "Let's all sing 'Row, Row, Row Your Boat' together." (Music Smart)
- "Turn to a partner and share something nice that happened to you this week." (People Smart)
- "Close your eyes and think about the happiest moment in your life—you won't have to share it with anybody." (Self Smart)
- "Look out the window and notice all the living things and natural formations you can see." (Nature Smart)

Adjust the activities to the ability level of your students, choosing ones that just about everyone can do and giving those who can't do them modified versions of the activities. You can use this approach either before or after explicitly describing the "eight kinds of smart." Make sure to ask students which activities they prefer, and remember to relate each activity to one or more of the eight intelligences.

Wall displays: If you walk into a typical U.S. classroom, you'll sometimes find a poster of Albert Einstein on the wall. Einstein is probably a good representative of multiple intelligences because he used several of them in his work, including Picture Smart, Body Smart, and Number/Logic Smart. Rather than just displaying this one poster, however, consider hanging eight posters on the wall, each representing a person especially proficient in one of the intelligences (see Gardner, 1993b, the "Biographies" section in this chapter, and Figure 4.2 for suggested names). Or hang a banner reading "Eight Ways to Learn" or "This Is How We Learn in School" and display photos of students using each of the intelligences.

Displays: Show products made by students in the school that required the use of each of the eight intelligences. Examples might include essays, stories, or poems (Word Smart); computer code (Number/Logic Smart); drawings and paintings (Picture Smart); musical scores (Music Smart); three-dimensional projects (Body Smart); collaborative projects (People Smart); individual projects (Self Smart); or naturalist investigations (Nature Smart). The products could be displayed on a shelf, in a glass case, or on a table, and rotated regularly so all students have a chance to display their achievements. Make sure each product is labeled with the intelligence or intelligences required to produce it to help reinforce MI theory with your class.

Readings: For high school students, you can assign readings from any of the numerous books and articles on the theory of multiple intelligences, including chapters from *Frames of Mind* (Gardner, 2011) or *7 Kinds of Smart* (Armstrong, 1999). Upper elementary and middle school students can read my book *You're Smarter Than You Think: A Kid's Guide to Multiple Intelligences* (Armstrong, 2014). Appendix B includes many more suggested readings.

MI tables: Set up eight tables in the classroom, each clearly labeled with a sign referring to one of the eight intelligences. On each table, place an activity card indicating what students are to do: At the Word Smart table, students can do a writing activity; at the Number/Logic Smart table, a math or science activity; at the Picture Smart table, a drawing activity; at the Body Smart table, a building activity; at the Music Smart table, a musical activity; at the People Smart table, a collaborative activity; at the Self Smart table, a self-reflection activity; and at the Nature Smart table, an activity that involves observing an animal or plant. Divide the class equally into eight groups, assigning each group to a particular table. Have the groups work at the activity for a designated amount of time (perhaps five minutes), and then use a musical signal (e.g., a bell) to indicate that it's time to move to the next table (moving clockwise). Continue until all students have been to each table and experienced each activity. Afterward, talk about students' preferences, relating each activity to its primary intelligence. (Chapter 7 deals more specifically with how to set up different types of activity centers that reflect a multiple intelligences perspective.)

Human intelligence hunt: If you're introducing MI theory at the beginning of the school year when students still don't know each other very well, a "human intelligence hunt" is a fun way to introduce students to the eight kinds of smart as well as to one another. The activity is based on the premise that each of us is a "treasure chest" filled with special gifts in the form of our intelligences. Sometimes, though, we're unaware of other people's gifts, so we have to go on a "treasure hunt"—in this case, an "intelligence hunt"—to discover one another's special talents. Each student receives a list of activities similar to those given in Figure 4.3 (for older students) or Figure 4.4 (for younger students). On a signal, students take the activity sheet along with a pen or pencil and find other students in the room who can do the activities listed. There are three basic rules: Students must actually perform the activities listed, not simply say they can do them; once a student performs an activity to the other treasure hunters' satisfaction, she should initial the blank space next to the activity on the sheet; and each student must have eight different sets of initials on her sheet (e.g., no using one person for more than one activity).

You can modify the activities listed in Figure 4.3 to include activities geared to your students' aptitudes and abilities. Figure 4.4 shows what it might look like for younger students. For emerging literacy learners, you can even create a hunt based entirely on pictures, which would involve students finding others who enjoy doing the kind of activity depicted in each picture. After the treasure hunt, talk about what students learned concerning one another's gifts or intelligences.

Figure 4.3
Human Intelligence Hunt (Older Students)

Find someone who can

- Hum a few bars of Beethoven's Fifth Symphony (Music Smart).
- Do a simple dance step (Body Smart).
- Recite four lines from a poem (Word Smart).
- Explain why the sky is blue (Number/Logic Smart).
- Briefly share a recent dream (Self Smart).
- Draw a picture of a horse (Picture Smart).
- Say they enjoy this activity (People Smart).
- Name five different types of birds found in the neighborhood (Nature Smart).

Figure 4.4
Human Intelligence Hunt (Younger Students)

Find someone who can

- Sing the "Happy Birthday to You" song (Music Smart).
- Touch their toes with the palms of their hands (Body Smart).
- Tell a funny joke or tongue twister (Word Smart).
- Complete the following sequence of numbers: 2, 4, 6, 8, ___ (Number/Logic Smart).
- Tell about one thing that she really does well (Self Smart).
- Find five blue things in the room (Picture Smart).
- Make a face that communicates to people the feeling that he is really happy (People Smart).
- Name the nonhuman living thing that is nearest to where she is standing (inside or outside) (Nature Smart).

Board games: Create a board game based on the eight intelligences. Take a manila file folder and a magic marker and draw a winding roadway divided into many small squares. Assign each intelligence a color and graphic symbol and then place an appropriately colored intelligence symbol on each square of the game board. You may use the symbols from the MI Pizza in Figure 4.1 or make up your own. Then, create eight sets of two-by-three-inch game cards from eight different hues of paper that match the colored symbols on the game board. On each set of game cards, type or write activities that involve using a specific intelligence. Here, for instance, are some activities for a Picture Smart game at the primary level:

- Draw a picture of a dog in less than 30 seconds.
- Find an object in the shape of a circle in the class.
- Tell us your favorite color.
- Describe four blue things you see in the room.
- Close your eyes and describe the pictures in your mind.

Make sure the activities are within the capabilities of most of your students. Then, get a pair of dice and some miniature plastic figurines to use as game pieces, and start playing! Alternatively, there are commercially available games that include activities that cover most of the multiple intelligences (e.g., the board game Cranium).

MI stories, songs, or plays: Be creative and make up your own story, song, or play for teaching the idea of multiple intelligences (your students can help you). You might, for example, create a story about eight children, each an expert in a particular intelligence, who don't get along very well and who are forced into an adventure that requires them to travel to distant magical lands. In each part of the story they encounter challenges that require the unique intelligence of a particular child. For example, the children might come to a land where, in order to be understood, people have to communicate through singing, so the Music Smart child guides them. In another land, they might fall into a hole and only get out through the Body Smart child's expertise. At the end of the story, the children are able to accomplish their task (to retrieve a golden jewel, perhaps) by drawing on the talents or intelligences of each one of them. This story can then be used as a metaphor for classroom behavior: we need to respect and find ways of celebrating the unique talents and gifts of each student. The story might be put on as a play, a puppet show, or a musical and performed for other students in the school.

There are undoubtedly many other activities that would help teach students about the theory of multiple intelligences. The development of such experiences should be an ongoing process throughout the year. After you have introduced a few activities, it may be helpful to prominently display a poster listing the eight intelligences, perhaps in the form of the MI Pizza. When something happens that seems to relate to one or more of the eight intelligences, you can then use the poster to help emphasize the relationship between what just happened and a particular intelligence. For example, if several students are working on a collaborative project, and one of the students is having trouble agreeing with the others, you can point out that most of the group wants to use their People Smart abilities while the individual student seems to want to use his Self Smart (and then you can decide whether to encourage the one student to see this as an opportunity to develop his People Smart, or, alternatively, suggest that he work individually using his Self Smart abilities). Commend a student who has created a particularly apt visual illustration for really exercising her Picture Smart in the work. By modeling the practical uses of MI theory frequently in the daily activities of the classroom, you will help students internalize the theory, and you should begin to see them use its vocabulary to make sense out of their own learning experiences.

For Further Study

1. Drawing upon the material in this chapter or activities of your own choosing, develop a way to introduce the theory of multiple intelligences to your students. Note students' initial reactions. Follow your introduction with supplementary activities. How long does it take before students begin to use MI terms themselves? Note two or three examples of how students used the theory to explain their own learning processes.

2. Create a mini-unit or special course for students on "learning about learning" that includes instruction in the theory of multiple intelligences (consider using my book *You're Smarter Than You Think: A Kid's Guide to Multiple Intelligences* [Armstrong, 2014] as a guide). Include readings, exercises, activities, and strategies designed to help students understand their thinking and learning processes so that they can learn more effectively.

3. Design a special wall display, bulletin board, or exhibit area where the eight intelligences are honored and celebrated. Include posters of famous people, photos of students engaged in MI activities, examples of products made by students that reflect different intelligences, or examples of other ways to convey the idea of the eight intelligences to students, teachers, parents, and members of the community.

5

MI Theory and Curriculum Development

We do not see in our descriptions [of classroom activity] . . . much opportunity for students to become engaged with knowledge so as to employ their full range of intellectual abilities. And one wonders about the meaningfulness of whatever is acquired by students who sit listening or performing relatively repetitive exercises, year after year. It appears to me that students spending 12 years in the schools we studied would be unlikely to experience much novelty. Does part of the brain just sleep, then?

—*John I. Goodlad*

MI theory makes its greatest contribution to education by suggesting that teachers need to expand their repertoire of techniques, tools, and strategies beyond the typical Word Smart and Number/Logic Smart abilities predominantly tapped in U.S. classrooms. Federal accountability laws such as No Child Left Behind and the Every Student Succeeds Act have created a climate in which Word Smart and Number/Logic Smart standardized tests, and the Word Smart and Number/Logic Smart methods to prepare for them, have overwhelmed the landscape in schools across the United States (see Ravitch, 2016). Similarly, the establishment of a standards movement that includes the Common Core State Standards and individual state variations on those standards has presented a challenge to educators in trying to create a pluralistic response to this one-size-fits-all mentality (Strauss, 2014); (see Appendix A for examples of multiple intelligences lesson ideas based on Common Core and other standards-based math, English, science, and arts benchmarks). In this context, the theory of multiple intelligences functions not only as a specific remedy to one-sidedness in teaching but also as a "metamodel" for organizing and synthesizing all the educational innovations that have sought to break out of this narrowly confined approach to learning. In doing so, MI theory provides a broad range of stimulating activities to "awaken" the slumbering brains of our disengaged "robo-students" (Connor & Pope, 2013).

The Historical Background of Multimodal Teaching

Multiple intelligences as a philosophy guiding instruction is hardly a new concept. Even Plato, in a manner of speaking, seemed aware of the importance of multimodal teaching when he wrote, "Do not use compulsion, but let early education be a sort of amusement; you will then be better able to find out the natural bent" (1952, p. 399). More recently, virtually all the pioneers of modern education developed systems of teaching based upon more than verbal pedagogy. The 18th-century philosopher Jean-Jacques Rousseau declared in his classic treatise on education, *Emile,* that the child must learn not through words but through experience: "You are alarmed to see him consume his early years doing nothing. What! Is it nothing to be happy? Is it nothing to jump, play, and run all day? He will never be so busy in his life" (Rousseau, 1979, p. 107). The Swiss reformer Johann Heinrich Pestalozzi (2013) emphasized an integrated curriculum that regarded physical, moral, and intellectual training as based solidly on concrete experiences. And the founder of the modern-day kindergarten, Friedrich Froebel (2005), developed a curriculum consisting of hands-on experiences with manipulatives ("gifts"), in addition to playing games, singing songs, gardening, and caring for animals. In the 20th century, innovators like Maria Montessori (1972) and John Dewey (1997) evolved systems of instruction based upon MI-like techniques, including Montessori's tactile letters and other self-paced materials and Dewey's vision of the classroom as a democratic microcosm of society.

By the same token, many recent alternative educational models essentially are multiple intelligences systems using different terminologies (and with varying levels of emphasis upon the different intelligences). Collaborative learning, for example, seems to place its greatest emphasis upon People Smart, yet specific activities can involve students in each of the other intelligences as well. Similarly, project-based learning and the "maker movement" engage students in Body Smart hands-on learning as well as Self Smart planning, Picture Smart designing, and Logic/Number Smart thinking.

MI theory essentially encompasses what good teachers have always done in their teaching: reaching beyond the text and the blackboard to awaken students' minds. Two exemplary movies about great teachers, *Stand and Deliver* (1987) and *Dead Poets Society* (1989), emphasize this point remarkably well. In *Stand and Deliver,* based on the true story of Jaime Escalante (played by Edward James Olmos), a high school mathematics teacher uses apples to introduce fractions, fingers to teach multiplication, and imagery and metaphor to clarify negative numbers (if one digs a hole in the ground, the hole represents negative numbers, and the pile of dirt next to it signifies positive numbers). John Keating (played by Robin Williams), the prep school instructor in *Dead Poets Society,* has students reading literary passages while kicking soccer balls and listening to classical music.

MI theory provides a way for *all* teachers to reflect upon their best teaching methods and to understand why these methods work (or why they work well for some students but not for others). It also helps teachers expand their current teaching repertoire to include a broader range of methods, materials, and techniques for reaching an ever wider and more diverse range of learners.

The MI Teacher

A teacher in an MI classroom contrasts sharply with a teacher in a traditional Word Smart and Number/Logic Smart classroom. In the traditional classroom, the teacher lectures while standing at the front of the classroom, writes on the blackboard or whiteboard, asks students questions about the assigned reading or handouts, and has students doing various types of written work often in workbooks or on worksheets. In the MI classroom, while keeping an educational objective firmly in mind, the teacher judiciously shifts the method of presentation from Word Smart to Picture Smart to Music Smart and so on, often combining intelligences in creative ways.

It's perfectly fine for an MI teacher to spend time lecturing and writing on the whiteboard at the front of the room. This, after all, is a legitimate teaching technique. Teachers have simply been doing too much of it. The MI teacher may draw pictures on the whiteboard or show a video clip to illustrate an idea. He may play music at some point during the day to set the stage for an objective, to make a point about the objective, or to provide an environment for studying the objective. The MI teacher may engage students in hands-on experiences, whether they involve getting students up and moving about, passing an artifact around to bring to life the material studied, or having students build something tangible to help integrate their understanding of the learning objective. The MI teacher may also have students interacting with each other in different ways (e.g., in pairs, small groups, or large groups); plan time for students to engage in self-reflection, undertake self-paced work, or link their personal experiences and feelings to the material being studied; and create opportunities for learning to occur through interactions with living things or systems.

Such characterizations of what the MI teacher may or may not do, however, should not serve to rigidify the instructional dimensions of MI theory. The theory can be implemented in a wide range of instructional contexts, from highly traditional settings where teachers spend much of their time directly teaching students, to open environments where students regulate most of their own learning. Even traditional Word Smart teaching can take place in a variety of ways designed to stimulate the eight intelligences. Teachers are using MI principles within a traditional teacher-centered perspective when they lecture with rhythmic emphasis (Music Smart), draw pictures on the board to illustrate points (Picture Smart), make dramatic gestures as they talk (Body Smart), pause to give students time to reflect (Self Smart), ask questions that invite spirited discussion (People Smart), and include references to nature in their lectures (Nature Smart).

Key Materials and Methods of MI Teaching

There are innumerable teaching tools in MI theory that go beyond the traditional teacher-as-lecturer mode of instruction. Figure 5.1 provides a quick summary of some of these MI teaching methods. The list on pages 58–61 provides a broader, but still far from complete, survey of techniques and materials that can be employed in teaching using the multiple intelligences. (Italicized items in the list are discussed more fully in Chapter 6.)

Figure 5.1
Summary of the Eight Ways of Teaching

Intelligence	Teaching Activities (Examples)	Teaching Materials (Examples)	Instructional Strategies	Sample Educational Movement (Primary Intelligence)	Sample Teacher Presentation Skill	Sample Activity to Begin a Lesson (Anticipatory Set)
Word Smart	Lectures, discussions, word games, storytelling, choral reading, journal writing	Books, audio recorders, stamp sets, audio books, word processing software	Read about it, write about it, talk about it, listen to it	Critical Literacy	Teaching through storytelling	Long, unfamiliar word on the blackboard
Number/ Logic Smart	Brainteasers, problem solving, science experiments, mental calculation, number games, Socratic teaching	Calculators, math manipulatives, science equipment, math games	Quantify it, think critically about it, put it in a logical framework, experiment with it, find logical patterns in it	Critical Thinking	Socratic questioning	A logical paradox
Picture Smart	Visual presentations, art activities, imagination games, mind mapping, metaphor, visualization	Graphs, maps, video, connector sets, art materials, optical illusions, photography, picture library	See it, draw it, visualize it, color-code it, mind-map it, make a video of it, take a photo of it	Expressive Arts Instruction	Drawing/mind-mapping concepts	Unusual or funny picture or photo on the overhead
Body Smart	Hands-on learning, drama, dance, sports that teach, tactile activities, relaxation exercises	Building tools, clay, sports equipment, manipulatives, tactile learning resources	Build it, act it out, touch it, dance it, fix it, hold it, invent it	Maker Movement	Using gestures/dramatic expressions	Mysterious artifact passed around the class
Music Smart	Rhythmic learning, rapping, singing, using songs that teach	Audio recorder, audio music collection, musical instruments	Sing it, rap it, listen to it, chant it, play it, dance to it	Orff Schulwerk	Using voice rhythmically	Relevant background music as students are coming into class

People Smart	Cooperative learning, peer or cross-age tutoring, community involvement, social gatherings, simulations	Board games, party supplies, props for role-plays, social spaces, social media	Teach it, collaborate on it, interact with respect to it	Collaborative Learning	Dynamically interacting with students	A pair-and-share on what each partner thinks will be the objective for the day.
Self Smart	Individualized instruction, independent study, electives, self-determination skill building	Use of self-checking materials (e.g., answer key), personal journals, materials, or equipment for project-based learning	Connect it to your personal life, make choices about it, reflect on it, become emotionally engaged to it	Individualized Instruction	Teacher sharing stories of own life to make an emotional impression	A personal reflection students are asked to make on a key idea for the lesson
Nature Smart	Nature study, ecological awareness, care of animals, gardening	Plants, animals, naturalists' tools (e.g., binoculars), gardening tools	Connect it to living things and/or natural phenomena and system	Ecological Studies	Linking subject matter to natural phenomena	An unusual plant, rock, shell, bone, insect, or animal to spark discussion

Word Smart

- *Audio recording*
- Books
- *Brainstorming*
- Choral reading
- Debates
- Extemporaneous speaking
- Individualized reading
- *Journal writing*
- Large- and small-group discussions
- Lectures
- Manuals
- Memorizing linguistic facts
- *Publishing*
- Reading to the class
- Sharing time
- *Storytelling*
- Student speeches
- Talking books
- Writing activities
- Word games

Number/Logic Smart

- *Calculations and quantifications*
- *Classifications and categorizations*
- Coding
- *Heuristics*
- Logic puzzles and games
- Logical problem-solving exercises
- Logical-sequential presentation of subject matter
- Mathematical problems on the board
- Piagetian cognitive exercises
- *Science thinking*
- Scientific demonstrations
- *Socratic questioning*

Picture Smart

- Art appreciation
- Charts, graphs, diagrams, and maps
- *Color cues*
- Computer graphics
- Construction kits
- Creative daydreaming
- *Graphic symbols*
- *Idea sketching*
- Imaginative storytelling
- Mind maps and other visual organizers
- Optical illusions
- Painting, collage, and other visual arts
- Photography
- Picture literacy experiences
- *Picture metaphors*
- Videos and movies
- Visual awareness activities
- Visual pattern seeking
- Visual puzzles and mazes
- Visual thinking exercises
- *Visualization*

Body Smart

- *Body answers*
- *Body maps*
- *Classroom theater*
- Competitive and cooperative games
- Cooking, gardening, and other "messy" activities
- Crafts
- Creative movement
- Field trips
- *Hands-on thinking*
- *Kinesthetic concepts*

- Math manipulatives
- Mime activities
- Physical awareness exercises
- Physical education activities
- Physical relaxation exercises
- Tactile materials and experiences
- Use of kinesthetic imagery
- Using body language/hand signals to communicate
- Virtual reality software

Music Smart

- Creating new melodies for concepts
- *Discographies*
- Group singing
- Linking music with concepts
- Listening to inner musical imagery
- *Mood music*
- Music appreciation
- Musical composition software
- *Musical concepts*
- Playing live music on piano, guitar, or other instruments
- Playing percussion instruments
- Playing recorded music
- *Rhythms, songs, raps, and chants*
- Singing, humming, or whistling
- *Supermemory music*

People Smart

- Academic clubs
- Apprenticeships
- *Board games*
- *Collaborative groups*
- Community involvement
- Conflict mediation
- Cross-age tutoring

- Group brainstorming sessions
- Interpersonal interaction
- Parties or social gatherings as context for learning
- *Peer sharing*
- *People sculptures*
- *Simulations*
- Social media

Self Smart

- *Choice time*
- Exposure to motivating materials
- *Feeling-toned moments*
- *Goal-setting sessions*
- Independent study
- Individualized projects and games
- Interest centers
- *One-minute reflection periods*
- Options for homework
- *Personal connections*
- Private spaces for study
- Self-esteem activities
- Self-paced instruction

Nature Smart

- Aquariums, terrariums, and other portable ecosystems
- Class weather station
- *Eco-study*
- Gardening
- Nature-oriented software
- Nature study tools (binoculars, telescope, microscope)
- Nature videos, films, and movies
- *Nature walks*
- *Pets in the classroom*
- *Plants as props*
- *Windows onto learning*

How to Create MI Lesson Plans

On one level, MI theory applied to the curriculum might best be represented by a loose and diverse collection of teaching strategies such as those listed on the preceding pages. In this sense, MI theory represents a model of instruction that has no distinct rules other than meeting the cognitive demands imposed by the intelligences themselves and the specific needs of the domain in which they are being used (e.g., math, science, literature). Teachers can pick and choose from the above activities, implementing the theory in ways suited to their own unique teaching style and congruent with their educational philosophy (as long as that philosophy does not declare that all children learn in the same way).

On a deeper level, MI theory suggests a set of parameters to help educators create new curricula. In fact, the theory provides a context within which educators can address any skill, content area, theme, or instructional objective and brainstorm at least eight ways to teach it. Essentially, MI theory offers a means of building daily lesson plans, weekly units, yearlong themes, and other programs in such a way that all students can have their strongest intelligences addressed at least part of the time.

The best way to approach curriculum development using the theory of multiple intelligences is by thinking about how to "translate" the material from one intelligence to another. In other words, how can we take a linguistic symbol system, such as the English language, and translate it into the languages of other intelligences, namely, pictures, physical or musical expression, logical symbols or concepts, social interactions, personal connections, and nature associations? The following seven-step procedure suggests one way to create lesson plans or curriculum units using MI theory as an organizing framework:

1. **Focus on a specific objective or topic.** You might want to develop a curriculum on a large scale (e.g., a yearlong theme) or create a program for reaching a specific instructional objective (e.g., for a student's IEP or individualized education program). Whether you have chosen "ecology" or "the *schwa* sound" as a focus, make sure you have clearly and concisely stated the objective. Place the objective or topic in the center of a sheet of paper, as shown in Figure 5.2 (you can also do this using Inspiration, Kidspiration, or another mind-mapping app).

Figure 5.2
MI Planning Questions

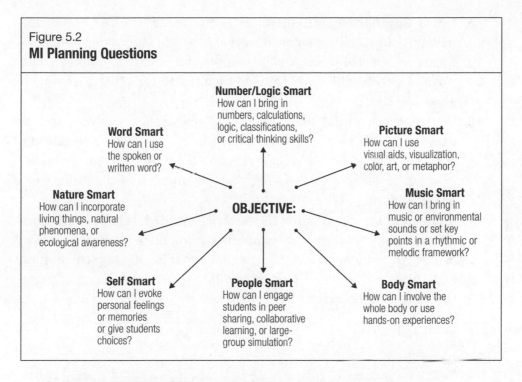

Number/Logic Smart
How can I bring in numbers, calculations, logic, classifications, or critical thinking skills?

Word Smart
How can I use the spoken or written word?

Picture Smart
How can I use visual aids, visualization, color, art, or metaphor?

Nature Smart
How can I incorporate living things, natural phenomena, or ecological awareness?

OBJECTIVE:

Music Smart
How can I bring in music or environmental sounds or set key points in a rhythmic or melodic framework?

Self Smart
How can I evoke personal feelings or memories or give students choices?

People Smart
How can I engage students in peer sharing, collaborative learning, or large-group simulation?

Body Smart
How can I involve the whole body or use hands-on experiences?

2. **Ask key MI questions.** Figure 5.2 shows the types of questions to ask when developing a curriculum for a specific objective or topic. These questions help prime the creative pump for the next steps.

3. **Consider the possibilities.** Look over the questions in Figure 5.2, the list of MI techniques and materials in Figure 5.1, and the descriptions of specific strategies in Chapter 6. Which of the methods and materials seem most appropriate? Think also of other possibilities not listed.

4. **Brainstorm.** Using an MI Planning Sheet like the one shown in Figure 5.3, begin listing as many teaching approaches as possible for each intelligence. You should end up with something like the sheet shown in Figure 5.4. When listing approaches, be specific about the strategy (e.g., "video clip of rain forest" rather than simply "video clip"). The rule of thumb for brainstorming is to list *everything* that comes to mind. Aim for at least 20 or 30 ideas, with a minimum of 2 or 3 for each intelligence. Brainstorming with colleagues may help further stimulate your thinking.

5. **Select appropriate activities.** Circle the ideas on your completed planning sheet that seem most workable within your educational setting. You can also use this mind-mapping technique to come up with ways of assessing knowledge (see Chapter 10 for other assessment ideas using MI theory).

6. **Set up a sequential plan.** Using the approaches you've selected, design a lesson plan or unit (or methods of assessment) around the specific topic or objective chosen. Figure 5.5 shows what an eight-day lesson plan might look like when 35 to 40 minutes of class time each day are allotted to the objective.

7. **Implement the plan.** Gather the materials needed, select an appropriate time frame, and then carry out the lesson plan. Modify the lesson as needed to incorporate changes that occur during implementation (e.g., based on feedback from students). Appendix A contains examples of standards-based MI lesson ideas.

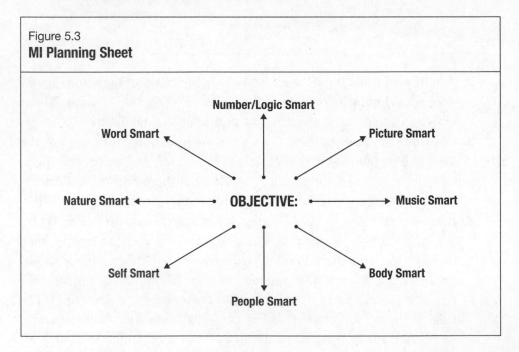

Figure 5.3
MI Planning Sheet

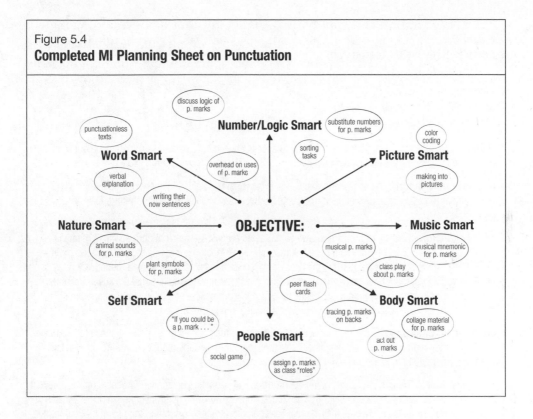

Figure 5.4
Completed MI Planning Sheet on Punctuation

MI and Interdisciplinary Instruction

Educators are increasingly recognizing the importance of teaching students from an interdisciplinary point of view. Although academic skill teaching or the teaching of isolated chunks of knowledge may provide students with competencies or background information that can prove useful to them in their further education, such instruction often fails to connect students to the world outside of school. Consequently, educators are turning toward models of instruction that more closely imitate or mirror life in some significant way. Such instruction is frequently *thematic* in nature. Themes cut through traditional curricular boundaries, weave together subjects and skills that are found naturally in life, and provide students with opportunities to use their multiple intelligences in practical ways. As Susan Kovalik (1993), developer of the Integrated Thematic Instruction (ITI) model (now called Highly Effective Teaching [HET]), puts it: "A key feature of *here*

Figure 5.5
Sample Eight-Day MI Lesson Plan

Level: 1st grade
Subject: English language arts
Standard: CCSS.ELA-LITERACY.L.1.2.B

Objective: To understand the function of, and differences between, four punctuation marks: the question mark, period, comma, and exclamation point.

Monday (Word Smart): Students listen to a verbal explanation of the function of punctuation marks, read sentences having examples of each mark, and complete a worksheet requiring them to fill in their own marks.

Tuesday (Picture Smart): The teacher draws on the board graphic images that correspond in meaning and form to each mark. Question mark = a hook because questions "hook" us into requiring an answer; exclamation point = a staff that you pound on the floor when you want to exclaim something; period = a point because you've just made your point, plain and simple; and a comma = a brake pedal because it requires you to temporarily stop in the middle of a sentence. Students can make up their own images and then place them as pictures in sentences (with different colors assigned to different marks).

Wednesday (Body Smart): The teacher asks students to use their bodies to form the shapes of the different punctuation marks as she reads sentences requiring them (e.g., a curved body posture for a question mark, a quick jump up and a stamping down for an exclamation mark).

Thursday (Music Smart): Play a clip of Victor Borge's use of phonetic punctuation (available on YouTube at www.youtube.com/watch?v=eixevXANKAo). Then, have students make up different sounds for the punctuation marks and use these sounds as they chorally read sample sentences requiring the use of the four marks.

Friday (Number/Logic Smart): Students form groups of four to six. Each group has a box divided into four compartments, each of which is assigned a punctuation mark. The groups sort sentence stubs with missing punctuation marks (one per sentence stub) into the four compartments according to the punctuation needed.

Monday (People Smart): Students form groups of four to six. Each student has four cards, each with a different punctuation mark written on it. The teacher places a sentence requiring a given punctuation mark on the whiteboard. As soon as students see the sentence, they toss the relevant card in the center of their group's circle. The first student in the group to throw in a correct card gets five points, the second four, and so on.

Tuesday (Self Smart): Students are asked to create their own sentences using each of the punctuation marks; the sentences should relate to their personal lives (e.g., a question they'd like somebody to answer, a statement they feel strongly about, a fact they know that they'd like others to know about).

Wednesday (Nature Smart): Students are asked to assign an animal and its respective sound to each of the punctuation marks (e.g., a period might be a dog barking; a comma, a duck quacking; a question mark, a cat meowing; and an exclamation point, a lion roaring). As the teacher (or a student) reads a passage, the students make the animal sounds corresponding to each punctuation mark encountered.

and now curriculum is that it is immediately recognized (by the student) as being relevant and meaningful. . . . Furthermore, it purports to teach our young about their world and the skills necessary to act within and upon it, thus preparing themselves for living the fast-paced changes of the [future]" (p. 5). Kovalik's thematic model is based in part on yearlong themes (e.g., "What Makes It Tick?") that are themselves made up of monthlong components (e.g., clocks/time, electrical power, transportation) and weekly topics (e.g., seasonal change and geologic time).

Other curricular approaches focus on other time frames, such as semester units or three-month themes. Regardless of the time interval selected, MI theory provides a context for structuring interdisciplinary curricula. It provides a way of making sure that the activities selected for a theme will activate all eight intelligences and thereby draw upon every child's inner gifts.

Figure 5.6 outlines the types of activities that might be used for the theme "Inventions." It shows how activities can be structured to address traditional academic subjects as well as integrate each of the eight intelligences. Significantly, this chart illustrates how science activities needn't focus only on Number/Logic Smart and how language activities (reading and writing) needn't focus only on Word Smart. They can, in fact, span all eight intelligences.

Keep in mind that MI theory can be applied to the curriculum in a variety of ways. There are no standard guidelines to follow. The ideas in this chapter are only suggestions. I invite you to create other forms or formulas for lesson planning or thematic development and encourage you to incorporate other formats, including those developed by educators such as Kovalik (1993), Madeleine Hunter (see Gentile, 1988), Grant Wiggins and Jay McTighe (2005), Carol Ann Tomlinson (2014), and Robert Marzano (2017). Ultimately, you should be guided by your deepest and sincerest attempts to reach beyond the intelligences you may currently be focusing on so that every child has the opportunity to succeed in school.

For Further Study

1. Look over the list of teaching strategies in this chapter. Circle the strategies you already use or have used in your instruction. Place a star next to the approaches that have worked best. Place an *x* next to the activities you think you use too much. Finally, place an upward pointing arrow to new activities you would like to try. Over

Figure 5.6

MI and Thematic Instruction
Sample Theme: Inventions

Intelligence	Math	Science	Reading	Writing	Social Studies
Word Smart	Read about a math equation used in creating an invention	Talk about the basic scientific principles involved in specific inventions	Read a book about the history of inventions	Write your personal autobiography as a "famous inventor"	Write about the social conditions that gave rise to certain inventions
Number/Logic Smart	Learn a math formula that served as the basis for an invention (e.g., $E=mc^2$)	Create a hypothesis for the development of a new invention	Read a book about the logic and math behind inventions	Write a word problem based on a famous invention	Create a time line of famous inventions
Picture Smart	Sketch the geometry involved in specific inventions	Draw a new or existing invention showing all working parts	Read a book with diagrams of the inner workings of an invention	Label the individual components of a drawing of your invention	Paint a mural showing inventions in social/historical context
Body Smart	Create an invention to measure a specific physical activity	Build your own invention based on sound scientific principles	Read the instructions for putting together an existing invention	Write instructions for building your own invention from scrap materials	Put on a play about how a certain invention came into existence
Music Smart	Study the math involved in the invention of musical instruments	Study the science behind the invention of electronic music	Read about the background to invention songs such as "John Henry"	Write the lyrics for a song promoting a new invention	Listen to music about inventions at different historical periods (e.g., John Henry)
People Smart	Join a study group that looks at the mathematics involved in specific inventions	Form a discussion group to study the science behind inventions	Read about the collaboration necessary for developing an invention (e.g., the Manhattan Project)	Write a collaborative play about inventions that can be dramatized by the class and presented to other classes	Hold a group discussion about how a certain invention came into existence
Self Smart	Write about the inventions you'd like to see invented that would positively change some metric in your life (e.g., money, weight)	Put together a project that investigates and presents on what you feel are the three greatest inventions of the 21st century	Read the biography of a famous inventor and compare his or her life to yours at the same age	Write about what you'd like to invent if you had the right resources	Think about this question: If you could invent a time machine, where would you go and what would you do?
Nature Smart	Investigate inventions used to measure positions of natural phenomena (e.g., astrolabe)	Study the scientific principles behind cloning and how a cloned human being may someday represent a biological "invention"	Read about "naturalist inventions" such as "wetware" (biological software) and genetically altered foods	Write an essay on your opinion of the use of animals in experiments to help develop of inventions	Design an invention that would contribute to the ecological welfare of the planet

the next few weeks, eliminate or scale back your use of some of the overused techniques, increase the time you spend using the starred approaches, and add some of the upward-arrow techniques to your teaching repertoire.

2. Select a specific skill or instructional objective that many of your students don't seem to be effectively mastering. Apply the seven-step planning process described in this chapter to generate a multiple intelligences lesson or series of lessons, and then teach your students using the activities you've developed. Afterward, reflect upon the lesson. Which strategies were most successful? Which were least successful? Ask students to reflect upon the lesson in the same way. What have you learned from this experience that can help you regularly teach through multiple intelligences?

3. Select a theme to serve as a basis for a curriculum in your class. Use the seven-step lesson-planning process described in this chapter to generate a basic framework of activities that includes all eight intelligences and each academic subject area. (Refer to Figure 5.6 for guidance in developing activities.)

4. Focus on an intelligence that you usually don't touch upon in your teaching, create a lesson plan that includes it, and teach the lesson to your students.

6

MI Theory and
Teaching Strategies

I suppose it is tempting, if the only tool you have is a hammer, to treat everything as if it were a nail.

—*Abraham Maslow*

MI theory opens the door to a wide range of teaching strategies that can be easily implemented in the classroom. In many cases, they are strategies that have been used for decades by great teachers. In other cases, the theory of multiple intelligences offers teachers an opportunity to develop innovative teaching strategies that are relatively new to the educational scene. MI theory suggests that no one set of teaching strategies will work best for all students at all times. All children have different proclivities in the eight intelligences, so any particular strategy is likely to be highly successful with one group of students and less successful with other groups. For example, teachers who use the Rhythms, Songs, Raps, and Chants strategy discussed in this chapter as a pedagogical tool will probably find that musically inclined students respond well while nonmusical students remain largely unmoved. Similarly, the use of pictures and images in teaching will reach students who are oriented more toward Picture Smart but perhaps have a different effect on those who are more Body Smart or Word Smart.

Because of these individual differences among students, teachers are best advised to use a broad range of teaching strategies in the classroom. As long as instructors shift their intelligence emphasis from presentation to presentation, there will always be a time during the period or day when a student has his most highly developed intelligence(s) actively involved in learning.

In this chapter, I present 40 teaching strategies, five for each of the eight intelligences. The strategies are designed to be general enough as to be applicable at any grade level, yet specific enough so that little guesswork is required to implement them. Keep in mind that these are only a sample of the strategies available (see Chapter 5 for a list of others). I encourage you to find or develop additional strategies or to develop your own unique adaptations of existing strategies.

Teaching Strategies for Word Smart

Word Smart is perhaps the easiest intelligence to develop strategies for, because so much attention has already been given to its cultivation in the schools. I do not include the traditional Word Smart strategies involving textbooks, worksheets, and lectures among the five strategies discussed here, however, simply because they have been overused. This is not to say that textbooks, worksheets, and lectures should never be used—they serve as adequate channels for effectively imparting certain types of information. But they are only *a tiny part* of a vast repertoire of teaching strategies— and not necessarily the most important part. Though used extensively by schools all over the United States, this trio of teaching techniques most easily reaches only a segment of the learning population: the most "book-oriented" and "lecture-gifted" students. The five strategies described here are accessible to a broader range of learners because they emphasize open-ended language activities that bring out the Word Smart in *every* learner.

Storytelling

Storytelling has traditionally been seen as entertainment for children in the public library or during special enrichment times in the classroom. However, it should be viewed as a vital teaching tool, as it has been an integral part of culture-making all over the world for thousands of years. When using storytelling in the classroom, teachers weave essential concepts, ideas, and instructional goals into stories that they tell directly to students. Although storytelling is usually thought of as a means of conveying knowledge in the humanities, it can be applied in mathematics and science as well. For example, to teach the idea of multiplication, teachers can tell students the story of brothers and sisters who have magical powers: whatever they touch multiplies (e.g., for the first child, it doubles; for the second, it triples; and so on). Or, to convey the notion of centrifugal force, you might take students on a mythical journey to a land where everything spins around very rapidly from the center outward.

Prepare for storytelling by listing the essential elements you'd like to include in the story. Then use your imagination to create a special land, a group of colorful characters, or a whimsical plot to carry the message home. It may help to visualize the story at first and then practice telling it to a spouse or to yourself in a mirror. Stories needn't be especially original or fabulous for children to benefit from them. Students are often impressed simply by a teacher's willingness to be creative and speak from the heart about a subject.

Brainstorming

Russian psychologist Lev Vygotsky once wrote that a thought is like a cloud shedding a shower of words. During brainstorming, students produce a torrent of verbal thoughts that can be collected and put on the board or an overhead projector or entered into a computer software program such as Inspiration or Kidspiration. The brainstorming can be about anything: words for a class poem, ideas for developing a group project, thoughts about a lesson being taught, suggestions for a class picnic, and so forth. The general rules for brainstorming are as follows: Participants share whatever comes to mind that is relevant, there are to be no put-downs or criticisms of any idea, and *every* idea counts. Place student ideas at random on the board or screen or use a special system such as an outline, a mind map, or some other graphic organizer for collecting them. After everyone has had a chance to share, look for patterns or groupings in the ideas, invite students to reflect on the ideas, or use the ideas in a specific project (such as a group poem). This strategy allows all students to receive special acknowledgment for their original thoughts.

Audio Recording

Audio recording devices are among the most valuable learning tools in any classroom, and they're usually included as a standard feature on most smartphones and tablets. They constitute a distinct asset because they offer students a medium through which to exercise their linguistic powers and help them employ verbal skills to communicate, solve problems, and express inner feelings. Students can use audio recorders to "talk out loud" a math problem they are attempting to solve or a history project they are planning to do. In this way, they're able to reflect metacognitively upon their own problem-solving processes. They can also use audio recorders to prepare for writing, dictating ideas that enable them to "loosen the verbal soil" of their topic. Students who are not good writers may also want to record their thoughts as an alternative mode of expression. Some students may use the audio recorder to send "oral letters" to other students in the class, both to share personal experiences and to get feedback about how they are coming across to others in the classroom.

Audio recorders can be used as *collectors* of information (e.g., in interviews) and as *reporters* of information (e.g., talking books). Audio recorders can also be used to provide information. For instance, a tablet with an audio recording app can be placed on a table in each activity center so students can listen to information about the topic in that center or receive instructions for doing an activity there. Every classroom should have audio recorders available, and teachers should plan on using them regularly to promote their students' language skills.

Journal Writing

Keeping a personal journal involves students in making ongoing written records related to a specific domain. The domain can be broad and open-ended ("Write about anything you're thinking about or feeling during the class day") or quite specific ("Use this journal to keep a simulated record of your life as a farmer during the 1800s as part of our history course"). Journals can be kept in math ("Write down your strategy for solving this problem"), science ("Keep a record of the experiments you do, hypotheses you're testing, and new ideas that emerge from your work"), literature ("Keep an ongoing record of your responses to the books you're reading"), and most other subjects. They can be kept entirely private, shared only between teacher and student, or regularly read to the class. They can also incorporate multiple intelligences by integrating drawings, sketches, photos, graphics, and other nonverbal information. (Note that this strategy also draws heavily upon Self Smart insofar as students work individually and use the journal to reflect upon their own lives.)

Publishing

In traditional classrooms, students typically complete assignments that are turned in, graded, handed back, and then thrown away (perhaps a linguistic ecologist should research the life cycle of a student paper!). Many students exposed to this type of routine begin to see writing as a meaningless process having no effect on the world outside of school. However, educators ought to be sending students a different message: that writing is a powerful tool for communicating ideas and influencing people and events. By providing students with opportunities to publish and distribute their work, we can make this point effectively.

Publishing takes many forms. Students can submit their writing to a class or school newspaper, a city newspaper, a children's magazine, or another publishing source that accepts student work. Students' writing can also be published using desktop publishing software such as Microsoft Publisher or Apple's Page, then bound in book form and made available in a special section of the class or school library. (Note that a number of companies provide their own book-making services, including Bookemon, Storybook, and Lulu.) Finally, students can publish their ideas on blogs, on websites, and through social networking channels such as Twitter or Facebook.

After publication, encourage interaction between authors and their readers. You might even hold a special student autographing party or convene book circles to discuss students' writings. When children see that others care enough about their writing to reproduce it, discuss it, and even argue about it, they become linguistically empowered and are motivated to continue developing their writing craft.

Teaching Strategies for Number/Logic Smart

Typically, Number/Logic Smart thinking is restricted to math and science courses. However, components of this intelligence are applicable throughout the curriculum. The critical thinking movement reflects one broad way in which Number/Logic Smart has been integrated into the social sciences and the humanities. Similarly, the calls for "numeracy" (the logical-mathematical equivalent of "literacy") in our schools, or for mathematics be applied to an interdisciplinary program, point to potential applications in every part of the school curriculum. The following are five key strategies for developing Number/Logic Smart that can be employed in all school subjects.

Calculations and Quantifications

In line with school reform efforts, teachers are being encouraged to discover opportunities to talk about numbers both inside and outside math and science classrooms. History and geography, for example, may put the focus on important statistics: the number of lives lost in wars, the populations of countries, and so forth. But how do we accomplish the same aim in literature? Though we shouldn't force connections that simply aren't there, it's surprising how many novels, short stories, and other literary works make reference to numbers, science, and logical thinking. In a novel by Virginia Woolf, *To the Lighthouse*, for example, there is a mention of a payment of 50 pounds to fix a greenhouse roof. How does that sum translate into U.S. dollars? What was a U.S. dollar worth in 1927 when the novel was published? In a short story by Nobel–prize winning author Doris Lessing, "Through the Tunnel," a boy must count to see how long he can stay underwater and then compare that to the amount of time it takes experienced divers to swim through a submerged tunnel. Each of these passages provides the basis for mathematical thinking.

Of course, we shouldn't feel compelled to make word problems out of great works of art—that would be stifling, to say the least. It is a good idea, however, to be alert for interesting numbers and intriguing math problems wherever they may be found. By tuning into the numbers in nonmathematical subjects, we can better engage highly logical students, and other students can learn to see that math belongs not just in math class but in the rest of life as well.

Classifications and Categorizations

The logical mind can be stimulated anytime information is put into some kind of rational framework, whether the data be linguistic, logical, visual, or of another kind. For example, in a unit on the effects of climate on culture, students might brainstorm a random list of geographic locations and then classify them by type of climate (e.g., desert, mountain, plains, tropical). Or, in a science unit on states of matter, the instructor might put the names of three categories—gas, liquid, solid—on the whiteboard and ask students to list examples of items belonging in each category. Other examples of logical frameworks include Venn diagrams; time lines; attribute webs that list the attributes of a person, place, or thing as "spokes" around the subject; 5W organizers that tabulate who, what, when, where, and why questions; and mind maps. Most of these frameworks are also Picture Smart in nature. The value of this approach is that disparate fragments of information can be organized around central ideas or themes, making them easier to remember, discuss, and think about. (A range of graphic organizers is available on the internet, including word cloud generators that size words based on their frequency and importance (see, e.g., Word It Out).

Socratic Questioning

The critical thinking movement has provided an important alternative to the traditional image of the teacher as dispenser of knowledge. In Socratic questioning, the teacher serves as an interrogator of students' points of view. The Greek sage Socrates is the model for this type of instruction. Instead of talking *at* students, the teacher participates in dialogues *with* them, aiming to uncover the rightness or wrongness of their beliefs. Students share their hypotheses about how the world works, and the teacher guides the "testing" of these hypotheses for clarity, precision, accuracy, logical coherence, or relevance through artful questioning. A history student who declares that World War II never would have happened if soldiers had actively resisted military service can have his point of view subjected to rigorous scrutiny in this approach to teaching. A student defending the motives of a character in *Huckleberry Finn* is carefully questioned to see if her stand is supported by the facts in the novel. The purpose is not to humiliate students or put them in the wrong but, rather, to help them sharpen their own critical thinking skills so that they no longer form opinions simply out of strong feelings or by mirroring the conventions of the day (see Paul, 1992).

Heuristics

The field of heuristics refers to a loose collection of strategies, rules of thumb, guidelines, and suggestions for logical problem solving that, while not necessarily leading to an exact answer, provide a "good enough" solution for the purpose at hand. Examples of heuristic strategies include finding analogies to the problem we wish to solve, separating the various parts of the problem, proposing a possible solution to the problem and then working backward, and finding an easier problem that's similar, solving it, and then using that method to solve the harder problem.

Although the most obvious applications of heuristics are in the math and science fields, heuristic principles can also be used in other subjects. In trying to envision solutions to the problems of government waste, for example, a student might seek analogies by asking himself what other entities create waste. While looking for the main idea in a reading passage, a student might separate out each part of the passage into sentences and subject each sentence to qualifying "tests" of a key point. Heuristics provides students with informal logical maps to help them find their way around unfamiliar academic terrain (see Polya, 2014).

Science Thinking

Just as teachers should look for mathematics in every part of the curriculum, so too should they seek out scientific ideas in courses other than science class. This strategy is especially important given research showing that up to 70 percent of adults lack a fundamental understanding of the scientific process (Recer, 2002). There are innumerable ways to spread science thinking across the curriculum. For instance, students can study the important influence scientific ideas have had on history (e.g., how the development and use of the atomic bomb influenced the outcome of World War II). They can read science fiction literature with an eye toward discovering whether the ideas described in them are feasible. They can learn about social science issues such as AIDS, overpopulation, and the greenhouse effect that require some science background to be well informed. In each part of the curriculum, science provides a supplemental point of view that can considerably enrich each student's perspective.

Teaching Strategies for Picture Smart

The cave drawings by prehistoric man are evidence that Picture Smart learning has been important to human beings for tens of thousands of years. Unfortunately, the "sensory channels" (VAKT) model of presenting information to students in visual as well as auditory ways often merely translates into writing words on the board, a practice that is actually Word Smart. Picture Smart has to do with *pictures and images*—either the pictures in our minds or the pictures in the external world, such as photos, videos, drawings, graphic symbols, maps, ideographs, and so forth. Here are five teaching strategies designed to make use of students' Picture Smart abilities for academic purposes.

Visualization

One of the easiest ways to help students translate book and lecture material into pictures and images is to have them close their eyes and picture whatever is being studied. One application of this strategy involves having students create their own "inner blackboard" (or movie or video screen) in their mind's eye. They can then place on this mental blackboard any material they need to remember: spelling words, math formulas, history facts, or other information. When asked to recall a specific body of information, students need only call up their mental blackboard and "see" the data inscribed on it.

A more open-ended application of this strategy involves having students close their eyes and visualize what they've just read or studied (e.g., a story or a chapter in a textbook). Afterward, they can draw or talk about their experiences. Teachers can also lead students through more formal "guided imagery" sessions as a way of introducing them to new concepts or material (e.g., by leading them on a "guided tour" through the circulatory system to learn anatomy, through the Battle of Gettysburg in history, or through the city of Verona in Shakespeare's *Romeo and Juliet*). Students may experience nonspatial content as well during these activities (e.g., kinesthetic images, verbal images, or musical images), which only serves to further enrich the experience.

Color Cues

Highly Picture Smart students are often sensitive to color. Unfortunately, the school day is usually filled with black-and-white texts, copy books, worksheets, and black or white chalkboards. However, there are many creative ways to use color in the classroom as a learning tool. Use different colors of chalk, markers, and transparencies when writing in front of the class, for example, or provide students with colored pencils, pens, or markers and colored paper on which to write assignments. Students can learn to use different colored highlighters to color-code material they are studying (e.g., by highlighting all the key points in red, all the supporting data in green, and all the unclear passages in orange). Use color to emphasize patterns, rules, or classifications during instruction (e.g., coloring all instances of *th* red in a phonics lesson, or using different colors to write about distinct historical stages in Greek history). Finally, students can use their favorite colors as a stress reducer when coping with difficult problems (e.g., "If you run into a word, problem, or idea you don't understand, imagine your favorite color filling your head; this can help you find the right answer or clarify things for you").

Picture Metaphors

A metaphor involves comparing one idea to another, seemingly unrelated idea. A picture metaphor expresses this concept visually. Developmental psychologists suggest that young children are masters of metaphor (Gardner, 1979). Sadly, this capacity often decreases as children grow older. However, educators can tap this underground stream (to use a metaphor!) to help students master new material. The educational value of using metaphors lies in establishing connections between what students already know and what they can learn. Think of the key point or main concept you want students to learn, then link that idea to a visual image. Construct the complete metaphor yourself (e.g., "How is the development of the colonies during early U.S. history like the growth of an amoeba?") or have students develop their own metaphors (e.g., "If the major organs in the body were animals, which ones would they be?").

Idea Sketching

A review of the notebooks of many eminent individuals in history, including Thomas Edison, Henry Ford, Marie Curie, and Charles Darwin, reveals that they often used simple drawings to develop many of their powerful ideas. Teachers should recognize the value that this kind of visual thinking can have in helping students articulate their understanding of subject matter. The Idea Sketching strategy involves asking students to *draw*, not write down, the key point, main idea, central theme, or core concept being taught. Neatness and realism should be de-emphasized in favor of quick sketches that help articulate an idea.

To prepare students for this type of drawing, it may be helpful to play the game Pictionary (or Pictionary Jr.) so students can get used to the notion of quick-drawing to convey central ideas. Then, begin to ask students to draw the concept or idea you want to focus on in a lesson. This strategy can be used to evaluate a student's understanding of an idea, to emphasize a concept, or to give students ample opportunity to explore an idea in greater depth. Here are some examples of subjects or concepts you might ask students to illustrate: the Great Depression, gravity, mathematical probability, fractions, democracy, pathos, an ecosystem, or continental drift. Follow up the drawing activity with a discussion of the relationship between the drawings and the subject matter. Don't evaluate the artistic quality of the drawings; instead, seek to "draw out" students' understanding using the sketches as a starting point.

Graphic Symbols

One of the most traditional teaching strategies involves writing words on a blackboard or whiteboard. Far less common, especially after primary school, is the *drawing of pictures* on the board. However, pictures may be critical to helping students master a skill or concept. Teachers reach a wider range of learners when they support their teaching with drawings and graphic symbols as well as words. This strategy, then, requires teachers to practice *drawing* at least some part of their lessons—for instance, by creating graphic symbols that depict the concepts to be learned. Here are some examples: showing the three states of matter by drawing a solid mass (heavy chalk marks), a liquid mass (lighter curvy marks), and a gaseous mass (little dots); indicating root words by adding little roots to the base of those words on the board; and drawing a time line for a novel's plot or historical event and marking it with pictures that symbolize the events.

You don't need superior drawing skills to use this strategy. Roughly drawn graphic symbols will suffice in most cases. The willingness to model imperfect drawing can actually serve as a model for students who feel shy about sharing their own drawings in class.

Teaching Strategies for Body Smart

Students may leave their textbooks and folders behind when they leave school, but they take their bodies with them wherever they go. Finding ways to help them integrate learning at a "gut" level can be very important in increasing their retention, understanding, and engagement in the learning process. Traditionally, physical learning has been considered the province of physical and vocational education. However, the following strategies show how easy it is to integrate hands-on and kinesthetic learning activities into traditional academic subjects like reading, math, and science.

Body Answers

Ask students to respond to instruction by using their bodies as a medium of expression. The simplest and most overused example of this strategy is asking students to raise their hands to indicate understanding or agreement. Instead of raising hands, students might smile, blink one eye, hold up fingers (one finger to indicate just a little understanding, five fingers to show complete understanding), make flying motions with their arms (to indicate confusion), and so forth. Students can provide "body answers" during a lecture ("If you understand what I've just said, put your finger on your temple; if you don't understand, scratch your head"), while going through a textbook ("Anytime you come to something in the text that seems outdated, I want you to frown"), or in answering questions that have a limited number of answers ("If you think this sentence has parallel construction, I want you to raise two hands high like a referee indicating a touchdown; if you think it's not parallel, put your hands together over your head like the peak of a house").

Classroom Theater

To bring out the actors in your students, ask them to enact the texts, problems, or other material to be learned by dramatizing or role-playing. For example, students might dramatize a three-step math problem by putting on a three-act play. Classroom Theater can be as informal as a one-minute improvisation of a reading passage or as formal as a one-hour play at the end of the semester that sums up students' understanding of a key learning theme. It can be done without any materials, or it may involve substantial use of props. Students may themselves act in plays and skits, or they may produce puppet shows or dramatizations in miniature (e.g., showing how a battle was fought by putting miniature soldiers on a painted plywood battle-field and moving them around to show troop movements). To help older students who may initially feel reluctant to engage in dramatic activities, try some warm-up exercises (see Spolin, 1986).

Kinesthetic Concepts

The game of charades has long been a favorite of partygoers because of how it challenges participants to express knowledge in unconventional ways. Similarly, the Kinesthetic Concepts strategy involves introducing students to concepts through physical illustrations or asking them to pantomime specific concepts or terms from the lesson. This strategy requires students to translate information from Word Smart or Number/Logic Smart symbol systems into purely Body Smart expressions. The range of subjects is end-less. Here are just a few examples of concepts that might be expressed through physical gestures or movements: soil erosion, cell mitosis, political revolution, supply and demand, subtraction (of numbers), the epiphany (of a novel), and biodiversity. Simple pantomimes can also be extended into more elaborate creative movement experiences or dances (such as dancing the periodic table of elements).

Hands-On Thinking

Students who are highly developed in the fine-motor aspect of Body Smart should have opportunities to learn by manipulating objects or by making things with their hands. Many educators have already provided such oppor-tunities by incorporating manipulatives (e.g., tangrams, geostix, Cuisenaire rods) into math instruction and by having students do experiments or lab work in science. In interdisciplinary projects, too, students can use hands-on thinking—for instance, in constructing adobe huts for a unit on American Indian traditions or in building dioramas of the rain forest for an ecology theme. One can extend this general strategy into many other curricular areas as well. At a rote level, students can study spelling words or new vocabulary words by forming them in clay or creating the letters with pipe cleaners. At a higher cognitive level, students can express complex concepts by creating clay or wooden sculptures, collages, or other assemblages. For example, students could convey an understanding of the term *deficit* using only clay (or some other available material) and then share their productions during a class discussion.

Body Maps

The human body provides a convenient pedagogical platform when used as a reference point or "map" for specific knowledge systems. One of the most common examples of this approach is the use of fingers in counting and calculating (elaborate finger-counting systems such as Chisanbop have been adapted for classroom use). We can map out many other domains onto the body. In geography, for example, the body might represent the continent of Africa (if the head represents Algeria, then the toes might represent South Africa, etc.). The body can also be used to map out a problem-solving strategy in math. For example, in multiplying a two-digit number by a one-digit number, the feet could be the two-digit number, and the right knee could be the one-digit number. Students could then perform the following actions in "solving" the problem: Tap the right knee and the right foot to get the first product (indicated by tapping the thighs); tap the right knee and the left foot to get the second product (indicated by tapping the stomach); tap the thighs and the stomach (to indicate adding the two products); and tap the head to indicate the final product. By repeating physical movements that represent a specific process or idea, students can gradually internalize the objective.

Teaching Strategies for Music Smart

For thousands of years, knowledge has been transmitted from generation to generation through the medium of singing or chanting. In the 20th century, advertisers discovered that musical jingles helped people remember their clients' products. Educators, however, have been slower to recognize the importance of music in learning. As a result, most of us remember hundreds of commercial musical jingles but have relatively few school-related musical pieces in our long-term memory. The following strategies will help begin the process of integrating music into the core curriculum.

Rhythms, Songs, Raps, and Chants

Take the essence of whatever you're teaching and put it into a rhythmic format that can be tapped, sung, rapped, or chanted. At a rote level, this might mean spelling words to the rhythm of a metronome or singing the times tables to the tune of a popular song. (When I taught, I wrote a song for my special education classes entitled "The Times Table Blues.") Teachers can also identify the main point they want to emphasize in a lecture, the main idea of a story, or the central theme of a concept and then place it in a rhythmic format. For example, to teach John Locke's concept of Natural Law, one-half of the class can chant "natural/law natural/law, natural/law, natural/law!" while the other half repeats "life/li-ber-ty/happ-i-ness! Life/li-ber-ty/happ-i-ness!" Inviting students themselves to create songs, raps, or chants that summarize, synthesize, or apply meanings from subjects they are studying moves students to an even higher level of learning. This strategy can also be enhanced through the addition of percussion or other musical instruments.

Discographies

Supplement bibliographies for the curriculum with lists of recorded musical selections that illustrate, embody, or amplify the learning content. In developing a unit about the U.S. Civil War, for example, collect songs related to that period in history (e.g., "When Johnny Comes Marching Home Again," "Tenting Tonight," "The Battle Hymn of the Republic," "The Night They Drove Old Dixie Down"). After listening to the recordings, discuss the content of the songs in relation to the themes of the unit.

Many recorded musical pieces can help sum up in a compelling way the key point or main message of a lesson or unit. For example, to illustrate Newton's first law of motion (a body remains in its state of rest unless it is compelled to change that state by a force impressed on it), you might play the first few lines of Sammy Davis Jr.'s version of "Something's Gotta Give" ("When an irresistible force such as you . . ."). Such "musical concepts" are often effective class openers, providing an anticipatory set or "hook" to a lesson. YouTube is a great resource for finding songs that both teach and engage students.

Supermemory Music

Thirty-five years ago, educational researchers in Eastern Europe discovered that students could more easily commit information to memory if they listened to the teacher's instruction against a musical background. Baroque musical selections in 4/4 time were found to be particularly effective (e.g., Pachelbel's Canon in D and the Largo movements of concertos by Handel, Bach, Telemann, and Corelli). Students should be in a relaxed state (heads on desks or lying on the floor) while the teacher rhythmically repeats the information to be learned (e.g., spelling or vocabulary words, history facts, science terms) against the musical background (see Rose, 1987).

Music Smart Concepts

Musical tones can be used to creatively express concepts, patterns, or schemas in many subjects. For example, to musically convey the idea of a circle, begin humming at a certain tone, drop the tone gradually (indicating the gradual slope of the circle) to a low note, and then gradually move up toward the original note again. Similar techniques can be used to express cosines, ellipses, and other mathematical shapes.

Rhythms can also be used to express ideas. For example, in a lesson on Shakespeare's *Romeo and Juliet,* use percussion instruments to pit the rhythms of the Montagues against those of the Capulets to suggest two families in conflict, and contrast this with two quieter musical patterns representing Romeo and Juliet. This strategy offers ample opportunity for creative expression from both teachers and students. How would you musically express some of the following ideas: political revolution, global warming, or the development of Jay Gatsby in *The Great Gatsby*?

Mood Music

Use recorded music to create an appropriate mood or emotional atmosphere for a particular lesson or unit. Such music can even include sound effects (nonverbal sounds are processed through the musical intellect), nature sounds, or classical or contemporary pieces that facilitate specific emotional states. For example, just before students are about to read a story that takes place near the sea, play a recording of sea sounds (waves crashing up against the shore, seagulls crying, etc.) or *La Mer* by Claude Debussy. (See Bonny & Savary, 1990 and Sacks, 2007 for more information on the effects of music on the mind.)

Teaching Strategies for People Smart

Some students need time to bounce their ideas off others when learning something new. These People Smart learners have benefited the most from the emergence of collaborative learning. Because all students are People Smart to one degree or another, all educators should be aware of teaching approaches that incorporate interaction with and among people. The following strategies can help tap each student's need for belonging and connection to others.

Peer Sharing

Peer sharing is perhaps the easiest of the MI strategies to implement. All you need to do is say to students, "Turn to a person next to you and share _____." You might want students to process material just covered in class ("Share a question you have about what I just presented"). Or, you might want to begin a lesson or unit with peer sharing to unlock students' existing knowledge about the topic under study ("Share three things that you know about the early settlers in the United States"). You can set up a buddy system so each student shares with the same person each time, or you may want to encourage students to share with as many different classmates as possible. Sharing periods can be short (30 seconds) or extended (an hour or longer). Peer sharing can also evolve into peer tutoring (one student coaching or teaching specific material to another student) or cross-age tutoring (an older student working with a younger student in a different class).

People Sculptures

Anytime students are brought together to collectively represent an idea in physical form, a *people sculpture,* otherwise known as a *tableaux vivant,* is one strategy to consider. If students are studying the skeletal system, they can build a people sculpture of a skeleton, with each person representing a bone or group of bones. For a unit on inventions, students can create people sculptures of different inventions, complete with moving parts. In algebra class, students can create people sculptures of different equations, with each person representing either a number or a function within the equation. In language arts, students can build people sculptures to represent spelling words (each person holding up a letter), sentences (each student representing a word), or whole paragraphs (each person taking responsibility for a complete sentence). Assign a student to help lead the activity, or let the components of the sculpture organize themselves. The beauty of this approach is in having people represent things that were formerly represented only in books or lectures (note: this strategy also taps Body Smart, making it doubly effective).

Collaborative Groups

The use of small groups working toward common instructional goals is the core component of the collaborative learning model. Such groups generally work most effectively when they have three to eight members. Students in collaborative groups can tackle a learning assignment in a variety of ways. Groups may work collectively on a written assignment, for example, with each member contributing ideas, much as screenwriters do when preparing a television episode or as scientists do in preparing a scientific paper. Alternatively, groups may divide up their responsibilities based on the structure of the assignment, with one member doing the introduction, another taking care of the middle section, and another contributing the conclusion. Or, groups may use a "jigsaw" strategy and assign each student (or group) responsibility for a particular book or subtopic.

Collaborative groups are particularly suitable for MI teaching because they can be structured to include students who represent the full spectrum of intelligences. For instance, a group charged with the task of creating a videotaped presentation might include a People Smart–oriented student to help organize the group, a Word Smart–inclined member to do the writing, a Picture Smart–motivated student to do the drawing, a Body Smart–focused student to create props or be a leading actor, and so forth. Collaborative groups provide students with a chance to operate as a social unit—an important prerequisite for success in real-life work environments.

Board Games

Board games represent a fun way for students to learn in the context of an informal social setting. On one level, students are chatting, discussing rules, throwing dice, and laughing. On another level, they are engaged in learning whatever skill or subject happens to be the focus of the game. Board games can be easily made using manila file folders, magic markers (to create the typical winding road or pathway), a pair of dice, and miniature cars, people, or colored cubes to serve as game pieces. Topics can range from math facts or phonics skills to science concepts or history questions.

The information to be learned (e.g., the math equation 5 x 7) should be placed on the individual squares of the winding road or on cards made from tag board or thick construction paper. Answers can be provided in a number of ways: on a separate answer key, from a specially designated "answer person," or on the board squares or cards themselves (glue a tiny piece of folded paper to each square; on the top flap write the question or problem, and on the bottom flap write the answer; players then simply open the flap to check the answer).

You can also design board games that involve quick open-ended or activity-oriented tasks. Simply place the directions or activities on each square or card (e.g., "Explain what you would do to control pollution if you were president of the United States" or "Look up the word *threshold* in an online dictionary").

Simulations

A simulation is a group of people coming together to create an "as if" environment. This temporary setting becomes the context for getting into more immediate contact with the material being studied. For example, students learning about a historical period might dress up in costumes of that era, turn the classroom into a place that might have existed then, and begin acting *as if* they were living in that time. Similarly, in learning about geographical regions or ecosystems, students could turn the classroom into a simulated jungle or rain forest.

Simulations can also be quick and improvisational in nature, with the teacher providing an instant scenario to act out ("Okay, you've just gotten off the boat from your trip to the New World from Europe in 1890 and you're all standing around together. Action!") Or simulations can be ongoing and require substantial preparation, such as acquiring or creating props or costumes.

Although this strategy involves several intelligences (including Body Smart, Word Smart, and Picture Smart), it is included in the People Smart section because the human interactions that take place help students develop a new level of understanding. Through conversation and other interactions, students begin to get an insider's view of the topic they are studying.

Teaching Strategies for Self Smart

Most students spend about six hours a day, five days a week in a classroom with 25 to 35 other people. For individuals who are Self Smart and/or have an introverted personality, this intensely social atmosphere can sometimes be a bit overwhelming. Hence, teachers need to build in frequent opportunities during the school day for students to experience themselves as autonomous beings with unique life histories and a deep sense of individuality. Each of the following strategies helps accomplish this aim in a slightly different way.

One-Minute Reflection Periods

During lectures, discussions, project work, or other activities, students should be given frequent "time-outs" for introspection or focused thinking. One-minute reflection periods offer students time to digest the information presented or to connect it to experiences in their own lives. These reflective periods also provide a refreshing change of pace that helps students stay alert and prepared for the next activity.

A one-minute reflection period can occur anytime during the school day, but it may be particularly useful after the presentation of information that is especially challenging or central to the curriculum. During this period (which can be extended or shortened to accommodate differing attention spans), no talking is allowed; students simply think about what has been presented in any way they'd like. Silence is usually the best medium for reflection, but occasionally you might try using background "thinking music" as an option. Though students should not feel compelled to share their thoughts during reflection, this activity can be combined with Peer Sharing to engage both Self Smart and People Smart capacities.

Personal Connections

The big question that accompanies the Self Smart part of students through-out their school career is "What does this have to do with *my* life?" Most students have probably asked this question in one way or another during their time in school. It's up to teachers to answer this question by continually making connections between what is being taught and students' personal lives. This strategy asks teachers to weave students' personal associations, feelings, and experiences into their instruction. You can do this through questions ("How many of you have ever...?"), statements ("You may wonder what this has to do with your life. Well, if you ever plan on..."), or requests ("I'd like you to think back in your life to a time when..."). For instance, to introduce a lesson on the skeletal system, you might ask, "How many people here have ever broken a bone?" Students then can share stories and experiences before going on to the anatomy lesson (suddenly, the topic of bones becomes much more relevant). Or, for a lesson on world geography, you might ask, "Has anybody ever been to another country? What country?" Students then can identify the countries they've visited and locate them on the map.

Choice Time

Giving students choices is a fundamental principle of good teaching and an excellent Self Smart teaching strategy. Essentially, choice time consists of building in opportunities for students to make decisions about their learning experiences. Making choices is like lifting weights: The more frequently students choose from a group of options, the thicker their "responsibility muscles" become. Choices may be small and limited ("You can choose to work on the problems on page 12 or 14") or significant and open-ended ("Select the kind of project you'd like to do this semester"). They can be related to content ("Decide which topic you'd like to explore") or to process ("Choose a method of presenting your final project from this list"). They may be informal and spur of the moment ("Would you rather stop now or continue talking about this?"), or they might be carefully developed and highly structured (as in the use of a learning contract for each student).

Assess the ways in which you currently provide for choice in your own classroom. Then, plan ways to expand the choice-making experiences that your students have in school.

Feeling-Toned Moments

All too often, teachers present information to students in an emotionally flat way. Yet we know that human beings possess an "emotional brain" consisting of several subcortical structures (see Armstrong, 2016). To feed that emotional brain, educators need to teach with feeling. This strategy suggests that educators are responsible for creating moments during lessons when students laugh, feel angry, express strong opinions, get excited about a topic, or feel a wide range of other emotions.

You can help create feeling-toned moments by expressing emotions yourself as you teach, by making it safe for students to have feelings in the classroom (giving permission, discouraging criticism, and acknowledging feelings when they occur), and by providing experiences (such as movies, books, and controversial ideas) that evoke emotional responses.

Goal-Setting Sessions

One of the characteristics of highly developed Self Smart learners is their capacity to set realistic goals for themselves. Because this is among the most important skills for leading a successful life, educators can help students immeasurably by providing them with opportunities to practice goal setting. Goals may be short term ("I want everybody to list three things they'd like to learn today") or long term ("Tell me what you see yourself doing 25 years from now"). The goal-setting sessions may last only a few minutes or involve in-depth planning over several months' time. The goals themselves can relate to academic outcomes ("What goals for grades are you setting for yourself this term?"), wider learning outcomes ("What do you want to know how to do by the time you graduate?"), or life goals ("What kind of occupation do you see yourself involved with after you leave school?"). Try to allow time *every day* for students to set goals for themselves. You may also want to show students different ways of representing their goals and of charting their progress along the way (e.g., through graphs, charts, journals, and time lines).

Teaching Strategies for Nature Smart

Most classroom instruction, in the United States at least, takes place inside a school building. For children who learn best through nature, this arrangement separates them from their most valued source of learning. There are two primary solutions to this dilemma. First, more learning should take place for these kids outside in natural settings. Second, more of the natural world needs to be brought *into* the classroom, so that Nature Smart students might have greater access to developing their Nature Smart skills while on the school campus. The strategies presented here are all drawn from one or both of these approaches.

Nature Walks

Nobel Prize–winning physicist Richard Feynman once wrote that he got his start as a scientist by taking walks in nature with his father as a child. It was from the kind of questions that his father would ask him as they walked along that his own scientific questioning attitude was formed (Feynman, 2005). Consider the benefits of a walk in the woods (or whatever other natural settings are available within walking distance of your school) for reinforcing learning. Virtually any subject lends itself to a nature walk. Science and math, of course, lend themselves to discussions about the growth of plants, the weather, the earth, and the living things that crawl or scurry about or fly above. If you're teaching a piece of literature or a history lesson that involves any type of natural setting (and most do), then you might use a nature walk as an opportunity to reconstruct a scene or two from the story or historical era ("Imagine that this is the meadow where the Pickwick Club had their ridiculous duel in Dickens's *Pickwick Papers*" or "Picture this as the setting of the Battle of Hastings just before the troops arrived on the scene"). Nature walks also make superb preparation for getting your class ready to do creative writing, drawing, or other activities.

Windows onto Learning

One of the classic images of an "inattentive" student is that of a child looking wistfully out the classroom window from her desk. All too often, students want to look out the window because what they see outside is more interesting than what is going on in the classroom. If this is true, then why not use this "off-task" tendency as a positive classroom strategy? Looking out a window provides us with many pedagogical possibilities, including weather study (have a class weather station to make measurements), bird-watching (have binoculars handy), understanding time (study the seasons' effects on the trees, grass, plants, etc.), and creative writing (have students create metaphors based on nature in their writing). Indeed, looking out a window can be used as a strategy for teaching just about any subject. As with nature walks, looking out a window can be used to set a scene for literature or history, or to make scientific observations. Other subjects that might be addressed in this way include geology or geography ("What nature features do you see in the earth or along the horizon?"), economics ("Investigate the cost of planting the trees just outside the window"), social studies ("How well designed is the landscaping just outside the window for human beings?"), and literature ("As we finish this story, I want you to look out the window and imagine our protagonist walking between the trees there in the distance").

If you don't have windows in your classroom or your windows look out onto other classrooms or expanses of concrete (a lamentable consequence of hiring architects who have little sense of Nature Smart), then it's not possible to fully realize the possibilities of this strategy. However, even then, you might have students employ the Picture Smart visualization strategy to imagine that they *do* have windows connecting them to the natural world.

Plants as Props

If you can't go out of the classroom on nature walks and don't have windows in your classroom through which to look at nature, one alternative is to bring nature into your classroom. Many teachers adorn their windowsills or shelves with house plants simply to create a positive ambiance for learning, but they can be used as learning tools as well. The fact that the petals of flowers in bloom, for example, often come in multiples allows us to examine the concept of multiplication in a natural setting. Plants can also make useful props as background scenery for the Classroom Theater and People Sculpture strategies described earlier in this chapter. In teaching about the branches of government, use a nearby branching plant as a naturalistic metaphor to illustrate the concept. In science and math, measure the growth of classroom plants. In history, study the uses of plants as medicines, foods, or even poisons. Assigning a particularly difficult child with Nature Smart the job of taking care of a plant in the classroom can be a useful way to redirect his energies.

I love the idea of using the image of plant growth as a metaphor for the learning process itself. At the beginning of the year, bring in a sprout of a plant, and at the end of the year, point out to students how much both they and the plant have grown!

Pets in the Classroom

Many elementary school classrooms keep a class pet such as a gerbil or a rabbit in a species-appropriate container. Having a pet in the classroom automatically creates a "safe place" where Nature Smart students can go to have a relationship with the natural world and feel a sense of caring for nature's beings (some of these kids may be our future veterinarians and forest rangers!). A pet in the classroom also creates the conditions for numerous learning opportunities. The scientific skill of observation can be developed by having kids keep notes on a pet's behavior. (The naturalist Jane Goodall traced her own love of animals back to an incident when she was 5 years old and stayed in a chicken coop for five hours just to see how chickens lay eggs! [Rundle, 2016]). Kids can keep math records on their pet's food intake, weight, and other vital statistics. In high school classrooms, teachers can use a class pet as a kind of "alter ego" for the classroom ("How do you think Albert the bunny would feel about the problem of world hunger?"). Students who relate best to the world through their love of animals might well use the pet's persona to give voice to their own thinking on the matter. Having a pet in the classroom creates a reality check for teachers and students alike, reminding us of our own connection to the animal world and our need to occasionally learn from the wisdom of our pets!

Eco-Study

This strategy encourages us to keep in mind the relevance of all subjects to ecology. "Ecology" shouldn't just be a unit, course, or topic isolated from the rest of the curriculum, but integrated into every part of the school day. So, for example, if the topic is fractions or percentages, the teacher can ask students to investigate how many specimens of an endangered species exist today as opposed to 50 years ago, or to calculate the percentage of rain forest left in Brazil compared to what was there in 1900. If the subject is how a bill becomes a law, students might explore the different stages required to pass a bill related to environmental conservation. In literature, consider assigning a work like Ibsen's *An Enemy of the People*—an ecological play written before our current awareness of environmental issues. Eco-study helps to draw in students who are especially sensitive to ecological issues while also stimulating their peers to take a deeper interest in the welfare of our planet.

For Further Study

1. Select three strategies from this chapter that intrigue you and that you haven't already used in your classroom. Do some background reading or consult with colleagues as needed to develop specific lesson plans that describe exactly how you will apply the strategies. Try out your lessons and then evaluate the results. What worked, and what didn't? How would you modify each strategy in the future to make it more successful?

2. Choose an intelligence that you usually don't address in your instruction, and research strategies not mentioned above to use in your teaching. (Consult the list of strategies in Chapter 5 for more ideas.)

3. Develop a curriculum unit for your students that incorporates at least one of the strategies from each of the eight sections of this chapter. For instance, you might develop a unit that involves body sculptures, mood music, feeling-toned moments, peer sharing, brainstorming, color coding, quantifications and calculations, and plants as props. Work alone or as part of an interdisciplinary team, and then evaluate the results. Did you see different groups of students respond in different ways to the eight strategies?

7

MI Theory and the Classroom Environment

Nowhere else [but in schools] are large groups of individuals packed so closely together for so many hours, yet expected to perform at peak efficiency on difficult learning tasks and to interact harmoniously.

—*Carol Weinstein*

For most Americans, the word *classroom* conjures up an image of students sitting in neat rows of desks facing the front of the room with a teacher either sitting at a large desk correcting papers or standing near a blackboard lecturing to students. This is certainly one way to organize a classroom, but it is by no means the only way or the best way. The theory of multiple intelligences suggests that the classroom environment—or classroom *ecology,* if you will—may need to be fundamentally restructured to accommodate the needs of different types of learners.

MI and Ecological Factors in Learning

At a minimum, MI theory provides a template through which educators can view some of the critical ecological factors in learning. Each intelligence, in fact, provides a context for asking some searching questions about those factors in the classroom that promote or interfere with learning, and those elements absent from the room that could be incorporated to facilitate student achievement and engagement. A review of the eight intelligences reveals some of the following questions:

Word Smart

- How are spoken words used in the classroom? Are the words the teacher uses too complex or too simple for the students' level of understanding, or is there a good match?
- How are students exposed to the written word? Are words represented on the walls (through posters, quotations, etc.)? Are written words presented through primary sources (e.g., novels, newspapers, historical documents) or through textbooks and workbooks written by committees?
- Is there "linguistic pollution" in class (i.e., ongoing exposure to worksheets and lecture), or are students being empowered to develop their own linguistic materials?

Number/Logic Smart

- How is time structured in the classroom? Do students have opportunities to work on long-term projects without being interrupted by school bells, or must they continually break off their activities to move on to a new course or a new room?
- Is the school day sequenced to make optimum use of students' attention spans (the morning generally being seen as best for focused academic work, and afternoon regarded as best for more open-ended activities), or do students have to perform under conditions that don't match their fluctuating attention spans?
- Is there some consistency to students' school days (e.g., routines, rituals, rules, effective transitions to new activities), or is there a sense of chaos or of reinventing the wheel with the start of each new school day?

Picture Smart

- How is the classroom furniture arranged? Are there different spatial configurations to accommodate different learning needs (e.g., desks for written work, tables for discussion or hands-on work, carrels for independent study), or is there only one arrangement (e.g., straight rows of desks)?

- Is the room attractive to the eye (e.g., artwork on the walls), or is it visually empty, boring, cluttered, or disturbing?
- Are students exposed to a variety of visual experiences (e.g., optical illusions, cartoons, illustrations, movies, YouTube videos, great art), or does the classroom environment function as a visual desert?
- Do the colors of the room (walls, floors, ceiling) stimulate or deaden students' engagement with learning?
- What types of illumination are used (fluorescent, incandescent, natural)? Do the sources of light refresh students or leave them feeling distracted or drained and depleted?
- Is there a feeling of spaciousness in the learning environment, or do students feel stressed due to overcrowding or lack of privacy?

Body Smart

- Do students spend most of their time sitting at their desks with little opportunity for movement, or do they have frequent opportunities to get up and move around (e.g., through exercise breaks, hands-on activities, role-play)?
- Do students receive healthy snacks and a well-designed breakfast or lunch during the day to keep their bodies active and their minds alert, or do they eat junk food during recess and have high-fat, low-nutrition cafeteria meals?
- Are there materials in the classroom that allow students to manipulate objects, build things, be tactile, or in other ways gain hands-on experience, or does a "don't touch" ethos pervade the room?

Music Smart

- Does the auditory environment promote learning (e.g., background music, white noise, pleasant environmental sounds, silence), or do disturbing noises frequently interfere with learning (e.g., loud buzzers or bells, aircraft overhead, traffic outside, industrial machines)?
- How does the teacher use his or her voice? Does it vary in intensity, inflection, and emphasis, or does it have a dull monotone quality

that puts students to sleep (like Ben Stein's voice in the movie *Ferris Bueller's Day Off*)?

People Smart

- Does an atmosphere of belonging and trust permeate the classroom, or do students feel alienated, distant, or mistrustful of one another?
- Are there established procedures for mediating conflict between class members, or must problems often be referred to a higher authority (e.g., the principal or the police) for resolution?
- Do students have frequent opportunities to interact in positive ways (e.g., through peer teaching, discussions, group projects, collaborative learning, end-of-term parties), or are students largely isolated from each other in class?

Self Smart

- Do students have opportunities to work independently, develop self-paced projects, or find time and space for privacy during the day, or is there a nonstop barrage of interpersonal demands placed on them?
- Are students exposed to experiences that heighten their self-concept (e.g., mindfulness meditation exercises, genuine praise and other positive reinforcement, frequent experiences of success in their school work), or are they subjected to put-downs, unredeemed failure, or other negative emotional experiences?
- Do students have the opportunity to share feelings in the classroom, or are their inner lives considered off-limits or dealt with punitively?
- Are students with emotional difficulties referred to mental health professionals for support, or are they simply left to fend for themselves?
- Are students given authentic choices in how they are to learn, or do they have only two choices: the teacher's way or the highway?

Nature Smart

- Are students given opportunities to do some of their learning outside of the school building in natural settings (e.g., through field trips, gardening, classes on the lawn), or do they remain isolated from the natural world during most of their school day?

- Does the classroom contain any living things aside from humans (e.g., pets, fish, gerbils, plants), or is the occasional fly the only nonhuman living thing to pass through its portals?
- Does the classroom have windows that look out onto the sky, clouds, trees, lawns, or other natural phenomena, or is it windowless and shut off from any contact with the world of nature?

The answers to these questions will provide a telling commentary on the quality of the learning environment available to students in school. If answers consistently tilt toward the negative side of the ledger, then learning is apt to be significantly impaired, even if students come into the classroom able, willing, and excited to learn. By contrast, answers that tend toward the positive will enhance a classroom environment to the point where even students who enter the room with significant academic, emotional, or cognitive difficulties will have an opportunity to feel stimulated toward making great strides in their learning.

MI Activity Centers

Although students can certainly engage in MI activities while seated at their desks, lengthy periods of seat time place significant limits on the kinds of MI experiences they can have. Restructuring the classroom to create "intelligence-friendly" areas or activity centers can greatly expand the parameters for student exploration in each domain. Activity centers can take a variety of forms, as illustrated in Figure 7.1. This figure shows MI activity centers along two axes: permanent to temporary (Axis A) and open-ended to topic-specific (Axis B).

Permanent Open-Ended Activity Centers

Quadrant 1 of Figure 7.1 represents permanent (usually yearlong) centers designed to provide students with a wide range of open-ended experiences in each intelligence. Here are some examples of such centers for each intelligence (with a very partial list of suggested items that might be found in such centers):

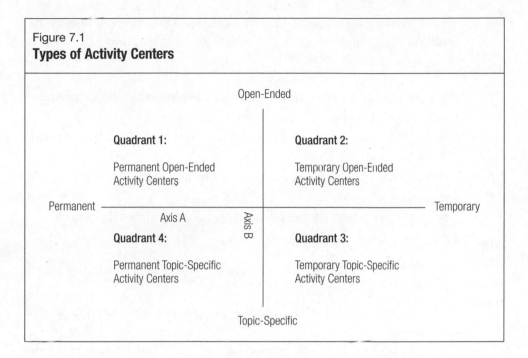

Figure 7.1
Types of Activity Centers

Word Smart

- Book nook or library area (with comfortable seating)
- Language lab (audio listening and recording devices, earphones, talking books)
- Writing center (word processing apps, varieties of paper and writing implements, magnet letters)

Number/Logic Smart

- Math lab (calculators, math manipulatives, measuring tools)
- Science center (chemistry equipment, microscope and slides, biology- and physics-related materials)

Picture Smart

- Art area (painting supplies, collage materials, drawing and painting apps)
- Visual media center (video playback and recording devices, animation apps, photography supplies)

- Visual-thinking area (maps, graphs, visual puzzles, picture library, 3-D building materials)

Body Smart

- Open space for creative movement (mini-trampoline, juggling equipment, stability balls)
- Hands-on center (clay, carpentry tools and supplies, construction blocks or connectors)
- Tactile-learning area (relief maps, mystery box with different textures, sandpaper letters)
- Drama center (stage for performances, props, puppet theater)

Music Smart

- Music lab (audio playback and recording devices, earphones, music recordings, composition apps)
- Music performance center (percussion instruments, audio recorder, metronome)
- Listening lab (stethoscope, walkie-talkies, small bottles that make different "mystery sounds" when shaken)

People Smart

- Round table for group discussions
- Desks paired for peer teaching
- Social area (board games, comfortable furniture for informal social gatherings)
- Computer area for social networking, Skype conferences, and so on

Self Smart

- Study carrels for individual work
- Loft (with nooks and crannies for privacy)
- Computer hutch (for self-paced study)

Nature Smart

- Plant center (seeds, gardening tools, supplies)
- Animal center (cage, terrarium, ant farm)
- Aquatic center (aquarium, tools for observing and measuring marine life)

Labeling each activity center with explicit MI nomenclature (e.g., "Word Smart Center," "Picture Smart Studio," "Nature Smart Corner") will reinforce students' understanding of MI theory. You may want to explain that the centers are named for the intelligence that is used *most often* in each center (remember from Chapter 1 that intelligences are always interacting, so students don't have to switch activity centers if, for example, they want to add a picture to the writing they're doing in the Word Smart Center).

Temporary Open-Ended Activity Centers

Quadrant 2 of Figure 7.1 represents activity centers for open-ended exploration that can be set up and taken down quickly. This type of center can be as simple as eight tables positioned around the classroom, each clearly labeled with an intelligence and holding intelligence-specific materials that invite students to engage in open-ended activities. Games lend themselves particularly well to temporary open-ended activity centers. Here are some examples of games that might be played in each center:

- **Word Smart**—Scrabble
- **Number/Logic Smart**—Monopoly
- **Picture Smart**—Pictionary
- **Body Smart**—Twister
- **Music Smart**—Encore
- **People Smart**—Family Feud
- **Self Smart**—The Ungame
- **Nature Smart**—Frank's Zoo

Temporary open-ended activity centers are especially useful for introducing students to the idea of multiple intelligences and for giving them experiences that illustrate each intelligence.

Temporary Topic-Specific Activity Centers

Quadrant 3 of Figure 7.1 represents topic-specific activity centers that change frequently and are geared toward a particular theme or subject. For example, if students are studying a unit on housing, you might create eight different centers that involve students in meaningful activities within each intelligence. The activities for the housing unit might include the following:

- **Word Smart**—A Reading Center where students read books on houses and write about what they've read
- **Number/Logic Smart**—A Computing Center where students compare the costs, square footage, or other statistical measurements of different houses
- **Picture Smart**—A Drawing Center where students design a futuristic house
- **Body Smart**—A Building Center where students create a model of a house using balsa wood and glue
- **Music Smart**—A Music Center where students listen to songs about dwellings (e.g., "This Old House," "Yellow Submarine") and make up their own songs
- **People Smart**—A Social Center where students "play house," simulating a home environment with peers
- **Self Smart**—A Reflection Center where students think, write, draw, and act out their personal experiences related to the homes they've lived in
- **Nature Smart**—A Landscape Architecture Center where students can design natural features to complement the house (e.g., lawn, bonsai garden, fountain, plants, aquarium)

Permanent Topic-Specific (Shifting) Activity Centers

Finally, Quadrant 4 of Figure 7.1 represents activity centers that are essentially a combination of Quadrant 1 (ongoing and permanent) and Quadrant 3 (topic-specific and temporary) activity centers. Permanent topic-specific activity centers are most appropriate for teachers working with yearlong themes along the lines of Susan Kovalik's (1993, 2001) Highly Effective Teaching (HET) model (formerly known as Integrated Thematic Instruction [ITI]). Each center exists year-round and includes permanent materials and resources that never change (e.g., art supplies in the Picture Smart Center, hands-on materials in the Body Smart Center). Within each center, however, are revolving "explorations" that change with every monthly component or weekly topic of the yearlong theme. So, for example, if the yearlong theme is "Does Everything Change?," a monthlong component might deal with the seasons, with a week devoted to each one. The activity centers might focus on winter one week, then shift to spring the next week, and to summer and fall in subsequent weeks. Every center might have activity cards posted that tell students what kinds of things they can work on either alone or collaboratively. For example, the activity cards for the topic of "summer" might read as follows:

- **Word Smart**—"Write a poem about what you plan to do during the summer. If this is a collaborative group activity, first choose a scribe to write down the poem. Then, each person should contribute a line to the poem. Finally, choose someone to read the poem to the class."

- **Number/Logic Smart**—"First, find out how many days there are in your summer vacation. Then, figure how out many minutes are in that number of days. Finally, calculate the number of seconds in your summer vacation. If this is a group activity, collaborate with the other members of your group on your answers."

- **Picture Smart**—"Make a drawing of some of the things you plan to do during the summer. If this is a group activity, do a group drawing on a long sheet of mural paper."

- **Body Smart**—"Create your own representation of 'summer' using a lump of clay. If this is a group activity, cooperate with the other members of your group to create a clay sculpture or quickly improvise a short play that includes the group's favorite summer activities."

- **Music Smart**—"Make up a rap, chant, or song about summer. If this is a group activity, collaborate on a group rap, chant, or song to present to the class, or brainstorm all the songs you can think of that have to do with summer and be prepared to sing a medley of them to the class."

- **People Smart**—"Have a group discussion about what you think makes for a *great* summer and select a spokesperson to summarize your conclusions in front of the class."

- **Self Smart**—"Make a list or a series of sketches of all the things you like about summer." (*Note:* Students work alone in this center.)

- **Nature Smart**—"Close your eyes and picture all the types of animals and plants you are likely to see this summer. Then, open your eyes and either draw them or create a story (or list) where they are all mentioned."

Student Choice and Activity Centers

Whether or not students should be able to choose which activity centers they work in depends on the types of activity centers (i.e., which quadrant the center belongs in) and the purpose of each center. Generally speaking, Quadrant 1 and 2 activity centers (those involving open-ended experiences) are best structured as "choice" activities. In other words, you can make them available to students during break times, recess, or special "choice times" after students have completed their other schoolwork. When used in this way, activity centers provide excellent assessment information about students' strengths in the eight intelligences. Students usually gravitate toward activity centers based on intelligences that they prefer or in which they feel most competent. For example, students who repeatedly go to the Picture Smart area and engage in drawing activities are sending a strong message to the teacher about the importance of Picture Smart in their lives.

Quadrant 3 and Quadrant 4 activity centers emphasize directed study. Consequently, when using these types of centers, you may want to let students choose the center they *start* with, then have them rotate clockwise until they've experienced all eight centers (I use a simple chime or bell to signal the movement from one center to the next). Using this rotation system also with Quadrant 1 and 2 activity centers will ensure that students have experiences across a wide spectrum of intelligences.

Activity centers provide students with the opportunity to engage in active learning. They serve as oases in the learning desert for many students who are thirsting for something other than boring worksheets, lectures, and standardized testing. MI theory allows you to structure activity centers in ways that activate a wide range of learning potentials in students. Though the descriptions here have been limited to centers based on individual intelligences, there is no reason why centers can't be structured to combine intelligences in different ways. In this sense, virtually any activity center that goes beyond simple reading, writing, or calculation activities qualifies as an MI center. A "Mechanic's Garage," for example, combines Number/Logic Smart, Picture Smart, and Body Smart, while a "Composer's Cabaret" combines Word Smart and Music Smart.

For Further Study

1. Survey your classroom environment using the questions on pages 97–100 as a guide. List the changes you would like to make in the ecology of your classroom. Prioritize these changes, putting those items that you'd like to change but can't on a separate list. Then, set about making those changes that you *can* make, one step at a time.

2. Set up MI activity centers in your classroom. First, decide which type of activity center you'd like to start out with (i.e., Quadrant 1, 2, 3, or 4). Then, list the materials you need and create a schedule for setting up the centers. Enlist the help of parent volunteers, students, or colleagues as necessary. If you've established permanent centers, assess the project after two or three weeks of use. If you've established temporary centers, assess their success immediately after students experience them. Use your evaluations to guide the design of future centers.

3. To introduce the idea of activity centers to your class, select a topic that engages students—for instance, fast food. Put up eight signs at various points around the room, each bearing the symbol for an intelligence. Under each sign, tape an activity card. Hand out slips of paper on which have been inscribed symbols for each of the eight intelligences (one symbol per slip) and have students go to the center that corresponds with their individual slip of paper. Students then need to read the activity for their area and cooperatively begin working on it. Set a time to reconvene so the groups can present their findings. Here are some suggestions for activities related to the topic of fast food:

   - **Word Smart**—"Create a manifesto (statement of basic principles) concerning student attitudes about fast food."
   - **Number/Logic Smart**—"Using the nutritional charts provided by the fast-food outlets you see here, develop a fast-food breakfast, lunch, or dinner that is as low in fat as possible; then, put together a fast-food breakfast, lunch, or dinner that is as high in fat as possible."
   - **Picture Smart**—"Create a mural that depicts people's fast-food eating habits."

- **Body Smart**—"Rehearse a role-play or commercial (with or without words) about people's fast-food eating habits and present it to the whole class."
- **Music Smart**—"Write a jingle or a rap about people's fast-food eating habits and present it to the whole class."
- **People Smart**—"Discuss the fast-food eating habits of your small group, then go out and poll the rest of the class about their fast-food eating habits. Select a scribe to record and report the results."
- **Self Smart**—"Think about these questions: If you could be any fast food, which would you be? Why? Choose a method for recording your thoughts (e.g., drawing, writing, pantomime). You may work alone or as a group."
- **Nature Smart**—"Make a list of all the plants and animals used in creating fast food. Discuss the potential effects of their consumption on the world's ecosystems (e.g., oxygen-producing rain forests may be cleared for raising the cattle used for the meat in hamburgers)."

8

MI Theory and Classroom Management

Nature endows a child with a sensitiveness to order. It is a kind of inner sense that distinguishes the relationships between various objects rather than the objects themselves. It thus makes a whole of an environment in which the several parts are mutually dependent. When a person is oriented in such an environment, he can direct his activity to the attainment of specific goals. Such an environment provides the foundation for an integrated life.

—*Maria Montessori*

A classroom is a microsociety complete with student citizens, many of whom have competing needs and interests. Consequently, rules, routines, regulations, and procedures—elements of *order*—are a fundamental part of the classroom infrastructure. Though MI theory doesn't prescribe a classroom management scheme per se, it offers beleaguered teachers a new perspective on the many types of management strategies that they have used or might use to "keep order" and ensure a smoothly running learning environment.

Gaining Students' Attention

Perhaps the best illustration of MI theory's utility in the area of classroom management can be seen in the ways in which teachers have sought to gain their students' attention at the beginning of a class or the start of a new learning activity. A comedy record some years ago (Cheech and Chong's "Sister Mary Elephant") humorously recounted one teacher's attempts to bring her class to order. After trying to get the class's attention in the usual way ("Class? Class?"), she yells "Shut up!" at the top of her voice. Everyone becomes quiet, and she says "Thank you" in a normal voice. But as she begins teaching, the students resume their chatter, which keeps building until once again the Sister yells "Shut up!," which makes the class quiet again and elicits once again her modest "Thank you," after which the cycle repeats itself again and again.

Teachers can laugh at this situation because many of us have had a similar experience. From a multiple intelligences perspective, however, the mere use of words to quiet a class—a Word Smart approach—might be regarded as the *least* effective way to gain the class's attention. Often, the teacher's Word Smart requests or commands (as "figure") dissolve in the students' Word Smart utterances (as "ground"). Students do not readily differentiate the teacher's voice from the other voices surrounding them. As a result, they fail to attend to directions. This phenomenon is particularly evident among students who have been diagnosed as having attention deficit hyperactivity disorder (ADHD), but it exists to a certain degree among most students.

A look at some of the more effective techniques used in the past by teachers to grab attention suggests the need to move to other intelligences. So, for example, we have the kindergarten teacher playing a piano chord to ask for silence (Music Smart), the 4th grade teacher flicking the lights on and off to call the class to order (Picture Smart), and the high school teacher using silence itself as an injunction to self-responsibility (Self Smart). Here are several other strategies for getting students' attention in the classroom:

- **Word Smart**—Write the words "Silence, please!" on the blackboard.
- **Music Smart**—Clap a short rhythmic phrase and have students clap it back.
- **Body Smart**—Put your finger against your lips to suggest silence while holding your other arm up. Have students copy your gestures until all hands are up.

- **Picture Smart**—Show a previously taken photo of the classroom being attentive on the whiteboard or media screen.
- **Number/Logic Smart**—Use a stopwatch to keep track of the time being wasted and write on the blackboard the number of seconds lost at 30-second intervals (time, perhaps, to be subtracted from a favored class activity).
- **People Smart**—Whisper in the ear of a student, "It's time to start again—pass it on," and then wait while students pass the message around the room.
- **Self Smart**—Start teaching the lesson and assume that the students will eventually take charge of their own behavior and become attentive.
- **Nature Smart**—Play a recording of a shrill bird whistle, or (even better) bring a live animal into the classroom. (Generally speaking, whenever there is an animal visitor in a classroom, that's where the attention will be!)

You can use similar strategies to initiate other types of classroom routines such as preparing students for transitions, starting activities, giving instructions, or forming small groups. Essentially, the underlying mechanism of each of these routines involves cueing students in such a way as to link aspects of one or more of the eight intelligences to specific instructions and behaviors. Teachers need to discover ways of getting students' attention not simply through the spoken word but through pictures or graphic symbols (Picture Smart), gestures and physical movements (Body Smart), musical phrases (Music Smart), logical patterns (Number/Logic Smart), social signals (People Smart), emotions (Self Smart), or natural world cues (Nature Smart).

Preparing for Transitions

To help prepare students for transitions, you can teach the class specific cues for each type of transition. When focusing on Music Smart, for example, you could explain that you will use different selections of music to signal recess (Beethoven's Pastoral Symphony), lunch ("Food, Glorious Food" from *Oliver!*), and dismissal (the "Goin' Home" movement from Dvořák's New World Symphony). Or, better yet, let the students choose the music for each transition. If Picture Smart is your focus, you might use graphic symbols: a photo of the class playing outside for recess, a photo of the class eating in the cafeteria for lunch, and a photo of the class boarding school buses or walking home for dismissal. For Body Smart, you might use specific gestures or body movements to signal the coming event. With this type of strategy, you begin the gesture and students then make the gesture back, indicating that they have "heard" the message (e.g., stretching and yawning for recess, rubbing stomachs and licking lips for lunch, and placing hands above the eyes and peering outside for dismissal). For Number/Logic Smart, you might display a large digital countdown clock that students can see from anywhere in the classroom, set it for the time left until the transition, and let students keep track of the time left. For People Smart, you could use a telephone-tree model: Simply give the cue to one student, who then tells *two* students, who each tell two students, and so forth, until all students are personally informed.

Communicating Class Rules

You can communicate the school or classroom rules for proper conduct through a multiple intelligences approach. Some possibilities include the following:

- **Word Smart**—Rules are written and posted in the classroom (this is the most traditional approach).
- **Number/Logic Smart**—Rules are numbered and referred to by number (e.g., "You're doing a great job of following rule number 4").
- **Picture Smart**—Written rules are accompanied by graphic symbols of what to do (e.g., "respect for others" might be symbolized by an image of two people holding hands).
- **Body Smart**—Each rule has a specific gesture; students show they know the rules by going through the different gestures (e.g., "respect for others" might be symbolized by waving and smiling at class members).
- **Music Smart**—Rules are set to music (either written by students or set to the melody of an existing song) or associated with relevant songs (e.g., "respect for others" might be connected to Aretha Franklin's version of the song "Respect").
- **People Smart**—Each rule is assigned to a small group of students who then have responsibility for knowing its ins and outs, interpreting it, and even enforcing it.

- **Self Smart**—Students are responsible for creating the class rules at the beginning of the year (with input from the teacher, of course) and developing their own unique ways of communicating them to others.
- **Nature Smart**—An animal symbol is assigned to each of the rules (e.g., "Respectful Rabbit"). Students learn the rules by imitating the sounds or movements of the animals.

Asking students to help create classroom rules is a common way of gaining their support of the rules. Similarly, asking students to help develop their own MI strategies or cues for classroom procedures is a useful way to establish effective cues. Students may want to provide their own music, create their own gestures, draw their own graphic symbols, or come up with their own animals to signal the class for different activities, transitions, rules, or procedures.

Forming Groups

Another application of MI theory to classroom management is in the forming of small groups. Although groups are often formed on the basis of arbitrary commands ("You, you, and you are in a group") or intrinsic factors (e.g., interest/ability groups), educators have increasingly seen the value of heterogeneous groups in collaborative instruction. MI theory provides a wide range of techniques for creating heterogeneous groups based on incidental features related to each intelligence. Some of the following ideas have been adapted from the book *Playfair: Everybody's Guide to Noncompetitive Play* by Joel Goodman and Matt Weinstein (1980):

- **Word Smart**—"Think of a vowel sound in your first name. Now make that vowel sound out loud. Go around the room and find three or four people who are making the same vowel sound, and that will be your group."
- **Number/Logic Smart**—"When I give the signal, I want you to raise between one and five fingers. Go! Now keep those fingers raised, and find three or four people whose raised fingers combined with yours add up to an odd number."
- **Picture Smart**—"Find three or four people who are wearing the same color clothes as you are."

- **Body Smart**—"Start hopping on one foot . . . now find three or four people who are hopping on the same foot."
- **Music Smart**—"What are some songs that everybody knows?" The teacher writes four or five titles on the board (e.g., "Row, Row, Row Your Boat," "Happy Birthday to You"). "Okay, I'd like you to file past me while I whisper one of these songs in your ear. Remember which one it is, and when I give the signal, I'd like you to sing your song and find all the others in the class who are singing it too. Go!" (Alternatively, students can decide themselves which song to sing.)
- **Nature Smart**—"Visualize a sheep, a pig, and a cow in a pasture. Suddenly, there is a loud noise and two of them run off. There is only one animal left. Start making the sound of that animal out loud, and then find three or four people who are making the same animal sound!"

You need not address *all* intelligences when developing a classroom management scheme. But by reaching beyond the traditional Word Smart approach and using some of the other intelligences (two or three at a minimum), you will be providing students with more opportunities for internalizing classroom routines in a fun way.

Managing Individual Behaviors

Regardless of how effectively you communicate class rules, routines, and procedures, there will always be students who—because of biological, emotional, or cognitive differences or difficulties—fail to abide by them. These few students may well take up much of your classroom time as you remind them (through several intelligences!) to sit down, stop throwing things, quit hitting, and start behaving. Although MI theory has no magical answer to their problems, it can provide a context for looking at a range of discipline systems that have proved effective with difficult behaviors. Naturally, MI theory suggests that *no one discipline approach is best for all kids*. In fact, the theory suggests that teachers may need to match different discipline approaches to different kinds of learners. What follows is a broad range of discipline methods matched to the eight intelligences:

- **Word Smart**—Talk with the student; provide books for the student to read that refer to the problem and point to solutions; help the student use "self-talk" strategies for gaining control.

- **Number/Logic Smart**—Use Dreikurs's (1993) logical-consequences approach; have the student quantify and chart the occurrence of negative or positive behaviors.
- **Picture Smart**—Have the student draw or visualize appropriate behaviors; provide the student with a metaphor to use in confronting challenges (e.g., "If people say bad things to you, see the bad things as arrows that you can dodge"); show the student videos that deal with the issue or that model the appropriate behaviors.
- **Body Smart**—Have the student role-play the inappropriate and appropriate behaviors and discuss the differences (these can be videotaped); teach the student to recognize red flags that indicate the beginning of a stressful situation that might erupt (e.g., tight chest, shortness of breath) and provide self-regulation strategies (e.g., taking a deep breath, tightening and relaxing muscles).
- **Music Smart**—Find musical selections that deal with the issue the student is facing; provide music that helps create the appropriate behavior (e.g., calming music for tantrums, stimulating music—"musical Adderall"—to help children labeled ADHD focus); teach the student to "play" his favorite music in his mind whenever he feels out of control.
- **People Smart**—Provide peer-group counseling; pair the student with a role model; have the student teach or look after a younger child; give the student other social outlets for her energies (e.g., leading a group).
- **Self Smart**—Teach the student to voluntarily go to a nonpunitive time-out area to gain control (see Nelsen, 1999); provide one-to-one counseling; develop a behavior contract (with the student's input); give the student the opportunity to work on high-interest projects; provide esteem-building activities.
- **Nature Smart**—Tell animal stories that teach about improper and proper behavior (e.g., "The Boy Who Cried Wolf" for a persistent fibber); use animal metaphors in working with difficult behavior (e.g., ask an aggressive student what sort of animal he feels like and how he can learn to "tame" it); use animal-assisted therapy to help with social, emotional, and cognitive functioning.

Behavioral strategies can be further tailored to the needs of students with specific kinds of difficulties. Figure 8.1 shows what some of these interventions might look like.

Figure 8.1

MI Strategies for Managing Individual Behaviors

Intelligence	Aggressive Student	Withdrawn Student	Hyperactive Student
Word Smart	Have the student read appropriate children's literature on the theme of anger management	Suggest that the student take up debate, oratory, or storytelling	Suggest books on the theme of hyperactivity (e.g., *The Boy Who Burned Too Brightly*)
Number/ Logic Smart	Use Dreikurs's natural and logical-consequences approach to discipline	Suggest that the student join a chess, coding, or science club	Provide the student with a way of self-monitoring time-on-task using a timer or timer app (e.g., Time Timer)
Picture Smart	Videotape the student in an aggressive situation, and one in an appropriate nonaggressive situation, then show him the videos in a nonjudgmental manner and discuss how he feels in each setting	Show the student a movie about a withdrawn child who befriends someone the same age	Recommend video games that help develop focus, control, and working memory
Body Smart	Provide instruction in martial arts training to channel aggression	Pair the student with a trusted mentor for walks, sports, games	Teach the student progressive relaxation, yoga, mindfulness meditation; recommend more play, exercise, recreation outdoors
Music Smart	Teach songs that promote nonaggressive ways of dealing with conflict that he could sing when he feels like he's going to lose control	Encourage the student to join a band, orchestra, choir, or other musical group	Provide the student's favorite music ("musical Adderall") to listen to with earphones if it helps him or her focus
People Smart	Suggest the student role-play the aggressive behavior and then role-play alternative ways of behaving, based on feedback from students and teacher	Refer the student for group counseling	Ask the student to tutor a younger child

Intelligence	Aggressive Student	Withdrawn Student	Hyperactive Student
Self Smart	Institute positive time-out (Nelsen, 1999) when the student feels close to a meltdown	Refer the student for one-to-one counseling/ psychotherapy	Teach the student emotional self-regulation strategies
Nature Smart	Suggest the student identify with an animal and consider how best to tame it as a metaphor for solutions to his aggressive behavior	Pair the child with an animal to take care of	Encourage the student to spend lots of time in nature

Taking a Broader Perspective

Of course, the above strategies are no substitute for a comprehensive professional team approach to a student's emotional problems or behavioral difficulties (e.g., Positive Behavioral Interventions and Supports, or PBIS). MI theory is valuable, however, because it provides teachers with the means to sort through a broad range of behavioral strategies and discipline systems and offers guidelines for selecting a limited number of interventions to try out based upon the student's proclivities.

Sometimes the best strategy for a student may be one matched to a poorly developed intelligence. For example, if a student has behavior problems because of his underdeveloped People Smart abilities, then he may benefit most from activities that seek to develop his social skills. In other cases, however, the best strategies will be in a student's areas of strength. For example, you probably would not want to assign reading to a student who has problems with both reading and "acting out" her frustrations. This strategy might only exacerbate the situation. By contrast, helping a student *master* a reading problem may be an important ingredient in improving her classroom behavior. For a student who acquires knowledge easily through the printed word, providing behavioral strategies geared to this strength would, generally speaking, be among the most appropriate choices.

Ultimately, MI theory used in conjunction with classroom management goes far beyond providing specific behavioral strategies and techniques. MI theory can greatly affect students' behavior in the classroom simply by creating an environment where individual needs are recognized and attended to throughout the school day. Students are less likely to be confused, frustrated, or stressed out when they begin to have consistent experiences of success and engagement. As a result, there is likely to be far less need for behavioral "tricks" or elaborate discipline systems, which often are initiated only when the student's learning environment has broken down around him. As Leslie Hart (1981) points out, "Classroom management, discipline, teacher burnout, student 'failures'—these are all problems inherent in the teacher-does-everything approach. Permit and encourage students to use their brains actively to learn, and the results can be astonishing" (p. 40).

For Further Study

1. Select a classroom routine that students are currently having trouble adapting to (e.g., moving from one activity to another, learning class rules) and develop different intelligence-specific cues to help them master it.

2. Try out nonverbal ways of getting students' attention through Music Smart, Picture Smart, Body Smart, People Smart, Number/Logic Smart, Nature Smart, or Self Smart intelligences. Develop alternative cues from those mentioned in this chapter.

3. Choose a student who has been particularly disruptive in class or whose behavior in some other way has proved difficult to handle. Establish criteria for knowing when her problems have been solved or significantly ameliorated. Determine her most developed intelligences (using identification strategies from Chapter 3). Then select and use behavioral strategies that match the student's most developed intelligences. Consider also using strategies in less developed intelligences that would help develop skills in areas of need. Evaluate the results according to your pre-established criteria.

4. Review the behavioral systems currently used in your classroom or school. Identify which intelligences they address and how they match or do not match your students' learning strengths.

5. Identify classroom management issues not specifically discussed in this chapter and relate MI theory to them in some tangible way (e.g., dealing with tantrums, swearing, coming to school late). What are the advantages of using MI theory in handling classroom management problems? What are its limitations?

9

The MI School

The school we envision commits itself to fostering students' deep understanding in several core disciplines. It encourages students' use of that knowledge to solve the problems and complete the tasks that they may confront in the wider community. At the same time, the school seeks to encourage the unique blend of intelligences in each of its students, assessing their development regularly in intelligence-fair ways.

—*Howard Gardner*

The implications of MI theory extend far beyond classroom instruction. At heart, the theory of multiple intelligences calls for nothing short of a fundamental transformation in the way schools are structured. It sends a strong message to educators everywhere that students who show up for school at the beginning of each day have the right to be provided with experiences that stimulate and develop all of their intelligences. During the typical school day, every student should be exposed to courses, projects, and/or programs that focus on developing each of their intelligences, not just the standard Word Smart and Number/Logic Smart abilities that for decades have been exalted above every other form of human achievement in school.

MI and the Traditional School

In most U.S. schools today, programs that concentrate on the neglected intelligences (Music Smart, Picture Smart, Body Smart, Nature Smart, People Smart, and Self Smart) tend to be considered electives and peripheral to the core academic courses. When a school district has a budget crisis, fiscal managers usually don't consider dropping the reading and math programs to save money. They begin by eliminating the music program, the art program, and the physical education program (see Hawkins, 2012). Even when these programs are still operating, they often show the subtle influence of Word Smart and Number/Logic Smart demands. John Goodlad (2004), commenting on observations from his monumental "A Study of Schooling," writes: "I am disappointed with the degree to which arts classes appear to be dominated by the ambience of English, mathematics, and other academic subjects. . . . They did not convey the picture of individual expression and artistic creativity toward which one is led by the rhetoric of forward-looking practice in the field" (pp. 219–220). Goodlad found the physical education classes similarly flawed: "Anything that might be called a program was virtually nonexistent. Physical education appeared to be a teacher-monitored recess. . . . " (p. 222).

Administrators and others who help structure programs in schools can use MI theory as a framework for making sure that each student has the opportunity every day to experience direct interaction with each of the eight intelligences in the specific domains where they figure most prominently (e.g., art, music, physical education). Figure 9.1 describes some of the programmatic features that span the eight intelligences in school, including traditional courses, supplementary programs or electives, and extracurricular offerings.

The Components of an MI School

Simply providing students with access to a diverse range of school subjects does not necessarily make a school an MI school. In his book *Multiple Intelligences: New Horizons in Theory and Practice*, Gardner (2006a) sets up one vision of the ideal multiple intelligences school, drawing on two non-school models:

Figure 9.1
MI in School Programs

Intelligence	Subjects	Electives and Supplementary Programs	Extracurricular Activities
Word Smart	• Reading • Language arts • Literature • English • History • Second languages • Speech	• Creative writing lab • Communication skills • Journalism • Public speaking • Sign language	• Debate • School newspaper • Yearbook • Language club • Honor society • Student radio broadcast
Number/ Logic Smart	• Science courses • Mathematics • Economics • Accounting • Electricity	• Critical thinking • Coding • Financial management • Business math	• Science club • Computer (coding) club • Math club • Chess club
Picture Smart	• Filmmaking • Photography • Drafting • Art history • Art appreciation	• Visual-thinking lab • Web design • Animation course • Interior design • Sculpture • Architecture • Ceramics	• Photography club • Audiovisual staff • Chess club • Student TV broadcast
Body Smart	• Physical education • Auto mechanics • Drama/theater • Driver's education • Personal hygiene class	• Fitness program • Ceramics • Dance • Yoga • CPR training • Nutrition • Jewelry making	• Team sports • Individual sports • Cheerleading • Walking program • Martial arts
Music Smart	• Music appreciation • Instrumental music • Music history • Voice	• Orff Schulwerk program • Kodaly method • Suzuki training • Dalcroze Eurhythmics	• Band • Orchestra • Chorus • Music club • Choir • Music production group (computer generated)

Continued

Figure 9.1 (*continued*)
MI in School Programs

Intelligence	Subjects	Electives and Supplementary Programs	Extracurricular Activities
People Smart	• Social sciences • Home economics • Business • Media studies • Sociology • Anthropology • Politics	• Social skills training • Substance abuse prevention • Diversity training • Counseling • Bullying prevention	• Glee club • Student government • Model United Nations • Future Homemakers of America • Service organizations • Human rights group
Self Smart	• Psychology • Career development • Research skills on the internet • Personal study skills	• Self-development programs • Counseling services • Philosophy • Religion • Career counseling	• Special-interest clubs • Hobby clubs • Honor society • Mindfulness meditation group • Entrepreneurship club • Blog- and website-building workshops
Nature Smart	• Biology • Zoology • Botany • Geology • Meteorology • Oceanography	• Gardening class • Camping expeditions • Landscaping class • Horticulture studies • Agricultural studies	• Future Farmers of America • Gardening club • Birdwatching club • Ecology groups

- *Contemporary children's museums*, which provide hands-on, interdisciplinary learning for visitors based on real-life contexts, set in an informal atmosphere that promotes free inquiry into novel materials and situations
- The age-old model of *apprenticeships*, whereby masters of a trade oversee ongoing projects undertaken by their youthful protégés

Gardner suggests that students in an MI school might spend their mornings working on traditional subjects in nontraditional ways. In particular, Gardner recommends the use of project-based learning, whereby students study a particular area of inquiry (a historical conflict, a scientific principle, a literary genre) and develop a project (photo essay, experiment, journal) that reflects an ongoing process of exploration of the many dimensions of the topic. Students then would go into the community during the second part of the day and further extend their understanding of the topics they are studying in school. Younger students might regularly go to children's museums, art or science museums, or other places where hands-on exploratory learning and play are encouraged and where interaction with docents and other expert guides takes place. Older students (past 3rd grade) could choose apprenticeships based upon an assessment of their intellectual proclivities, interests, and available resources. They could then spend their afternoons studying with community experts on specific arts, skills, crafts, physical activities, or other endeavors.

Fundamental to Gardner's vision of an MI school are the activities of three key members of the school staff, representing functions that are currently absent from most schools. In Gardner's model, every MI school would have staff filling the following roles:

1. **Assessment specialist:** This staff member would be responsible for developing an ongoing record of each child's strengths, challenges, and interests in all eight intelligences. Using intelligence-fair assessments, the assessment specialist would document each child's school experience in many ways (through observation, informal assessments, and multimedia documentation) and provide parents, teachers, administrators, and students themselves with an overview of their proclivities in each of the eight intelligences. (See Chapter 10 for an MI perspective on testing and assessment.)

2. **Student–curriculum broker:** This person would serve as a bridge between the student's gifts and abilities in the eight intelligences and the available resources in the school. The student–curriculum broker would match students to specific courses and electives and provide teachers with information about how particular subjects might best be presented to a student (e.g., through video, hands-on experiences, books, music). This staff member would be responsible for maximizing the student's learning potential given the available materials, methods, and human resources.

3. **School–community broker:** This staff person would be the link between the student's intellectual proclivities and the resources

available in the broader community. A school–community broker would possess a wealth of information about the kinds of apprentice-ships, organizations, mentorships, tutorials, community courses, and other learning experiences available in the surrounding area. This person would then seek to match a student's interests, skills, and abilities to appropriate experiences beyond the school walls (e.g., finding an expert cellist to guide a student's burgeoning interest in playing the cello).

According to Gardner, MI schools are far from utopian pipe dreams, but they do depend upon the confluence of several factors, including (1) assessment practices that engage students in the actual materials and sym-bols of each intelligence, (2) curriculum development that reflects real-life skills and experiences, (3) teacher training programs that reflect sound educational principles and that have master teachers working with students committed to the field, and (4) a high level of community involvement from parents, business leaders, museums, and other learning institutions.

A Model MI School: New City School

Although the first school to fully implement multiple intelligences, The Key Learning Community in Indianapolis, Indiana, closed its doors in 2016—a victim of the push in American education for higher standardized test scores—it helped to inspire what became the second school to adapt MI theory in the United States: New City School in St. Louis, Missouri. After reading Gardner's *Frames of Mind* and visiting the Key School (as it was then called) in 1988, Tom Hoerr, the Head of School at New City School, began to meet regularly with his teachers to study Gardner's work and to determine how best to implement its theories in their school. Soon thereafter, they began to modify their teaching and assessment methods to reflect the eight intelligences. In the 1990s, they convened four national conferences on MI theory and their staff wrote two books on multiple intelligences: *Celebrating Multiple Intelligences: Teaching for Success* (Faculty of New City School, 1994) and *Succeeding with Multiple Intelligences: Teaching Through the Personal Intelligences* (1996).

Now, over two decades later, New City School, a highly diverse pri-vate school meeting the needs of students from age 3 to 6th grade at all socioeconomic levels, is still going strong, and has implemented MI theory in some of the following ways:

- **MI-integrated curriculum:** At the kindergarten level, for example, as the school's website points out, "Students role-play stories and practice letter and number formations using their bodies, play dough, chalk, paint, and pencils (Body Smart). They sing and listen to literacy and math songs (Music Smart). Children observe and interact with nature both inside and outside of our classroom. They use these experiences in drawing and writing activities as well as to identify patterns (Nature Smart). The children study artist styles, illustrate their own stories and math problems, construct puzzles, and create tactile letters and numbers (Picture Smart). Students also reflect on their work, make choices, and teach each other. They work alone, with a partner, or in a group (Self Smart and People Smart)" (MI in the Classrooms, 2013-2017).

- **An MI library:** Carrying 13,000 volumes of high-quality children's literature, this library, designed with input from Howard Gardner, has many connections to the seven intelligences beyond Word Smart as well. It includes an amphitheater for storytelling and drama; an Exploratorium with dry-erase walls, a sink, and a tile floor that allows for art projects and other types of "messy" work; and a Games Program that lets students explore MI problem-solving strategies while playing games such as checkers, chess, Othello, and Boggle. It also has MI Centers that are set up on a weekly basis on various themes, including small performances of stories that have been read, art projects inspired by a particular illustrator, and the use of tangrams to further explore stories.

- **The Evan Delano Gallery:** This is an art gallery just outside the MI Library that serves as a venue for art created by students, parents, and other creative individuals in the community. Exhibit themes have included "Full Steam Ahead," showing student work inspired by the science and art initiative (STEAM) in education; "AlphaART," showing work inspired by a letter or letters of the alphabet; and "Sew Loved," a presentation of student-designed and student-created soft sculpture and textile art.

- **Service Learning:** New City School's commitment to developing Self Smart and People Smart is revealed perhaps most powerfully in its contributions to both the local and the global communities. The preschoolers create art, write letters, and sing songs to share with senior citizens at a local retirement center. Second graders are involved in a community outreach program where they help clear annual plants, loosen the soil in preparation for planting bulbs, and harvest vegetables at Forest Park, which they then donate to Operation Food Search, an organization that distributes food to needy families in the St. Louis metropolitan area.

New City School demonstrates what is possible when a group of committed teachers and a highly motivated administrator work together with the community to create learning opportunities for students that span all eight intelligences. For a guide to how the school came into being, see Tom Hoerr's book *Becoming a Multiple Intelligences School* (Hoerr, 2000). You can also contact him directly for more information about the school at trhoerr@newcityschool.org.

MI Schools of the Future

The New City School experience should by no means be taken as the only way, or even necessarily the preferred way, to develop a multiple intelligences school. There may be as many possible types of MI schools as there are groups of educators, parents, administrators, and community leaders committed to putting MI principles into action. Regardless of how they are structured, MI schools of the future will undoubtedly continue to expand the possibilities for unleashing student potential in all the intelligences. Perhaps MI schools of the future will look less like schools and more like the world outside, with traditional school buildings serving as conduits through which students move on their way to meaningful experiences in the community. Programs will arise that specialize in the development of one or more of the intelligences (they have already in magnet schools that specialize in science and the arts)—although we must be quick to guard against a "brave new world" of multiple intelligences that could seek to identify individual students' strongest intelligences early in life so as to exploit them and channel them prematurely into a small niche of society.

Ultimately, what will enrich the development of MI theory is its implementation in interdisciplinary ways that reflect the ever-changing demands of an increasingly complex society. As society changes—and perhaps as we discover new intelligences to help us cope with these changes—MI schools of the future may reflect features that are beyond our wildest dreams.

For Further Study

1. Evaluate your school in terms of its implementation of MI theory. During the course of a school day, ask yourself: Does each student have the opportunity to develop each of the eight intelligences for its own sake (not merely as a medium for teaching academics)? Specify programs, courses, activities, and experiences that develop the intelligences. How could the school's programs be modified to better incorporate the broad spectrum of intelligences?

2. Assuming you had an unlimited amount of money and resources available to you, what kind of multiple intelligences school would you develop? Plan your vision of the ideal MI school. What will the physical plant look like? Draw a floor plan of the school to illustrate. What types of courses will be offered? What will the functions of teachers be? What types of experiences will students have? Develop a scenario of a typical student going through a typical day at such a school.

3. Contact schools that are now using multiple intelligences theory and compare and contrast their different ways of applying the model (use the online search terms "schools" and "multiple intelligences"). Which aspects of each program are applicable to your own school or classroom? Which components are not?

4. Discuss some of the problems that schools might have in implementing MI theory as part of a broader reform movement (e.g., the push for higher standardized test scores). How can MI theory best fit into a school's restructuring process? What elements can be included in staff development to improve the chances for this model's success?

10

MI Theory and Assessment

I believe that we should get away altogether from tests and correlations among tests, and look instead at more naturalistic sources of information about how peoples around the world develop skills important to their way of life.

—*Howard Gardner*

The kinds of changes in instructional practice described in the previous nine chapters require an equivalent adjustment in our approach to assessing learning progress. It would be the height of hypocrisy to ask students to participate in a wide range of experiences spanning all eight intelligences, only to then assess them using tests that focus narrowly on Word Smart or Number/Logic Smart competencies. Educators would clearly be sending the message that these two intelligences take priority over the others.

MI theory proposes a fundamental restructuring of the way in which educators assess their students' learning progress. It suggests a methodology that relies far less on standardized or other formal types of tests (normative or traditional assessment) and far more on measures that compare students to their own past performances (ipsative assessment), represent meaningful expressions of the students' learning process (authentic assessment), and involve students themselves as an integral part the assessment process (student voice).

The MI philosophy of assessment is closely aligned with the perspective of a growing number of leading educators who have argued that authentic measures of assessment probe students' understanding of material far more thoroughly than do multiple-choice or fill-in-the-blank tests (see Gardner 1993b, 2006a; Popham, 2008; Ravitch, 2016). Authentic measures allow students to show what they've learned in context—that is, in a setting that closely matches the environment in which they would be expected to show their learning in real life. By contrast, standardized measures almost always assess students in artificial settings far removed from the real world. Figure 10.1 lists a number of ways in which authentic measures prove superior to standardized benchmarks in promoting educational quality.

Another distinction worth discussing is the one between summative and formative assessments. The goal of summative assessments is to measure student proficiency against a given benchmark or standard; summative assessments include high-stakes standardized tests, standards-aligned tests, and grades given at the end of a course. Formative assessments focus on gathering information about student learning for the purpose of helping both students and teachers improve the level, pace, and quality of instruction, as well as to give feedback that can be part of the student's own learning process (Fisher & Frey, 2014; Moss & Brookhart, 2009).

Summative assessments can be used in a formative way, by using a standardized test not to compare students, but to probe a student's understanding of the material covered. Formative assessments can be used in a summative way, for example, by evaluating a student's learning portfolio against a benchmark or assigning a score to a final product. Both formative and summative assessments can be used as authentic measures, such as when students keep journals or portfolios to track their learning processes (formative assessment), or when they create a final project or performance that represents the culmination of a term-long or yearlong period of study (summative assessment). Both formative and summative assessments can also be used in nonauthentic or traditional ways, such as when pop quizzes are used to see where students are in their understanding of a subject (formative assessment) and those quiz results help determine the final grade in a course (summative assessment). Figure 10.2 illustrates the different interrelationships that can exist among the four categories of assessment.

Figure 10.1
Standardized Testing Versus Authentic Assessment

Standardized Testing

- Reduces children's rich and complex lives to a collection of scores, percentiles, or grades
- Creates stresses that negatively affect a child's performance
- Creates a mythical standard or norm requiring that a certain percentage of children fail
- Pressures teachers to narrow their curriculum to only what is tested on an exam
- Emphasizes one-shot exams that assess knowledge in a single mind at a single moment in time
- Tends to place the focus of interpretation on errors, mistakes, low scores, and other things that children *can't* do
- Focuses too much importance on single sets of data (i.e., test scores) in making educational decisions
- Treats all students in the same way
- Discriminates against some students because of cultural background and learning preferences
- Judges the child without providing suggestions for improvement
- Regards testing and instruction as separate activities

Authentic Assessment

- Gives the teacher a "felt sense" of the child's unique experience as a learner
- Provides interesting, active, lively, and exciting experiences
- Establishes an environment where every child has the opportunity to succeed
- Allows teachers to develop meaningful curricula and assess within the context of that material
- Assesses on an *ongoing* basis in a way that provides a more accurate picture of a student's achievement
- Puts the emphasis on a student's *strengths;* tells what they *can* do and what they're *trying* to do
- Provides *multiple* sources of evaluation that give a more accurate view of a student's progress
- Treats each student as a unique human being
- Provides a *culture-fair* assessment of a student's performance; gives everyone an equal chance to succeed
- Provides information that is *useful* to the learning process
- Regards assessment and teaching as two sides of the same coin

Figure 10.2
Assessment Quadrant with Examples

	Formative Assessments	Summative Assessments
Traditional Assessments	Teacher-created pop quiz that guides teachers in what needs to be retaught or guides students in what needs to be studied	High-stakes standardized test
Authentic Assessments	Student-generated portfolio of ongoing learning progress	End of term "celebration of learning" presentation

Varieties of Assessment Experience

Authentic assessment covers a wide range of instruments, measures, and methods. One of the most important prerequisites to authentic assessment is *observation*. Howard Gardner (1993a, 1993b, 2006a) has pointed out that we can best assess students' multiple intelligences by observing students manipulating the symbol systems of each intelligence (for instance, by observing students play a logical board game, interact with a machine, dance, or cope with a dispute in a cooperative learning group). Observing students solving problems or fashioning products in real-life contexts provides the best picture of student competencies across the broad range of subjects taught in school.

The next most important component in implementing authentic assessment is the *documentation* of student products and problem-solving processes. Here are some examples of effective ways to document student performance:

- **Anecdotal records:** Keep a journal with a section for each student in which you record important academic and nonacademic accomplishments, interactions with peers and learning materials, and other relevant information.

- **Work samples:** Keep a file for each student that contains samples of the student's work in subjects for which you are responsible. The samples can be photocopies if the student wishes to keep the originals.

- **Audio files:** Have students read and summarize stories out loud that are captured by an audio recorder. You might also have them record jokes, stories, riddles, memories, opinions, and other samples of oral language. In addition, you could include examples of students' Music Smart abilities (e.g., singing, rapping, playing an instrument).

- **Video:** Use video to record a child's intelligences in areas that are hard to document in other ways (e.g., acting in a school play, catching a pass in a football game, demonstrating how a machine was repaired, introducing an ecology project), and to record students presenting summative projects they've completed.

- **Photography:** Use your smartphone to snap photos of things kids have made that might not be kept around very long (e.g., 3-D constructions, inventions, science and art projects).

- **Student journals:** Have kids keep ongoing journals of their experiences in school, including text, diagrams, doodles, scrapbook items, and drawings.
- **Student-kept charts:** Encourage students to keep records of their academic progress in the form of graphs or charts.
- **Sociograms:** Keep a visual record of student interactions in class, using symbols to indicate affiliations, negative interactions, and neutral contacts between class members.
- **Teacher-created informal (formative) assessments:** Create non-standardized tests to elicit information about a student's ability in a specific area. Focus on building a qualitative picture of the student's understanding of the material rather than devising a method to expose the student's ignorance in a subject.
- **Informal (or formative) use of summative assessments such as standardized tests:** Administer standardized tests without following the strict administration guidelines. Focus on specific items rather than on the total score. Relax time limits, read instructions to the student, ask the student to clarify responses, and provide opportunities for the student to answer using pictures, three-dimensional constructions, music, and movement. Find out what the student really knows; probe errors to find out how the student is thinking. Use the test as a stimulus to engage the student in a dialogue about the content.
- **Student interviews:** Periodically meet with students to discuss their school progress, their broader interests and goals, and other relevant issues. Keep a record of each meeting in a student's file. Meetings can also be videotaped.
- **Criterion-referenced assessments:** Use measures that evaluate students not on the basis of a norm but with respect to a given set of skills (such as the Common Core State Standards)—assessments that specify in concrete terms what the student can and cannot do (e.g., add two-digit numbers with regrouping, write a three-page story on a subject that interests the student). This type of evaluation is authentic when students are allowed to demonstrate their understanding through different intelligences (see Appendix A for standards-based multiple intelligences lesson ideas).

- **Checklists:** Keep a checklist of important skills or content areas used in your classroom and check off competencies as students achieve them.

MI Assessment Projects

There have been a number of assessment projects congruent with the fundamental philosophy of MI theory over the years, some under the direction of Howard Gardner and his colleagues at Harvard University's Project Zero. Two prominent studies coming out of Project Zero were Project Spectrum and Arts PROPEL.

Project Spectrum: This was a preschool and early primary program piloted at the Eliot Pearson Children's School at Tufts University in Medford, Massachusetts. The program used several assessment instruments that were themselves rich and engaging activities forming an integral part of the Spectrum curriculum. They included creative movement experiences (Body Smart, Music Smart); a dinosaur board game involving rolling dice, counting moves, and calculating strategies (Number/Logic Smart); and a storyboard activity requiring students to create a miniature three-dimensional world and then tell a story about it (Picture Smart, Word Smart). The program also made use of art portfolios and teachers' observations of children engaged in activities in the different centers (e.g., the storytelling area, the building center, the naturalist's corner). In addition to looking for proclivities in the eight intelligences, teachers assessed each student's characteristic working styles, looking, for example, at whether students were confident or tentative, playful or serious, reflective or impulsive in their way of approaching different learning settings. (For books that focus on Project Spectrum assessment instruments, learning activities, and strength-building strategies, see Gardner, Feldman, & Krechevsky, 1998a, 1998b, 1998c.)

Arts PROPEL: This was a five-year high school arts project piloted in the Pittsburgh Public Schools in Pennsylvania. The project focused on two elements: (1) domain projects—a series of exercises, activities, and productions in the visual arts, music, and creative writing designed to develop student sensitivity to compositional features; and (2) process folios—ongoing collections of students' artistic productions, such as drawings, paintings, musical compositions, and creative writing, from initial idea through rough drafts to final product. Evaluation procedures included self-assessments (requiring student reflection) and teacher assessments that probed students' technical and imaginative skills and their ability to benefit from self-reflection and critique from others (see Foote, 1991; Scripp, 1990).

Assessment in Eight Ways

MI theory provides its greatest contribution to authentic assessment by suggesting multiple ways to evaluate students. The biggest shortcoming of most traditional assessments, including standardized tests, is that they require students to show what they've learned in a narrowly defined way. Standardized tests usually demand that students be seated at a desk, that they complete the test within a specific amount of time, and that they speak to no one during the test. The tests themselves usually contain Word Smart or Number/Logic Smart questions or test items that students must answer by filling in bubbles on computer-coded forms. MI theory, however, supports the belief that students should be able to show competence in a specific skill, subject, content area, or domain in any variety of ways. And just as the theory of multiple intelligences suggests that any instructional objective can be taught in at least eight different ways, so too does it support the idea that any subject can be assessed in at least eight different ways.

If, for example, the objective is for students to demonstrate an understanding of the character of Huck Finn in Mark Twain's *Adventures of Huckleberry Finn,* a summative assessment might require students to complete the following task on a testing form:

Choose the word that best describes Huck Finn in the novel:
(a) Sensitive
(b) Jealous
(c) Erudite
(d) Fidgety

Such an item demands that students know the meanings of each of the four words and that every student's interpretation of Huck Finn coincides with that of the test maker. For instance, although "fidgety" might be the answer the testers are looking for, "sensitive" might actually be closer to the truth, because it touches on Huck's openness to a wide range of social issues. But a standardized test provides no opportunity to explore or discuss this interpretation. Students who are not particularly Word Smart may know a great deal about Huck Finn, yet not be able to show their knowledge on this test item.

MI theory suggests a variety of ways in which students could demonstrate their understanding:

- **Word Smart**—"Describe Huck Finn in your own words, either orally or in an open-ended written format."
- **Number/Logic Smart**—"If Huck Finn were a scientific principle, law, or theorem, which one would he be? Explain."
- **Picture Smart**—"Draw a quick sketch showing something that you think Huck Finn would enjoy doing that's not indicated in the novel."
- **Body Smart**—"Pantomime how you think Huck Finn would act in a classroom."
- **Music Smart**—"If Huck Finn were a musical phrase, what would he sound like? What song would he be?"
- **People Smart**—"Who does Huck Finn remind you of in your own life (friends, family, other students, TV characters)?"
- **Self Smart**—"Describe in a few words how you are similar or different from Huck Finn."
- **Nature Smart**—"If Huck Finn were an animal, plant, or weather pattern, which one would he be? Explain."

By linking Huck Finn to pictures, physical actions, musical phrases, scientific formulas, social connections, personal feelings, or natural phenomena, we offer students more opportunities to think about the character of Huck Finn in a truly comprehensive way.

Many students who are expected to do well on summative assessments such as standardized tests may not have the means to show what they've learned if the only setting available for demonstrating competency is narrowly focused on Word Smart or Number/Logic Smart capabilities. Figure 10.3 shows other examples of how students can show competence with respect to specific academic topics. Here are a few other ways to assess:

- Through a thorough exposure to all eight performance tasks in an attempt to discover the areas in which they are most successful.
- By assigning performance tasks based on the teacher's understanding of each student's most developed intelligence.

Figure 10.3

Examples of the Eight Ways Students Can Show Their Knowledge About Specific Topics

Intelligence	Factors Associated with the South Losing the Civil War	Development of a Character in a Novel	Principles of Molecular Bonding
Word Smart	Give an oral or written report	Do an oral interpretation from the novel with accompanying commentary	Explain the concept verbally or in writing
Number/ Logic Smart	Present statistics on the number of dead and wounded, availability of supplies and weapons	Present sequential cause-effect chart of character's development	Write down appropriate chemical formulas and show how they were derived
Picture Smart	Draw maps of important battles	Develop a flowchart or series of sketches showing the rise and fall of character	Draw diagrams that show different patterns of molecular bonding
Body Smart	Create 3-D maps of important battles and act them out with miniature soldiers	Pantomime the character's role from the beginning of the novel to the end, showing changes in attitude, outlook, or personality	Build several molecular structures with multicolored pop-beads
Music Smart	Assemble Civil War songs that point to causal factors	Present the development of a character as a musical composition	Orchestrate a dance showing different molecular bonding patterns
People Smart	Design a class simulation of important battles	Discuss underlying motives and moods relating to the character's development	Demonstrate molecular bonding using classmates as atoms
Self Smart	Develop a unique way of demonstrating competency	Relate the character's development to one's own life history	Create a scrapbook demonstrating competency in understanding molecular bonding
Nature Smart	Examine how the geographical features of the North and South contributed to end result	Compare the development of the character to the evolution of a species or the history of an ecosystem	Use animal analogies to explain the dynamics of bonding (e.g., animals that attract and don't attract, symbiotic relationships in nature)

Figure 10.4
"Celebration of Learning" Student Sign-Up Sheet

To show that I know _____, I would like to

- Write a report
- Do a photo essay
- Compile a scrapbook
- Build a model
- Put on a live demonstration
- Design a group project
- Create a statistical chart
- Develop a multimedia computer presentation
- Keep a journal
- Record interviews
- Design a mural
- Create a discography
- Give a talk
- Develop a simulation
- Create a series of sketches/diagrams
- Set up an experiment
- Engage in a debate or discussion
- Do a mind-map
- Produce a video
- Create an ecology project
- Write a musical
- Create a rap or song
- Teach the topic to someone else
- Choreograph a dance
- Other:_____

Brief description of what I intend to do:

_____   _____
Signature of Student   Date

_____   _____
Signature of Teacher   Date

- By letting students choose the manner in which they'd like to be assessed. (Figure 10.4 contains a sample form that suggests how students might "contract" to be assessed in a specific subject area.)

MI Assessment in Context

MI theory expands authentic formative and summative assessment settings considerably to include a wide range of possible contexts within which students can express competence in specific areas. It suggests that both the manner of presentation and the method of response will be important in determining a student's competence. If a student is highly developed in Picture Smart, yet is exposed only to Word Smart strategies when learning new material, then she will probably not be able to demonstrate full mastery of the subject. Similarly, if a student is physically oriented (Body Smart), yet has to demonstrate mastery through a paper-and-pencil test, then he probably will not be able to optimally express what he knows. Figure 10.5 indicates some of the many combinations possible that combine method of presentation and method of response in structuring assessment contexts.

Typical formative and summative assessment settings for students in schools take in only one or two of the 64 contexts shown in Figure 10.5 (e.g., "Read a book, then write a response"). Yet even the contexts listed in Figure 10.5 are but a fraction of the potential settings that could be used for assessment purposes. For example, "Listen to a talking book" could be substituted for "Read a book," and "Tell a story" might replace "Write a response." There are also many opportunities for variety even within each of the combinations shown in Figure 10.5. For example, the performance of a student who chooses to "go on a field trip, then build a model" will vary depending on where the field trip is taken, what kind of mediating experiences are provided during the trip, and how the model-building activity is structured. These factors would give rise to a multiplicity of contexts, some of which might be favorable to a student's demonstration of competency (e.g., a field trip to a place the student is interested in or has had prior experience with) and others that might be unfavorable (e.g., the use of modeling materials the student doesn't like or has no familiarity with, or their use in a setting with peers with whom the student doesn't get along).

Clearly, you do not need to develop 64 different assessment contexts for everything you evaluate, but Figure 10.5 does suggest the need to provide

Figure 10.5
64 MI Assessment Contexts

Activity/ Assessment	Word Smart Activity	Number/Logic Smart Activity	Picture Smart Activity	Music Smart Activity	Body Smart Activity	People Smart Activity	Self Smart Activity	Nature Smart Activity
Word Smart Assessment	Read a book, *then write a response.*	Examine a statistical chart, *then write a response.*	Watch a movie, *then write a response.*	Listen to a piece of music, *then write a response.*	Go on a field trip, *then write a response.*	Have a group discussion, *then write a response.*	Think about a personal experience, *then write a response.*	Observe nature, *then write a response.*
Number/ Logic Smart Assessment	Read a book, *then develop a hypothesis.*	Examine a statistical chart, *then develop a hypothesis.*	Watch a movie, *then develop a hypothesis.*	Listen to a piece of music, *then develop a hypothesis.*	Go on a field trip, *then develop a hypothesis.*	Have a group discussion, *then develop a hypothesis.*	Think about a personal experience, *then develop a hypothesis.*	Observe nature, *then develop a hypothesis.*
Picture Smart Assessment	Read a book, *then draw a picture.*	Examine a statistical chart, *then draw a picture.*	Watch a movie, *then draw a picture.*	Listen to a piece of music, *then draw a picture.*	Go on a field trip, *then draw a picture.*	Have a group discussion, *then draw a picture.*	Think about a personal experience, *then draw a picture.*	Observe nature, *then draw a picture.*
Body Smart Assessment	Read a book, *then build a model.*	Examine a statistical chart, *then build a model.*	Watch a movie, *then build a model.*	Listen to a piece of music, *then build a model.*	Go on a field trip, *then build a model.*	Have a group discussion, *then build a model.*	Think about a personal experience, *then build a model.*	Observe nature, *then build a model.*
Music Smart Assessment	Read a book, *then create a song.*	Examine a statistical chart, *then create a song.*	Watch a movie, *then create a song.*	Listen to a piece of music, *then create a song.*	Go on a field trip, *then create a song.*	Have a group discussion, *then create a song.*	Think about a personal experience, *then create a song.*	Observe nature, *then create a song.*

Continued

Figure 10.5 (continued)
64 MI Assessment Contexts

Activity/ Assessment	Word Smart Activity	Number/Logic Smart Activity	Picture Smart Activity	Music Smart Activity	Body Smart Activity	People Smart Activity	Self Smart Activity	Nature Smart Activity
People Smart Assessment	Read a book, then share what you've learned with a friend.	Examine a statistical chart, then share what you've learned with a friend.	Watch a movie, then share what you've learned with a friend.	Listen to a piece of music, then share what you've learned with a friend.	Go on a field trip, then share what you've learned with a friend.	Have a group discussion, then share what you've learned with a friend.	Think about a personal experience, then share what you've learned with a friend.	Observe nature, then share what you've learned with a friend.
Self Smart Assessment	Read a book, then relate it to your own life.	Examine a statistical chart, then relate it to your own life.	Watch a movie, then relate it to your own life.	Listen to a piece of music, then relate it to your own life.	Go on a field trip, then relate it to your own life.	Have a group discussion, then relate it to your own life.	Think about a personal experience, then relate it to your own life.	Observe nature, then relate it to your own life.
Nature Smart Assessment	Read a book, then do an ecology project.	Examine a statistical chart, then do an ecology project.	Watch a movie, then do an ecology project.	Listen to a piece of music, then do an ecology project.	Go on a field trip, then do an ecology project.	Have a group discussion, then do an ecology project.	Think about a personal experience, then do an ecology project.	Observe nature, then do an ecology project.

students with authentic assessment experiences that include access to a variety of methods of presentation (inputs) and means of expression (outputs). The types of assessment experiences that MI theory proposes—particularly those that are project-based and thematically oriented—offer students frequent opportunities to be exposed to several of these contexts at one time (as the Project Zero programs described earlier illustrate). For example, if students are developing a video to show their understanding of the effects of pollution on their local community, they may have to read books (Word Smart), do fieldwork (Body Smart), listen to environmental songs (Music Smart), and engage in collaborative activities (People Smart) to assemble a montage of pictures, music, dialogue, and words. This complex project provides the teacher with a context-rich document (the video) within which to both formatively and summatively assess a student's ecological competencies through a variety of intelligences.

MI Portfolios

As students increasingly engage in multiple intelligence projects and activities, the opportunities for documenting their learning process in MI portfolios expand considerably. In the past, portfolio development among reform-minded educators has often been limited to work requiring Word Smart and Number/Logic Smart (e.g., writing and math portfolios). However, MI theory suggests that, when appropriate, portfolios ought to include materials from each of the eight intelligences. Figure 10.6 lists some of the types of documents that might be included in an MI portfolio.

Figure 10.6
What to Put in an MI Portfolio

To document Word Smart

- Prewriting notes
- Preliminary drafts of writing projects
- Best samples of writing
- Written descriptions of investigations
- Audio recording of debates, discussions, problem-solving processes

---

Continued

Figure 10.6 (*continued*)
What to Put in an MI Portfolio

To document Word Smart (continued)

- Final written work
- Audio files of dramatic interpretations
- Reading skills checklists
- Audio recording of reading or storytelling
- Samples of word puzzles solved

To document Number/Logic Smart

- Math skills checklists
- Samples of best math work
- Notes from computations/problem-solving processes
- Write-ups of science lab experiments
- Documentation of science fair projects (e.g., awards, photos, videos)
- Samples of logic puzzles or brainteasers solved
- Samples of coding created or computer programming language learned

To document Picture Smart

- Photos of projects
- Three-dimensional mock-ups
- Diagrams, flowcharts, sketches, or mind-maps of thinking
- Samples or photos of collages, drawings, paintings, or other art objects
- Video recordings of visually based projects
- Samples of visual-spatial puzzles solved

To document Body Smart

- Video recordings of hands-on demonstrations
- Photos or videos of the process of creating a project
- Photos of hands-on materials created
- Videos of theater, drama, athletics, craftsmanship, or other bodily-kinesthetic products and productions

To document Music Smart

- Audio recordings of musical performances, compositions, musical medleys
- Samples of written scores (performed or composed)
- Lyrics of raps, songs, or rhymes written by student
- Discographies compiled by student
- Audio files of soundtrack music used in multimedia presentation

To document People Smart

- Letters to and from others (e.g., letter to an expert in the field)
- Collaborative reports
- Written feedback from peers, teachers, and experts
- Teacher–student conference reports (summarized or transcribed)

To document People Smart (*continued*)
- Parent–teacher–student conference reports
- Peer evaluations
- Photos, videos, or write-ups of collaborative learning projects
- Documentation of community service projects (e.g., certificates, photos, videos)

To document Self Smart

- Self-assessment inventories (e.g., multiple intelligences, emotional intelligence)
- Transcribed interviews related to goals and plans
- Interest inventories
- Photos or videos showing outside hobbies or activities
- Student-kept progress or goal charts
- Personal notes or journaling involving self-reflection on one's learning

To document Nature Smart

- Field notes from nature expeditions
- Records of 4-H or similar club participation
- Photos or videos displaying the care of animals or plants
- Video of project presentation on naturalist theme
- Records and notes of volunteer work with ecological organizations
- Personal writings about experiences in nature (e.g., poetry, stories, memoir, novel)
- Photos of nature collections (e.g., leaves, rocks, insects, fossils)

Naturally, the types of materials placed in an MI portfolio will depend upon the educational purposes and goals of each project. There are at least five basic uses for portfolios, which I refer to as "the Five Cs of Portfolio Development":

1. **Celebration**—To acknowledge and validate students' products and accomplishments during the year (authentic summative assessment)
2. **Cognition**—To help students reflect upon their own work (authentic formative assessment)
3. **Communication**—To let parents, administrators, and other teachers know about students' learning progress (authentic formative and summative assessment)
4. **Collaboration**—To provide a means for groups of students to collectively produce and evaluate their own work (authentic formative assessment)
5. **Competency**—To establish criteria by which a student's work can be compared to that of other students or to a standard or benchmark (traditional and authentic summative assessment)

The checklist in Figure 10.7 can help you clarify some of the uses to which portfolios might be put in the classroom.

Figure 10.7
MI Portfolio Checklist

How will you use the portfolio?

- For student self-reflection (Cognition)
- As part of regular school evaluation/report card (Competency)
- At parent conferences (Communication, Competency)
- In IEP/SST meetings (Communication, Competency)
- In communicating to next year's teacher(s) (Communication, Competency)
- In curricular planning (Competency)
- In acknowledging students' accomplishments (Celebration)
- In creating collaborative learning activities (Collaboration)
- Other:_____

How will it be organized?

- Chronologically
- Finished pieces from a variety of subjects
- Documentation from least satisfactory work to best work (teacher determined)
- Documentation from least satisfactory work to best work (student determined)
- Documentation of progress from first idea to final realization
- Representative samples of a week's/month's/year's work
- Only best work
- Include group work
- Other:_____

What procedures will you use in placing items in the portfolio?

- Select regular times for pulling student work
- Teach students criteria for self-selecting
- Pull items that meet preset criteria
- Random approach
- Other:_____

What will the portfolio look like?

- Box or other container
- Scrapbook
- Diary or journal
- Manila folder
- Bound volume
- Electronic text (e.g., CD, Word document, PowerPoint file)
- Audio (CD or audio file)
- Video (DVD or video file)

What will the portfolio look like? (*continued*)
- Website or blog
- Posting on a social networking platform (e.g., Facebook, Instagram)
- Other:_____

Who will evaluate the portfolio?

- Teacher
- Teacher working in collaboration with other teachers
- Student as part of a self-evaluation process
- Peers
- Other:_____

What factors will go into evaluating the portfolio?

- Number of entries
- Range of entries
- Degree of self-reflection demonstrated
- Improvement from past performances
- Achievement of preset goals (student's, peer's, teacher's, school's)
- Interplay of production, perception, and reflection
- Responsiveness to feedback/mediation
- Depth of revision
- Group consensus (among student, peers, teachers)
- Willingness to take risks
- Development of themes
- Use of benchmarks, rubrics, or standards
- Other: _____

The process of evaluating MI portfolios and other MI performances presents the most challenging aspect of their use. Reforms in assessment have emphasized the development of benchmarks, rubrics, or other methods by which complex performances and works can be evaluated (see Johnson, Mims-Cox, & Doyle-Nichols, 2006). In my estimation, benchmarks and the like are best suited only for the competency dimension of portfolio development—that is, for summative assessment. For the other four components, emphasis should be placed less on comparison and more on student self-evaluation, on ipsative measures (assessment that compares a student's current and past performances), and on authentic formative assessment (evaluation that contributes to learning and better teaching). Unfortunately, some teachers use assessment techniques to reduce students' rich and complex works to holistic scores or rankings like these: Portfolio A is a 1, Portfolio B is a 3; Child C's art project is at a "novice" level, while Child D's project is at a "mastery" level.

This misappropriation of an authentic formative assessment as a traditional summative assessment ends up looking very much like standardized testing. I suggest that we instead initially focus our attention in MI assessment on examining individual students' work in depth in terms of the unfolding of each student's uniqueness (for appropriate formative assessment models of this kind, see Carini, 1977 and Edwards, Gandini, & Foreman, 2011).

Ultimately, MI theory provides an assessment framework within which students can have their rich and complex lives acknowledged, celebrated, and nurtured. Because MI assessment and MI instruction represent two sides of the same coin, MI approaches to authentic formative assessment are not likely to take more time to implement as long as they are seen as an integral part of the instructional process. As such, assessment experiences and instructional experiences should begin to appear virtually indistinguishable from one another (a key feature of formative assessment). Moreover, students engaged in this process should begin to regard the assessment experience not as a gruesome "judgment day" (expressed in a traditional summative assessment) but, rather, as simply another opportunity to learn.

For Further Study

1. Choose an educational outcome that you are preparing students to achieve. Then, develop an MI-sensitive authentic summative assessment that will allow students to demonstrate competency through two or more of the eight intelligences.
2. Help students create "celebration portfolios" that include elements from several intelligences (see Figure 10.6 for examples of what to put in a portfolio). Develop a set of procedures for selecting material (see Figure 10.7) and a setting within which students can reflect on their portfolios and present them to others.
3. Put on a "Celebration of Learning" fair at which students can demonstrate competencies and show products they've made that relate to the eight intelligences.
4. Focus on a method of documentation that you'd like to explore, develop, or refine (including photography, video, audio, or electronic duplication of student work) and begin documenting student work using this medium more often.

5. Keep a daily or weekly diary in which you record your observations of students demonstrating competency in each of the eight intelligences. Reflect on how these observations help you to create more individualized strategies for students.

6. Experiment with the types of inputs (methods of presentation) and outputs (methods of expression) you use in constructing assessments. Use Figure 10.5 as a guide in developing a variety of assessment contexts.

7. Develop an ipsative assessment approach (i.e., one that compares students' current performance to their past achievements) and reflect on its usefulness compared with traditional summative methods of assessment and evaluation (e.g., standardized tests, benchmarked performances, holistically scored portfolios).

11

MI, Neurodiversity, and Special Education

Neurodiversity may be every bit as crucial for the human race as biodiversity is for life in general. Who can say what form of wiring will prove best at any given moment? Cybernetics and computer culture, for example, may favor a somewhat autistic cast of mind.

—*Harvey Blume*

The theory of multiple intelligences has significant implications for special education. By focusing on a wide spectrum of abilities, MI theory places the whole issue of "disabilities" in a broader context. Using MI theory as a backdrop, educators can begin to perceive children with special needs as whole persons possessing strengths in many intelligences. Over the history of the special education movement in the United States and elsewhere in the world, educators have had a disturbing tendency (gifted educators excepted) to work from a deficit paradigm—focusing on what students *can't* do—in an attempt to help students succeed in school and life. In speaking about special education, Paugh and Dudley-Marling (2011) point out that "'deficit' constructions of learners and learning continue to dominate how students are viewed, how school environments are organized, and how assessment and instruction are implemented" (p. 819). Yet we know from various psychological research effects, including the Pygmalion effect, the Hawthorne effect, the halo effect, the placebo effect, and fixed-versus-growth mindsets, that self-expectations and the expectations of others can have a huge effect on behavior and achievement (see, e.g., Dweck 2007; Rosenthal & Jacobson, 2004). MI theory provides a learning model that celebrates the abilities of students with special needs and offers specific strategies and tools to help address these students' challenges with learning, behaving, attending, and achieving in school.

Neurodiversity: The Future of Special Education?

The concept of neurodiversity emerged from the autism rights movement in the 1990s (Blume, 1998; Singer, 1999) and is now being used as a way of understanding and helping students with a wide range of challenges, including autism spectrum disorder, ADHD, and learning and intellectual disabilities. Briefly defined, neurodiversity is the idea that atypical (neurodivergent) neurological development is a normal human difference that is to be recognized and respected as much as any other natural human variation. This view contrasts with a disability point of view, which increasingly has framed special education labels within the context of underlying neurobiological disorders (see Figure 11.1). The irony is that educators teach kids to celebrate biodiversity and cultural diversity, but when it comes to differences among human brains, they still fall back on models based on disorder, damage, and dysfunction. We don't say that a calla lily has petal deficit disorder; we appreciate its unique contribution to the floral community. Similarly, we need to honor and value the unique differences that kids with special needs have to contribute to the classroom and the broader society.

A growing body of research validates the view that kids with special needs have strengths in certain intelligences even as they have difficulties in others. Here, for example, is a brief summary of some of the "smarts" that have been associated with four different diversity categories:

Autism spectrum disorder (ASD): Research suggests that people with an ASD diagnosis:

- Are better than "neurotypical" individuals at finding details in complex designs (i.e., Picture Smart; Baron-Cohen, 1998).

Figure 11.1

The Disability Paradigm Versus the Diversity Paradigm in Special Education

The Disability Paradigm

- Labels individuals in terms of specific impairment (e.g., learning disabilities, attention deficit hyperactivity disorder, intellectual disabilities).
- Diagnoses specific impairment using a battery of standardized tests focusing on errors, low scores, and areas of weaknesses.
- Attempts to remediate impairments using specialized treatment strategies that are usually removed from any real-world context.
- Often separates individuals from regular classroom activities for specialized treatment in segregated classes, groups, or programs.
- Uses a proprietary collection of tests, programs, kits, materials, and workbooks that are different from those found in general classrooms.
- Segments the individual's life into specific behavioral, cognitive, or educational objectives that are regularly monitored, measured, and modified.
- Creates programs that run on a parallel track with general education programs (e.g., teachers from the two tracks rarely meet except at IEP meetings).

The Diversity Paradigm

- Uses labels only for administrative purposes; students are defined in the classroom primarily by their own strengths, challenges, and uniqueness.
- Assesses the needs of students using authentic assessment approaches within a naturalistic context focusing primarily on strengths.
- Helps students learn and grow by using a rich and varied set of interactions with real-life activities, skills, and events.
- Seeks to enrich students' connections with others by helping facilitate a rich and diverse social network system.
- Uses materials, strategies, and activities that are good for *all* kids.
- Applies the understandings from biodiversity and cultural diversity to the neurodiversity needs of each student.
- Establishes collaborative models that enable specialists and regular classroom teachers to work closely together as much as possible in inclusive classrooms with both neurodiverse and neurotypical students.

- Prefer to work with systems (such as computer or mathematical systems) rather than with people (Number/Logic Smart; Baron-Cohen, 2003).
- Perform 30 to 70 percent better on the Raven's Progressive Matrices, which emphasizes Picture Smart and Number/Logic Smart abilities, compared with the more frequently administered Wechsler Intelligence Scale for Children (Mottron, 2011).

- May possess savant-like abilities in one or more of the multiple intelligences (e.g., a Number/Logic Smart person who can calculate numbers rapidly; Tammet, 2007).
- Frequently have special interests that may involve one or more of the eight intelligences (Kluth, 2008).

Dyslexia: Research suggests that people with a dyslexia diagnosis:

- Often display three-dimensional Picture Smart thinking abilities, skills that are necessary for success in a wide range of fields such as genetics, surgery, and biochemistry (Diehl et al., 2014; Karolyi, Winner, Gray, & Sherman, 2003).
- Possess global Picture Smart perceptual capabilities that are helpful for interpreting "fuzzy data" such as x-rays and pictures of the cosmos (Schneps, Brockmole, Sonnert, & Pomplun, 2012).
- Show proclivities toward Self Smart entrepreneurial activities (Warren, 2008).

ADHD: Research suggests that people with an ADHD diagnosis:

- Have proclivities for "wandering around" as a way of acquiring new information (Body Smart; Hartmann, 1997).
- Seek novelty—an important component of creative perception and expression (White & Shaw, 2011).
- Demonstrate evidence of neoteny (i.e., the holding of youthful characteristics into later development), which makes them more playful and flexible in their thinking and behavior (Montagu, 1988; Shaw et al., 2007).
- See their symptoms decrease when they are in natural settings (Nature Smart; Kuo & Taylor, 2004).

Intellectual disabilities: Although the low I.Q. scores that are the basis for a diagnosis of intellectual disabilities reflect difficulties in Word Smart and Number/Logic Smart, these students often show strengths in one or more of the other intelligences:

- Individuals with a diagnosis of Down syndrome demonstrate greater personal charm (Self Smart) and friendliness (People Smart) than many neurotypical kids (Dykens, 2006).

- People with a diagnosis of Williams syndrome show greater musical interest and aptitude in Music Smart compared with neurotypical individuals. They also possess strengths in Word Smart (possessing interesting vocabularies) and People Smart (demonstrating gregariousness; Lenhoff, Wang, Greenberg, & Bellugi, 1997).
- Students with a diagnosis of Willi-Prader syndrome display strong nurturing tendencies (People Smart) that can make them excellent caregivers (Dykens, 2006).

Positive Niche Construction and MI Theory

I've borrowed a concept from evolutionary biology—niche construction—to suggest the type of approach that educators should use in helping kids with special needs succeed in the classroom and life. *Niche construction* is defined as helping to ensure the thriving of an organism by directly modifying the environment in such a way that it enhances that organism's chances for survival. This is something that animals do all the time in the natural world: birds build nests, ants create anthills, spiders spin webs, beavers build dams. I suggest that in the classroom, educators need to build positive niches for students with special needs that provide synergistic ecological components within which they can achieve and succeed. Typically, educators try to change the student with special needs to adapt or fit in with the surrounding environment. Positive niche construction, by contrast, suggests that the environment be changed to fit the students' unique ways of being in the world. Both approaches are necessary, of course, but since there has been far less focus on the construction of positive niches, more work needs to be done to promote it in the schools. I've identified seven components of positive niche construction:

1. Strength awareness: The first and most important step for educators is to find out as much as they can about a student's strengths, including their multiple intelligences. The MI checklist provided in Chapter 3 (Figure 3.2) and the Multiple Intelligences Diagnostic Assessment Scales (MIDAS; Shearer, 1994) are two useful instruments for doing this. There are a number of other informal assessment approaches that can also be used, including observation of students demonstrating their most developed intelligences, and documentation of student strengths through photos, work samples, and videos (see Chapter 10 for a wider discussion of these and other assessment tools).

2. Positive role models: Neurodivergent students need to see that there are people in the world who have been diagnosed with their "disorder" and have succeeded in life. This will enable them to construct a positive mindset (e.g., If they can do it, so can I!) Figure 11.2 provides a list of well-known role models in several special needs categories. Role models can also come from the school, the local community, and even from the student's own extended family.

3. Assistive technologies and Universal Design for Learning (UDL) methodologies: These strategies and tools can help students achieve success by "working around" their difficulties so that their problems don't stand in the way of accomplishing their learning goals. For example, speech-to-text software can enable a student to write an essay without going through what might be the frustration of writing by hand or typing on a computer. Figure 11.3 provides a sample list of assistive technologies and UDL tools and the intelligences that they address.

4. Strengths-based learning strategies: This component is related to the wide range of learning strategies available to teachers that make the most of a student's strengths to help them develop in areas of difficulty. Students who are Picture Smart but have Word Smart difficulties, for example, might learn the alphabet through pictures (e.g., an S shaped like a snake) or, in the higher grades, do a written assignment that includes photos, pictures, animation, or cartooning. Figure 11.4 gives other examples of strengths-based strategies related to the eight intelligences.

5. Enhanced social resource networks: This is essentially a People Smart approach to shoring up a student's relationships with others, both in the school as well as in the extended family and the local community. It consists of four primary interventions:

- Eliminating or lessening the influence of negative social connections (e.g., bullies, gangs)
- Strengthening existing positive relationships (e.g., by using more collaborative learning)
- Creating new positive relationships (e.g., through a buddy program or cross-age tutoring)
- Repairing existing negative relationships (e.g., improving a poor relationship with a student's regular classroom teacher).

Figure 11.2
High-Achieving People Facing Personal Challenges

Neurodiverse Challenge / Most Developed Intelligence	Learning Difficulties	Communicative Difficulties	Emotional Difficulties	Physical Difficulties	Hearing Difficulties	Sight Difficulties
Word Smart	Agatha Christie	Demosthenes	Virginia Woolf	Alexander Pope	Samuel Johnson	James Joyce
Number/Logic Smart	Albert Einstein	Michael Faraday	John Nash	Stephen Hawking	Thomas Edison	Johannes Kepler
Picture Smart	Leonardo da Vinci	Marc Chagall	Vincent Van Gogh	Frida Kahlo	Granville Redmond	Otto Litzel
Body Smart	Auguste Rodin	Marilyn Monroe	Vaslav Nijinsky	Sudha Chandran	Marlee Matlin	Tom Sullivan
Music Smart	Sergei Rachmaninoff	Carly Simon	Robert Schumann	Itzhak Perlman	Evelyn Glennie	Stevie Wonder
People Smart	Whoopi Goldberg	Winston Churchill	Princess Diana	Franklin Roosevelt	King Jordan	Harry Truman
Self Smart	General George Patton	Aristotle	Friedrich Nietzsche	Joan of Arc	Helen Keller	Aldous Huxley
Nature Smart	Linnaeus	Charles Darwin	Gregor Mendel	Jean Jacques Rousseau	Johannes Kepler	E.O. Wilson

Figure 11.3

Assistive Technologies and Universal Design for Learning Methods Using MI

Assistive Technologies and Universal Design for Learning Methods / Area of Difficulty	Word Smart Strategies and Tools	Number/Logic Smart Strategies and Tools	Picture Smart Strategies and Tools	Music Smart Strategies and Tools	Body Smart Strategies and Tools	People Smart Strategies and Tools	Self Smart Strategies and Tools	Nature Smart Strategies and Tools
Word Smart	Speech-to-text apps, text-to-speech apps	Spelling/grammar check apps	Ideographic reading strategies (e.g., Peabody Rebus Reading Program)	Karaoke machine	Braille	Tutors, reading specialists, cross-age peer teaching, member of family who loves to read	Personal journaling, self-paced reading programs	Books and reading apps with nature themes
Number/Logic Smart	Calculators	Khan Academy videos	Cognitive organizers	MIND Research Institute Math+Music Program	Abacus, Cuisenaire rods, and other math manipulatives	Math tutor, math specialist, math study groups	Self-paced math or science apps	Scientific instruments to observe nature (e.g., microscope)
Picture Smart	Enlarged print books; audio books	GPS device	Magnifiers, enlarged Internet screens	Walking cane with tone sensor	Walking cane with Mowat sensor	Personal guide, sight impaired support group	Practice in navigating the perimeters of one's world and recognizing personal cues	Canine companion
Body Smart	How-to books (e.g., *Juggling for the Complete Klutz* and other books from Klutz Press)	Virtual and augmented reality software	How-to videos on YouTube	Neurofeedback using tones	Mobility devices (e.g. motorized wheelchair), Wii sports and fitness games	Personal caregiver	Apps for setting personal goals and charting progress	Canine companion

Figure 11.3 (continued)

Assistive Technologies and Universal Design for Learning Methods Using MI

Assistive Technologies and Universal Design for Learning Methods/Area of Difficulty	Word Smart Strategies and Tools	Number/Logic Smart Strategies and Tools	Picture Smart Strategies and Tools	Music Smart Strategies and Tools	Body Smart Strategies and Tools	People Smart Strategies and Tools	Self Smart Strategies and Tools	Nature Smart Strategies and Tools
Music Smart	Audio recordings of rhythmic poetry	Apple's Garage Band app for composition	Machine that translates music into a sequence of colored lights	Music CDs, music video streaming	Playing percussion instruments, dancing lessons	Piano or other musical instrument teacher, voice teacher	Self-paced music lessons online (e.g., piano instruction)	Recordings of nature sounds (e.g., bird calls); musical pieces in nature settings (e.g., The Moldau by Smetana)
People Smart	Bibliotherapy on interpersonal themes	Cognitive-behavioral therapy	Films on interpersonal themes	Involvement in music groups (e.g., choir)	Involvement in group fitness classes	Recovery/self-help support groups	Individual psychotherapy	Sierra Club group expeditions
Self Smart	Self-help books	Mood tracker apps, self-organization apps, goal-setting apps	Art therapy	Music therapy	Personal fitness trainer	Psychotherapist	Retreats, sabbaticals, periods of solitude for reflection	Vision quest in nature
Nature Smart	Field guides, National Geographic magazine	Taxonomies and classification systems	Video nature programs (e.g., Discovery Channel, Animal Planet)	Audio recordings of bird songs and other nature/animal sounds	Nature walks	Nature guide, volunteer experiences for ecological organizations	Taking care of a pet, planting a garden, or other solo nature projects	Camping and hiking experiences

Figure 11.4

Examples of MI IEP Strategies for Specific Objectives

Instructional Objective/Strategy	Correct the Letter Reversals *b* and *d*	Understand the Three States of Matter	Understand the Value of Simple Fractions
Word Smart Remedial Strategy	Identify through context in words or sentences	Give verbal descriptions, assign reading matter	Use storytelling, word problems
Number/Logic Smart Remedial Strategy	Play anagrams or other word-pattern games	Classify substances in the classroom in these three categories	Show math ratios on a number line
Picture Smart Remedial Strategy	Color code every *b* and *d*; use stylistic features unique to each letter; create "pictures" out of letters (e.g., "bed" where the stems are the posts)	Draw pictures of different states; look at pictures of molecules in different states (e.g., www.chem.purdue.edu/gchelp/liquids/character.html)	Draw "pies" and slice them in different fractions (e.g., halves, thirds, fourths)
Body Smart Remedial Strategy	Use kinesthetic mnemonic (put fists together, thumbs upraised, palms facing you—this makes a "b-e-d"")	Act out the three states of matter in a dance; do hands-on lab experiments; build 3-D models of three states	Put together manipulative fraction puzzles for different values
Music Smart Remedial Strategy	Sing songs (while reading lyrics) that have lots of highlighted *b*s and *d*s in them to help differentiate	Make up a song about the three states	Listen to a teacher-created song about fractions on YouTube such as "Fractions-Fractions"
People Smart Remedial Strategy	Give letter cards with *b*s and *d*s randomly to students; have them find others who are making the sound (aurally) and then check answers visually with cards	Create the three states as a class in a three-part dance (each person as a molecule); solid, liquid, gas	Divide the class into different fraction groups (e.g., thirds, fourths, fifths), and then have individual kids in a group stand up with other students determining the fraction made

Figure 11.4 (continued)

Examples of MI IEP Strategies for Specific Objectives

Instructional Objective/ Strategy	Correct the Letter Reversals *b* and *d*	Understand the Three States of Matter	Understand the Value of Simple Fractions
Self Smart Remedial Strategy	List favorite words that begin with *b* and *d*	Examine the three states of matter as they exist in one's body, home, and neighborhood	Examine fractions in one's own life (e.g., What fraction am I of my whole family? What fraction of school books did I bring yesterday?)
Nature Smart Remedial Strategy	List favorite animals and plants that begin with *b* and *d*	Study the three states of matter as they exist in nature (e.g., clouds, rain, sand)	Divide apples or other food items into equal segments, and then name the fraction represented by one or more slices

My book *Neurodiversity in the Classroom* (2012) provides more examples of how to create enhanced social resource networks for neurodiverse students.

6. Affirmative career aspirations: All too often, students in special education are perceived as having slim prospects for finding a decent job. A key component in creating positive niches for these students involves matching their MI strengths to careers in the community that need people with those particular abilities. For example, a student diagnosed with ADHD who has a penchant for moving around and does best in highly stimulating environments may be well matched in a job as a firefighter or an emergency room worker (see Archer, 2015), while a student diagnosed with ASD who has a Number/Logic Smart knack for computers and coding may find opportunities available in the IT field (see Wang, 2014).

7. Positive environmental modifications: This component reflects actual structural changes in the environment such as stability balls (Body Smart) for students diagnosed with ADHD, colored gels (Picture Smart) for students diagnosed with dyslexia, and the elimination of disturbing sounds (and addition of positive sounds) for Music Smart students diagnosed with ASD who have sensory sensitivities.

Potential Positive Outcomes of Integrating MI Theory with Neurodiversity

Several positive outcomes can emerge from a concerted attempt to integrate MI theory with neurodiversity in special education, including the following:

- **Greater use of positive assessment instruments:** In addition to the MIDAS, there is a wide range of assessments available to the special educator that help discover strengths and abilities in students, including the Gallup organization's Strengths Explorer (Gallup Youth Development Specialists, 2007), the VIA Strengths Survey for Children (www.viacharacter.org), the Search Institute's 40 Developmental Assets (www.search-institute.org), and the Torrence Tests of Creative Thinking (www.ststesting.com/ngifted.html). The type of assessments that are more typically used in a Gifted and Talented program should be used throughout the special education system with all neurodiverse students.

- **More positive IEP meetings:** With a greater emphasis on diversity and multiple intelligences, IEP meetings will have more opportunities for engaging in positive dialogue about students' strengths, talents, and abilities and how these can be used to improve students' school success (as well as facilitate a successful transition into the workplace for older students). One helpful model, Appreciative Inquiry, (Cooperrider, 2001) has been successfully implemented for use in IEP meetings (Kozik, 2008).

- **Greater reflection of strengths in IEPs:** Since the federal Individual with Disabilities Education Improvement Act (IDEA) requires strengths to be a part of the IEP process, educators can integrate MI theory and other strengths-based approaches into the actual wording of IEP objectives. See Figure 11.5 for examples of how this might be done.

- **More successful implementation of inclusive practices in schools:** One of the chief barriers to the successful inclusion of students with special needs into regular classrooms is the perception by regular classroom teachers that the incoming neurodiverse students represent a greater burden to their teaching load. If these students are instead perceived as possessing a range of strengths, interests, and capabilities in one or more of the eight intelligences, then they are more likely to be welcomed and integrated into the classroom by both teachers and fellow students.

Ultimately, if the goal of special education is to help students with special needs achieve success in school and life, then the more educators learn about the conditions that incline each student toward success, the better able they'll be to bring about that positive result. The theory of multiple intelligences provides both a sound theoretical framework for an understanding of strengths and special needs and a practical repertoire of strategies, resources, and tools to meet the needs of every neurodiverse student in the classroom.

Figure 11.5
Sample MI Plans for Individualized Education Programs

Subject: Reading

Short-Term Instructional Goal: When presented with an unfamiliar piece of children's literature with a readability level of beginning 2nd grade, the student will be able to effectively decode 80 percent of the words and answer four out of five comprehension questions based on its content.

Plan 1: For a Child with Highly Developed Body Smart and Picture Smart
IEP Strategies:

- Act out (mime) new words and the content of new stories.
- Make new words into pictures (e.g., drawing street lights on the word "street").
- Sculpt new words and their meanings using modeling clay.
- Draw pictures expressing the content of books at readability level.

Assessment: Student is allowed to move his body while reading the book; student can answer content questions by drawing answers rather than (or in addition to) responding orally.

Plan 2: For a Child with Highly Developed Music Smart and People Smart
IEP Strategies:

- Make up songs using new words.
- Play board games or card games with others that require learning new words.
- Use simple songbooks as reading material (singing lyrics accompanied by music).
- Read a book with a peer who is at a higher reading level.
- Teach a child at a lower reading level using beginning 2nd grade texts.

Assessment: Student is allowed to sing while reading a book; student may demonstrate competency by reading a book to another child or answering content questions posed by a peer.

For Further Study

1. Develop a curriculum unit for a regular or special-needs classroom that focuses on famous individuals who were diagnosed with disabilities. Include biographies, videos, posters, and other materials. Discuss with students how a disability accounts for only one part of an individual's life experience. Use MI theory as a model for understanding both the strengths and the challenges in our lives.

2. Identify a neurodiverse student who is currently not succeeding in the school system. Assess the student's strengths in terms of MI theory (see Chapter 3 for assessment tools). Brainstorm as many strengths as possible, including strengths that combine intelligences. Then discuss with colleagues how this process of strengths assessment can affect their overall view of the student and generate solutions in the classroom.

3. Read my book *Neurodiversity in the Classroom* (2012) and integrate the strategies and examples in that book with the eight intelligences in MI theory. Consider, for example, how the computer interests of a student diagnosed with ASD might be linked to Number/Logic Smart and integrated into the curriculum, or how the personal charm and friendliness (Self Smart and People Smart) of a student with intellectual disabilities might be leveraged to help them learn Word Smart and Number/Logic Smart skills.

4. Write MI strategies into a student's IEP based upon the student's strengths in one or more intelligences. Use Cooperrider's group dynamics model of Appreciative Inquiry and Kozik's IEP protocol to help guide IEP meetings based on strengths-based objectives (Kozik's protocol is reprinted in Armstrong [2012, p. 156]).

5. Read some of the literature cited in this chapter on the strengths and abilities of neurodiverse individuals and communicate this information to other educators in your school. Discuss the implications of strengths-based research for our changing understanding of students with special needs, to our provision of appropriate strengths-based learning strategies, and to our better envisioning of the transition opportunities available to them.

6. Work individually with one or more neurodiverse children and help them become aware of their special strengths in terms of MI theory (see Armstrong, 2014). How does a knowledge of their strengths and abilities affect their attitudes toward themselves? Toward their schoolwork? Toward their future?

12

MI Theory, Personalization, and Deeper Learning

The more people participate in the process of their own education . . . the more [they] participate in the development of their selves. The more the people become themselves, the better the democracy.

—*Paulo Freire*

Up to this point in the book, I have presented MI theory strategically as a way to enrich virtually any style of teaching or system of learning. In this chapter, however, I'd like to look at the emerging personalization movement and examine how MI theory can help to deepen its practice.

Let me be clear about what I mean by *personalization*. First, I am not talking about personalization in the way corporate education companies that tout "personalized" programs and products do. In essence, these programs use algorithms to collect data about students as they work through computerized course material, and then proceed to customize modules and assignments based on student inputs. There is little of the "person" in any of this (education critic Diane Ravitch calls these "de-personalization" programs on her blog at http://dianeravitch.net). Second, I'm not speaking of teacher-directed programs where instructors assess student interests, preferences, and learning styles and craft curriculum around those factors (the primary focus of this book up to this point). When I use the term personalization in this chapter, I'm referring to student-centered, student-driven projects and activities that strongly emphasize student voice and student choice.

Real personalization respects students' aspirations and feeds students' desire for mastery over real-world challenges. The reason this approach is so important to the lives of students is that it represents the best preparation they can receive for life. As Ron Berger, the chief academic officer of Expeditionary Learning (EL) Education puts it,

> In all of my years sitting in classrooms as a student, in public schools that were highly regarded, I never once produced anything that resembled authentic work or had value beyond addressing a class requirement. My time was spent on an academic treadmill of turning in short assignments completed individually as final drafts—worksheets, papers, math problem sets, lab reports—none of which meant much to anyone and none of which resembled the work I have done in the real world. Although I received good grades, I have no work saved from my days in school, because nothing I created was particularly original, important or beautiful. Yet when we finish school and enter the world of work, we are asked to create work of value—scientific reports, business plans, websites, books, architectural blueprints, graphic artwork, investment proposals, medical devices and software applications. This work is created over weeks or months with team consultation, collaboration and critique, and it goes through multiple revisions. The research, analysis, and production involve multiple disciplines, such as reading, writing, mathematics, science, engineering and design. (Berger, 2013)

It stands to reason, then, that the type of curriculum students should be engaged with in school reflects to a reasonable degree what they're going to be doing once they get out into the workforce. Implementing personalized learning is the best way to ensure this.

MI Theory's Contribution to Personalized Learning

Here are some ways in which MI theory can help guide the personalization process.

MI theory places Self Smart and People Smart front and center. Instead of regarding Word Smart and Number/Logic Smart as the foundation of school learning, personalized projects require, more than anything else, intrapersonal and interpersonal intelligences. In order to do the envisioning, planning, and organization required to launch personalized projects, students need to frankly assess their own strengths and weaknesses, engage in realistic goal setting, and adjust their goals as the project unfolds. Similarly, in personalized team projects, students must learn how to collaborate and participate in the give-and-take necessary to effectively implement their plans and envision the social connections needed to accomplish their goals.

Here's an example. A senior at Avalon Charter School in St. Paul, Minnesota, decided to engage in a project related to theater production. In the course of the project, he analyzed plays, took a class on stagecraft at a local university, built stage sets, and produced, directed, and acted in plays for the school community. Another senior at Avalon spent more than 800 hours working with a nonprofit educational advocacy group to help pass legislation in Minnesota expanding opportunities for individualized learning programs in the state (Traphagen & Zorich, 2013). Although both of these projects also involved the other intelligences (Logic Smart to analyze, Body Smart to dramatize, Picture Smart to visualize), the key driving power was supplied by the students' use of the personal intelligences.

MI theory helps both students and teachers envision the broad spectrum of possibilities available in developing a personalized project. A teacher who limits her understanding of learning to just words and numbers may facilitate deeply authentic personalized projects in a classroom where students choose their readings and decide on their writing genres and topics. But if this is all that is available to students, then potential gifts that they may possess in musical expression, artistic ability, dramatic sensibility, or ecological sensitivity may go untapped. When we suggest to students the possible tools available to them in developing a personalized project—words, numbers, music, audio, video, drama, nature, photos, and much more—they are more likely to be fully engaged. Figure 12.1 provides a menu of processes that students might select from in developing a project or personalized learning plan.

Figure 12.1

Processes for Personalized Learning Projects

Word Smart	Number/ Logic Smart	Picture Smart	Body Smart	Music Smart	People Smart	Self Smart	Nature Smart
Writing	Analyzing	Drawing	Building	Composing	Mentoring	Reflecting	Classifying nature
Reading	Collecting data	Photographing	Dramatizing	Performing	Interning	Choosing	Collecting nature
Journaling	Graphing	Videotaping	Crafting	Creating musical	Apprenticing	Organizing	Observing nature
Speaking	Measuring	Painting	Making (Maker	instruments	Job shadowing	Goal-setting	Preserving nature
Listening	Quantifying	Sculpting	Movement)	Listening to music	Volunteering	Envisioning	Gardening
Editing	Coding	Visualizing	Performing	Conducting	Interviewing	Self-evaluating	Farming
Publishing	Thinking critically	Cartooning	Miming	Analyzing music	Marketing	Planning	Ranching
Blogging	Calculating	Sketching	Role-playing	Singing	Persuading	Meditating	Raising or caring
Translating	Inventing	Animating	Coaching	Synthesizing	Mediating	Dreaming	for animals
Proofing	Using heuristics	Designing	Dancing	Recording	Counseling	Self-monitoring	Conserving
Storytelling	Generating statistics	Doodling	Touching	Broadcasting	Consulting	Self-regulating	Advocating
Debating	Experimenting	Observing	Simulating	Rapping	Leading	Getting in touch	
Recording (words)		Mapping	Mimicking	Chanting	Group organizing	with one's deepest	
Orating		Envisioning	Sculpting		Discussing	feelings	
Memorizing		Collaging	Creating mock-ups		Collaborating		
		Showing (e.g., at a gallery)			Sharing		

MI theory can help teachers integrate personalized student-driven activities and projects into the traditional curriculum. Many teachers are hesitant to wade into the deep waters of authentic student-centered projects because they fear losing contact with the standards, requirements, and content that form the core of their teaching responsibilities. Kallick and Zmuda (2017) view personalized learning as a continuum, teacher-directed at one end and student-driven at the other. Furthermore, they apply this continuum to several components of the personalized learning process, including goal setting, idea generation, tasks, and evaluation. Students may lead the way in some of these areas, while the teacher takes responsibility for the others. Certainly, many teachers will want to test the waters before they engage in a full-fledged student-directed program. Figure 12.2 suggests how activities in traditional content areas might be designed to begin the process of personalizing work in each of the eight intelligences.

MI theory provides a way to contextualize the learning that unfolds during student-directed projects. Understanding that truly personalized learning reflects the fact that students may change direction as they develop their projects, MI theory provides a conceptual map that can help both teachers and students understand which intelligences are being activated and how they can be further extended into the learning process.

An excellent model being used to personalize learning is the Genius Hour, which emerged from Google's injunction to employees that 20 percent of their work time should be spent on creating their own unique ideas for helping the organization. In Genius Hour classrooms across the United States, teachers have set aside a specific amount of time per day or week for students to engage in passion projects that reflect their own deepest interests. For example, Spencer (2017) writes about a student who focused on studying the history of skateboarding and ultimately designed a model of a hybrid skateboarding museum and skate park. This project integrated the Word Smart, Body Smart, Picture Smart, and Number/Logic Smart intelligences into a Self Smart–directed project. Another student curated (Self Smart) her favorite recipes from around the world (Word Smart, Body Smart) and integrated them with interviews she conducted with immigrants (People Smart). A group of students collaborated (People Smart) on rating (Number/Logic Smart) existing roller coasters and eventually designed (Body Smart, Picture Smart) their own model ride.

Figure 12.2

Personalized Learning and MI Theory

Personalized Learning MI Integration	My Community (1st Grade Social Studies)	Geology (4th Grade Science)	Expressive Arts (8th Grade Art)	The Novel (11th Grade English-Language Arts)
Word Smart	Make a book about your favorite things in the community	Read self-chosen books and articles on geology; keep a "geologist's journal" of your explorations	Create art from words and letters in English and other languages spoken by you or your family	Read self-chosen novels
Number/Logic Smart	Choose things to count in your community (e.g., houses on your block, street lamps downtown)	Become familiar with field guide tools and strategies used to analyze rocks; study the molecular structure/elemental composition of rocks	Create art from mathematical representation of personal data (e.g., scatter plot art based on the times you went to bed each night plotted against your test score results the following day)	Create databases to keep track of books read and films watched (with a data field for personal reactions and interpretations)
Picture Smart	Take photos of your town and put them together in a photography exhibit	Put together a photo display of local rocks (for use to help others in their identification)	Put together a "mood collage" representing your feelings during a typical day	Watch films based on novels read
Body Smart	Go on field trips to different areas of your community and create "social stories" of the trips	Learn appropriate techniques for breaking rocks for analysis	Create a self-portrait sculpture	Put on a play, mime show, or improvisation based on scenes from novels read

Personalized Learning MI Integration	My Community (1st Grade Social Studies)	Geology (4th Grade Science)	Expressive Arts (8th Grade Art)	The Novel (11th Grade English-Language Arts)
Music Smart	Make an audio recordings of the sounds heard around your community	Write a song based on your favorite rock or rocks ("rock music")	Use composition software to create an instrumental work representing your opinion about some controversial topic	Create a musical composition that tells the most interesting stories from each novels
People Smart	Contact a local historian who can visit the school and talk about the history of your community; interview members of the community about the history of your town	Establish a "rock hound" club; meet with a geologist; share rock collection with a lower grade	Get together with a small group of peers to create a drama that acts out a topic of keen interest to participants	Create a book study group; e-mail or Skype with authors
Self Smart	Make a list of all the things you like most about your community and all the things you like least about it	Put together a rock display of your favorite found specimens	Choose an art form and a topic of special passion and create the work	Choose the novels you wish to read; work at your own pace; decide how to present each book to others
Nature Smart	Create a garden to produce food to give to the neediest people in your community	Study the geology of the local area where you live	Create a work of art expressing your personal philosophy using only natural materials	Create a bibliography of novels where nature is one of the key "characters"

Yes, But How Deep Is the Learning?

Naturally, a big concern of teachers relates to how much learning is actually going on during these student-driven projects. Some teachers have aligned personalized learning exercises directly to state or district standards or developed benchmarks to assess student learning progress. Whether a teacher decides to do this or not, it can be helpful to have some measure of the *level* of learning going on at any given stage of the personalized learning process. Webb's (1997) Depth of Knowledge (DOK) schema provides a template to help educators gauge how deep a student project may go in terms of cognitive complexity for any given learning activity. It consists of the following four levels (Hess, 2013):

1. **Recall and Reproduction**—includes listing, defining, calculating, memorizing, reporting, and identifying;

2. **Skills and Concepts**—includes inferring, categorizing, predicting, interpreting, summarizing, and predicting;

3. **Strategic Thinking and Reasoning**—includes critiquing, appraising, investigating, testing, hypothesizing, assessing, and revising; and

4. **Extended Thinking**—includes initiating, designing, collaborating, researching, synthesizing, self-monitoring, critiquing, producing, and presenting.

It's important to keep in mind that we're not talking here about "good, better, or best" learning or thinking. Each of these levels has significance in its own right. For example, a student's plan during a Genius Hour to learn Mandarin Chinese may exist at Level 1 of Webb's model, but would be more intellectually challenging than another student's Level 4 project to research the background and significance of songs popular during World War I.

Webb's model allows teachers to monitor levels of thinking processes and use that information to help students self-evaluate and improve their learning plans. In the course of developing a robotics project, for example, a student may realize he needs to master a Level 1 skill in coding as a prerequisite for programming the robot for a Level 4 navigation routine. The fact that students can themselves learn to self-monitor the cognitive complexity of their work (and, in addition, understand their multiple intelligences) represents an important metacognitive skill that can carry over into everyday life. Figure 12.3 provides examples of how MI theory can be understood in relation to Webb's DOK model.

Figure 12.3
Examples of Webb's Depth of Knowledge Model Integrated with MI Theory

Intelligences	DOK-1 – Recall and Reproduction *What is the knowledge?*	DOK-2 – Basic Application of Skills and Concepts *How can the knowledge be used?*	DOK-3 – Strategic Thinking *Why can the knowledge be used?*	DOK-4 – Extended Thinking *How else can the knowledge be used?*
Word Smart	Learn the correct orthographic spelling of English words	Write a poem, short story, or novel	Analyze an author's writing style to help improve one's own writing abilities	Create a weekly radio show based on research done during the previous week
Number/ Logic Smart	Memorize algo-rithms to use in doing math problems	Use heuristic strategies in solving math problems	Design a science experiment to measure the amount of sugar in various fast food beverages	Set up a school weather station and monitor data over a period of several weeks or months
Picture Smart	Learn about and reproduce graphic images for an artwork	Use knowledge of graphic software to create a website	Use a graphic arts app to create an architectural design that integrates two architectural styles	Curate a visual art show made up of contributions from the school and local community
Body Smart	Master a motoric routine for a gymnastics class	Execute winning backhand volleys while playing a game of tennis	Choreograph a dance	Develop a football game playbook that can be used by the school's varsity team
Music Smart	Learn how to read musical notation for the piano	Play a violin sonata by Mozart	Compose a piece of music for the electronic synthesizer	Organize a concert where you will perform or conduct your composition and give a lecture afterward on its creation

Figure 12.3
Examples of Webb's Depth of Knowledge Model Integrated with MI Theory

Intelligences	DOK-1 – Recall and Reproduction	DOK-2 – Basic Application of Skills and Concepts	DOK-3 – Strategic Thinking	DOK-4 – Extended Thinking
	What is the knowledge?	*How can the knowledge be used?*	*Why can the knowledge be used?*	*How else can the knowledge be used?*
People Smart	Remember and reproduce proper social behaviors in the classroom	Lead a small-group discussion using acquired interpersonal strategies that maximize collaboration	Create, provide, and evaluate a survey that polls student opinion on the topic of school bullying	Plan, create, and lead a student voice campaign in school
Self Smart	Recall and be able to express past memories of failures and successes in school	Write or create in nonverbal media an autobiographical account of your life	Create and lead an activity to teach 1st grade students about their multiple intelligences	Develop a yearlong project to plan and direct your independent learning in school based on Joseph Campbell's hero's journey
Nature Smart	Memorize the taxonomy of living things created by Linneaus	Use Linneaus's taxonomy to classify arthropods in the field	Design an experiment to evaluate the quality of the local drinking water	Plan and lead a coordinated school–community campaign to test and monitor the water pollution in the local community

Ultimately, authentic personalized learning should be regarded as a delicate balance between a student's own motivations, interests, and aspirations and the teacher's knowledge of the terrain that can be covered in a learning adventure. The student provides the passion, the background, and the forward motion in exploring an area of great interest, while the teacher brings to the table her own skill set of strategies, resources, suggestions, and feedback. A knowledge of MI theory provides a cognitive map that can help lead a student's personalized learning journey toward a successful and meaningful conclusion.

For Further Study

1. Set aside a specific amount of time each day or week for a Genius Hour when students can explore a topic, issue, or pursuit of great interest to them (for more information on setting up a program, go to www. geniushour.com). As students choose their projects, notice whether there is a match or mismatch between a student's most developed intelligences and the intelligences required to do the project or the intelligences that will be strengthened as a result of the project. Talk with colleagues who are implementing the Genius Hour about the pros and cons of students choosing projects based on their desire to improve a difficult intelligence, their wish to continue developing a preferred intelligence, or the impetus to explore an intelligence they may only be dimly aware of possessing.

2. Evaluate the level at which your current classroom teaching integrates authentic personalized instruction (not computer-based or teacher-enforced). Consider how you might bring more student-driven personalization into your program and how you could integrate the theory of multiple intelligences into the projects or pursuits that students choose to explore.

3. Develop a student-directed personalized program, or take curricula you've already developed and use Webb's DOK schema and MI theory to keep track of which intelligences are being used and what levels of learning are being engaged. List additional activities that might enhance the intellectual breadth and cognitive depth of the program.

13

MI Theory and New Learning Technologies

I think it's fair to say that personal computers have become the most empowering tool we've ever created. They're tools of communication, they're tools of creativity, and they can be shaped by their user.

—*Bill Gates*

If we look at the history of the computer over the past 50 years or so, we can see a progression in the number of intelligences that have been integrated as the technology became more and more sophisticated. In the beginning, the world of computer technology was restricted to those Number/Logic Smart individuals who could read and write in one or more programming languages such as BASIC, COBOL, or FORTRAN. In 1980, the emergence of word processing hardware and software opened up the world of computers to Word Smart individuals. Then when Apple's icon-driven graphical user interface appeared in 1983, computers began to become accessible to Picture Smart people. From that point on, the rapid development of the computer industry brought with it tools and technologies that drew upon each of the other intelligences as well, with e-mail, chat rooms, and social media engaging People Smart users; gaming, robotics, touch-screen technology, and virtual reality activating Body Smart minds; music file sharing, streaming, and playlists incorporating Music Smart capabilities; simulations and self-paced learning programs of all types incorporating Self Smart capacities; and nature simulations, GPS technology, and ecologically oriented software involving Nature Smart abilities.

A similar process of expansion has occurred in education as the role of technology has grown from the use of computer applications for developing what were essentially electronic worksheets, tests, and other Number/Logic Smart and Word Smart materials to the present day when, to put it mildly, educators everywhere are presented with an embarrassment of riches in programs, apps, software, hardware, and other tools that can be used with all eight intelligence areas to engage students in the classroom. In this chapter, we'll examine a few of the many opportunities that exist for educators to use new learning technologies to advance learning.

Teaching to the Picture Smart Individual

One of my "crusades" in education over the past 40 years has been to advocate for the needs of Picture Smart learners who all too often are overwhelmed by an onslaught of Word Smart and Number/Logic Smart methods of learning, never getting the chance to exercise their most highly developed intelligence by engaging with learning materials in a visual-spatial way. Although some educators, to their detriment, may continue to rely only on Word Smart and Number/Logic Smart techniques, there has never been a more advantageous time to use Picture Smart in learning something new. For example, Google Images provides a way for a student to learn vocabulary words by seeing pictures of them. A student who's reading a Victorian novel and runs across the word *brougham* has only to search Google Images (or one of the many other image libraries online) to see the cute little carriages that carried people around in the 19th century. Similarly, a teacher who is teaching a unit in history can usually find a three- to five-minute documentary with historical footage that can grab Picture Smart learners and excite them enough to engage with the material in the classroom textbook.

Students have so many ways to activate creative projects and presentations that rely upon Picture Smart know-how combined with other intelligences. The day of the traditional book report is now over. Instead, students have a wide range of Picture Smart options to use in making their understanding of a book come alive. Students can use PowerPoint or Prezi presentation software, for example, to enhance their own oral commentary with sound, visuals, animation, and music. They can use iMovie to integrate video, images, text, and sound into a multimedia presentation of their book. They can use the video feature of their smartphones to record a panel discussion of several students, who can compare and contrast their ideas about the narrative in each novel they are reading. They can create their own interactive book reports by blogging or creating a website with links to other sites that give further information, images, videos, or music about the book's themes. They can even create three-dimensional images (using, e.g., 123D Capture) to illustrate their knowledge of a book's characters or historical setting.

Exercising the Body Smart Mind

A typical image of computers in education is of a classroom of students sitting at their workstations busily tending to computerized assignments on their keyboards. Such a picture doesn't give much allowance for physical movement beyond the wiggling of fingers. Dig deeper into the world of new learning technologies, however, and you'll find a wealth of applications that engage two fundamental Body Smart components: the movement of the whole body and use of the hands. The field of robotics, for example, provides students with the opportunity to build or modify working robots and then operate them using a coding language such as Lego Mindstorms. Similarly, Nintendo's Wii applications connect student movements to onscreen avatars so that they can virtually golf, bowl, or play tennis while their fellow students use Number/Logic Smart to keep score, or go on safaris and take photos of the animals they encounter in the wild.

Another emerging learning technology that has Body Smart integration features is virtual reality (VR). In virtual reality, students wear headgear (e.g., Google Cardboard, Sony Playstation VR, Oculus Rift) to gain access to a 360-degree view of scenic worlds they might never encounter in their lives, including the ancient pyramids of Egypt, the enigmatic statues on Easter Island, and the marine biomes of the Great Barrier Reef. Using VR technology, students have been able to dissect animals, study chemical structures, investigate the human heart, and take virtual trips to Verona, Italy, as part of a unit on *Romeo and Juliet*. The virtual reality experience will continue to develop its Body Smart potential as it adds other peripherals such as data gloves and walking pads.

Augmented reality is another technology that offers a 3-D Picture Smart experience and Body Smart engagement with the objective world. It refers to the overlaying of computer images onto real objects by viewing them through a smartphone or tablet. For example, the Guinness Book of World Records has an app that allows viewers to see sharks leaping from its pages, take control of carnivorous dinosaurs and walk them around the page, and compare themselves to the tallest and shortest people in the world.

Computer-Based Technologies with People Smart Potential

Another innovation that has emerged from the development of computer technology is the ability to initiate interpersonal communication across large distances in both one-on-one and group situations. From e-mail to internet chat rooms to the wealth of opportunities currently available via social media channels, People Smart individuals have a wide range of options available to them for interacting and collaborating with each other.

Through videoconferencing portals such as Skype and Google Hangouts, students have the opportunity to converse with authors of the books they're reading; communicate with experts in history, science, math, art, or other subjects they are studying; or link up with classrooms in other countries to collaborate on projects and topics of mutual concern. Programs and websites like Google Docs and Wikispaces provide platforms for students to post documents, images, and other materials, and work on them jointly. Students can use social media channels such as Twitter to comment on each other's work or a teacher's lecture, use hashtags to follow a particular topic being tweeted online, communicate with students or experts around the world by following their Twitter feeds, and keep their different Twitter streams all together in one place by using an app such as TweetDeck. Finally, students can create their own websites, blogs, and other web-based projects to share projects, ideas, assignments, and experiences with others.

Exploring the Digital World of Music

The rapid expansion of the internet over the past 25 years has brought with it a wide range of resources for Music Smart students. Teachers can spice up their lesson plans by searching on YouTube, iTunes, Spotify, or Pandora for music files and create music playlists tied to specific historical eras, literary themes, math and science topics (e.g., using musical mnemonics), or other content. Students can add music or sound effects to their presentations using features in presentation software or by looking for audio files on the internet (YouTube has its own sound effects library). They can create their own musical compositions as part of a project-based learning activity using software such as GarageBand or Fruity Loops. Using the game-based interactive platform Wii Music, students can experiment with more than 60 different virtual instruments ranging from bagpipes to the ukulele, play mini-games such as Handbell Harmony and Pitch Perfect, and jam as part of an ensemble. There's also an app for teachers called Pocket Pied Piper that lets them download and store musical selections to use as classroom management cues (e.g., "line up," "clean up," "back to desks," and "thinking time").

Developing Self Smart Skills Through Technology

Since the beginning of computerized instruction, one important Self Smart component has been self-paced learning. Being able to work on programmed materials at one's own pace and receive instantaneous feedback makes self-paced learning a great alternative for independent-minded Self Smart students. In teacher-directed environments, academic work has to be completed within a fixed time period, and feedback on learning performance often does not occur until tests are corrected and handed back to the student—sometimes days, weeks, or even months later. Today's digital "personalized" learning systems (not to be confused with the personalization strategies discussed in Chapter 12) have become much more sophisticated in applying algorithms that adapt student responses to tailored learning materials that take into consideration students' interests and backgrounds.

Following are some other apps that assist students with self-management skills:

- MyHomework helps students organize their homework assignments.
- Corkulous is a virtual cork board where students can "pin" to-do lists, brainstorms, notes, and other data.
- Evernote lets students store articles, photos, handwritten notes, and other information for easy retrieval at a later date.

- Time Timer is a simple time-management tool that provides a 60-minute clock face showing in red the amount of time left to work on an assignment.

- SoundNote provides students with the ability to take notes; if they have difficulty keeping up, they can write a word on specially treated paper, and later listen to the missed portion of the lecture by tapping on that word.

- Flashcards Deluxe allows students to create their own flashcards or download premade sets from a library of over four million cards.

- StayOnTask lets students set an audiovisual signal to appear randomly during study periods to provide reminders to stay on task.

- EpicWin is a goal-setting app. When goals are achieved, students can "blow them up" through an animation feature.

- How Would You Feel If . . . asks users the question and presents them with 56 different life situations designed to initiate discussions on how to handle emotions (for example, "How would you feel if your favorite football team lost a game?").

High-Tech Nature Smart Apps

Although technology has been criticized for keeping kids indoors and in front of screens when they should be outdoors enjoying the wonders of nature (see, e.g., Louv, 2008), there exists a wide range of apps for nurturing a love of nature:

- North Face Trailhead consists of a database of hiking routes that outdoor enthusiasts have shared at the website EveryTrail.com, featuring information on a hike's level of difficulty and other trailblazing tips.

- Florafolio is an interactive field guide to trees, shrubs, perennials, ferns, vines, and grasses (versions are currently available for the Northeast and Southern United States and Eastern Canada).

- iBird Plus Guide to Birds provides data for identifying 938 species of birds.

- Leafsnap features an extensive directory of North American plants.

- MyNature Animal Tracks allows users to identify animal movements.

- iNaturalist allows you to record your observations of nature and contribute them to iNaturalist.org, a social media network for naturalists.
- Project Noah lets user upload photos to a database to share their experience of nature's diversity.

There are also numerous opportunities for budding naturalists and ecologists to work online with researchers in the field to contribute knowledge to ongoing studies and programs (see Adria & Mao, 2017).

This chapter has only touched the tip of the iceberg when it comes to digital learning technologies that use and develop the multiple intelligences. Hopefully, it has given you a glimpse of the tremendous potential for e-learning to be much more than just electronic worksheets and assignments. Instead, it represents thousands of different opportunities for students to engage in creative ways with words, numbers and logic, images, physical experiences, music, social interaction, personal exploration, and nature adventures (see Figure 13.1 for a list of just some of the resources available).

Figure 13.1

Resources for Integrating New Learning Technologies (examples are in parentheses)

Word Smart	Word processing (Microsoft Word) Podcast production (Spotify, Audacity) Speech-to-text apps (Dragon Naturally Speaking) Text-to-speech apps (TextAloud) Translation (Google Translate) Website builder (Weebly) Blog authoring (Blogger) Note-taking (SoundNote)
Number/Logic Smart	Spreadsheets (Microsoft Excel) Coding (Tynker) Math skills platform (Khan Academy) Logic games (Rubik's App) Critical thinking apps (Opposing Views) Database management (Microsoft Access) Financial management (Quicken Deluxe) Science apps (Coaster Physics) Math apps (Monster Math)

Picture Smart	Video sources (Watch/Know/Learn; YouTube) Video creation (iMovies) Sandbox video games (Minecraft) Image library (Google Images) 3-D image generator (123D Catch) Image curation (Pinterest) Graphic organizers (Kidspiration) Mapping platforms (Google Earth, Google Maps) Storyboarding apps (Storyboard Composer) Animation software (Stykz) Draw and paint apps (Sketchbook) Clip art sources (www.schoolclipart.com)
Body Smart	Robotics and coding (Lego Mindstorms) Interactive exercise games and sports (Wii Fitness, Wii Sport) Virtual reality adventures (Google Cardboard) Augmented reality experiences (Aurasma) Touchscreen technology (iOS, Android) Motion simulation games (Aerofly 2)
Music Smart	Musical signals for classroom management (Pocket Pied Piper) Soothing background music (iZen Garden) Music composition (GarageBand) Music playlists or sound effects library (YouTube) Interactive music games (Wii Music) Music notation apps (Noteflight) Music tutors (Staff Wars)
People Smart	Collaborative conferencing (Skype) Collaborative mind-mapping (Coggle) Collaborative document-sharing platforms (Google Docs) Social writing platform (wikispaces.com) Augmentative and alternative communication (Proloquo2Go) Cloud-based collaboration (Voice Thread) Social media platforms (Twitter) Genealogy programs (Family Tree Maker)
Self Smart	Presentation apps (Prezi) Multimedia book creation (Book Creator) Self-organization apps (iStudiez) Time management (Time Timer) Goal-setting (EpicWin) Emotional self-regulation (How Would You Feel If. . .) Emotional self-monitoring (Mood Meter)

Continued

Figure 13.1 (*continued*)
**Resources for Integrating New Learning Technologies
(examples are in parentheses)**

Nature Smart	Interactive Nature Adventure (Wii Wild Earth: African Safari)
	Interactive field guides (Florafolio)
	GSP apps (Google Maps)
	Nature-based networking (iNaturalist)
	Environmental apps (Kid Weather)
	Topological mapping (Park Maps); hiking guides (Every Trail)
	Astronomy apps (Star Walk)

For Further Study

1. Conduct an assessment of the learning technologies you currently use in your classroom or school, and note which intelligences are associated with each of them. Determine what your needs are in terms of acquiring additional software, apps, or other e-resources that make use of intelligences currently underrepresented in your collection of technological tools.

2. Using a project-based learning approach, guide your students in choosing and designing multimedia projects that incorporate several of the intelligences. Ask students to evaluate whether the tools they choose are associated with their most developed intelligences or reflect instead intelligences that they are more interested in developing.

3. Select one or more of the computer programs or apps listed in this chapter (or ones similar to them) that you haven't used in the classroom, and design a strategy for integrating it into an existing curriculum unit or lesson plan. Evaluate its success or failure in enriching the unit or lesson and determine how it might be better used next time. Repeat this process with other apps, links, or software that are new to you.

14

MI Theory and Existential Intelligence

[Existential intelligence] has been valued in every known human culture. Cultures devise religious, mystical, or metaphysical systems for dealing with existential issues; and in modern times or in secular settings, aesthetic, philosophical, and scientific works and systems also speak to this ensemble of human needs.

—*Howard Gardner*

Howard Gardner has written about the *possibility* of a ninth intelligence—the existential (Gardner, 1995, 1999)—so I would like to examine what some of the potential applications of this intelligence candidate might be in the curriculum. Gardner defines *existential intelligence* as "a concern with ultimate life issues" and describes it as "the capacity to locate oneself with respect to the furthest reaches of the cosmos—the infinite and the infinitesimal—and the related capacity to locate oneself with respect to such existential features of the human condition as the significance of life, the meaning of death, the ultimate fate of the physical and the psychological worlds, and such profound experiences as love of another person or total immersion in a work of art" (Gardner, 1999, p. 60). Gardner explicitly states that he is *not* proposing here a spiritual, religious, or moral intelligence based upon any specific "truths" that have been advanced by different individuals, groups, or institutions (see Gardner, 1999, pp. 53–77, for a fuller discussion of why he has decided not to propose a spiritual or moral intelligence). Instead, he is suggesting that any rendering of the spectrum of human intelligences should probably address humanity's long-standing efforts to come to grips with such ultimate questions of life as "Who are we?" "What's it all about?" "Why is there evil?" "Where is humanity heading?" and "Is there meaning in life?" There is room in this inclusive definition for explicitly religious or spiritual roles (theologians, pastors, rabbis, shamans, ministers, priests, yogis, lamas, imams) as well as nonreligious or nonspiritual roles (philosophers, writers, artists, scientists, and others who are grappling with these deeper questions as a part of their creative work).

Gardner has considered including existential intelligence in MI theory (at times he's quipped that he currently has 8½ intelligences) because it appears to fit quite well with most of his criteria for an intelligence:

- **Cultural value**—Virtually all cultures have belief systems, myths, dogmas, rituals, institutions, and/or other structures that attempt to come to grips with ultimate life issues.

- **Developmental history**—A look at the autobiographies of great philosophical, religious, spiritual, scientific, or artistic individuals often shows an increasing progression from inklings of cosmic concerns in childhood through apprenticeship stages to more advanced levels of understanding or comprehension of these issues in adulthood.

- **Symbol systems**—Most societies historically have developed different types of symbols, images, or "maps" with which to communicate to their members about existential themes (witness, e.g., key symbols used by the world's major religions such as the cross for Christianity, the star and crescent for Islam, the star of David for Judaism).

- **Exceptional individuals (savants)**—In many parts of the world, there are to be found individuals who are said by the local populace to possess a deeper wisdom or understanding, or a unique capacity to ask existential questions, while at the same time having a low I.Q. or lacking substantially in the capacities of the other intelligences (the titular figure from the movie *Forrest Gump* is perhaps the best-known representation of this phenomenon in Western popular culture; for an Eastern perspective, see Donkin, 2001).

- **Psychometric studies**—Certain personality assessments purport to measure traits of "religiosity" or "spirituality," although there are certain problems inherent in obtaining quantitative measures of experiences that are by definition ineffable.
- **Evolutionary plausibility**—There is evidence for an awareness of existential themes in the hunting and burying rituals of prehistoric humans.
- **Brain research**—Individuals who have temporal-lobe epilepsy sometimes show signs of hyperreligiosity, and identical twins reared apart show a strong link in terms of their religious attitudes, suggesting the possibility of heritability; however, there are problems involved in subjecting existential concerns to bioreductionism.

Although the existential intelligence is not a perfect fit in terms of Gardner's criteria (which is why he has still not fully qualified it for entry into the pantheon of multiple intelligences theory), there are enough points of confluence to warrant its being taken seriously by educators as a strong contender for a new intelligence.

Some educators may feel a certain reluctance to address the existential intelligence for fear of running into controversy from the community, abridging constitutional protections of the separation of church and state, or violating their own consciences or belief systems or those of their students. It is therefore important to emphasize that this intelligence does not involve promoting religion, spirituality, or any specific belief system. Rather, it is dedicated to examining the ways in which humanity has addressed existential concerns (both religious and nonreligious) since the beginning of recorded time. There are clear constitutional protections for teaching *about* religion in public schools (objectively and neutrally) and important pedagogical reasons for doing this regularly across the curriculum (see Nord & Haynes, 1998).

Potential applications of the existential intelligence to the curriculum are bound to be more selective than they are for any of the other intelligences. I don't see any advantage in attempting to apply existential intelligence to every possible educational objective (e.g., there seems to me to be no point in searching for an existential strategy for teaching, say, the times tables or phonemic awareness). For this reason, I think that the existential intelligence—even if fully endorsed by Howard Gardner as an "official" intelligence someday—will always maintain a somewhat special status within MI theory, somewhere on the periphery of the day-to-day workings of the model.

I believe that attempts to assess existential intelligence in students, or to develop existential methods for assessing regular school topics, are not going to be at all productive or useful in an educational context because they will tend to force educators into creating criteria that are far too limiting and artificial to be of any pedagogical value (and are conversely likely only to incite controversy and confusion). I also believe that attempts to create "existential strategies" to teach curriculum in specific areas (e.g., having students re-create a religious ritual during a multicultural unit or telling them to do a closed-eyes meditation on the significance of death in a biology class) are likely to violate the consciences of some students and possibly be unconstitutional in a public school setting as well. Consequently, I feel that the most appropriate way to bring existential intelligence into the classroom is by integrating content into the curriculum that helps students think about the existential dimensions of whatever they are studying (and why scientists, artists, politicians, writers, and others have incorporated existential concerns into their own work). I suggest that educators read the book *Taking Religion Seriously Across the Curriculum* (Nord & Haynes, 1998) for a solidly grounded, legally based, and pedagogically sound approach to teaching about religious issues in the classroom. For a look at how children are natural philosophers, I would suggest *The Philosophy of Childhood* (Matthews, 1996).

Following are some of my own suggestions for how existential intelligence can intersect with different areas of the curriculum and be integrated into the classroom in a way that does not violate separation of church and state and the belief systems of individual students.

Science and the Exploration of the Unknown

Although the logical foundation of the scientific method may seem to preclude the possibility of entertaining existential issues, the inner core of science is very much alive to metaphysical concerns. Recall that modern science emerged in the 17th century out of philosophy, religion, alchemy, and other fields that dealt with existential issues. Many of the great scientists of the modern era, including Newton, Boyle, and Einstein, have been motivated in part (sometimes in large part) by religious, spiritual, or cosmic concerns (e.g., Einstein, rejected the indeterminacy of quantum physics by famously saying that he did not believe that God would play dice with the universe). Teachers can address science existentially in the classroom by highlighting those areas that involve, as Gardner (1999) puts it, "the furthest reaches of the cosmos—the infinite and the infinitesimal" (p. 60)—that is, theories about the origins of the universe, subatomic physics, and so forth. An excellent book that vividly demonstrates these extreme limits is *Powers of Ten* (Morrison & Morrison, 1994), which takes readers from the edges of the universe to subatomic particles by successive powers of 10 (it is also available as a nine-minute film produced by Charles and Ray Eames at www. youtube.com/watch?v=0fKBhvDjuy0).

In the biological sciences, teachers can similarly approach the origins of life in an existential way by helping students wonder about the distinctions between inanimate forms (rocks and minerals) and animate ones (plants and animals). Many current controversies in science, from human cloning to nuclear weapons research, raise opportunities for deep reflection upon the nature and destiny of humanity. In fact, wherever science is working at its own frontiers with unanswered questions, there is plenty of room for existential concerns to be brought to the fore in the curriculum.

The Magic of Mathematics

Like science, mathematics has been entwined for thousands of years with existential issues. One of the first Western philosophers, the Greek thinker Pythagoras, was a mathematician and a mystic who believed that number patterns revealed the ultimate harmony of the cosmos. Following Pythagoras, Plato believed that mathematical reasoning was closer to ultimate reality than the unreliable data gathered by the human senses. The mystic traditions of Judaism, Islam, and other great religions view numbers and mathematical reasoning as doorways into the secrets of the mysteries of the universe. In the classroom, teachers can add a multicultural emphasis to mathematics lessons that addresses some of these historical connections. There are also opportunities to touch upon existential themes when discussing math concepts like zero or infinity, very large or very small numbers, negative numbers, irrational numbers, imaginary numbers, and probability and topology.

The Role of Religious Thinking in History

It is simply not possible to discuss human history to any substantial degree without bringing in factors related to existential concerns, especially those involving religion. Consider U.S. history. The motivation for many settlers to come to North America in the 17th century was to seek freedom from religious oppression. Consequently, it's important for history students to have a sense of what Puritans believed, for example, and how their own beliefs differed from the Church of England (and, similarly, how the Church of England came to split off from Roman Catholicism in the 16th century).

Many if not most of the wars in human history have come about at least partially as a result of religious differences, so students need to know something about the nature of those religions in order to understand the causes of those conflicts. At the same time, students need to be familiar with trends in philosophy and other existential domains to fully appreciate the dimensions of many world events (e.g., the effects of the Enlightenment on the French Revolution). Then there are events such as the Holocaust that transcend any particular point of view and force us to confront the nature of evil, suffering, and death in ways that can shake up our own personal belief systems and cause us to transform our views about human existence.

Existential Themes in Literature

The clearest connection in the West between literature and existential intelligence can be seen in the influence of the Hebrew and Christian Bibles on subsequent writers in history. One can't fully understand or appreciate many of the great books of our culture—including most of Shakespeare's plays, Bunyan's *Pilgrim's Progress,* Melville's *Moby-Dick,* Faulkner's *Absolom, Absolom,* and many, many more—without understanding how biblical or religious sources informed them. I'm willing to make the claim that virtually all great literature deals with issues of ultimate life concern and cannot be understood apart from them: from the existential crisis of Gilgamesh after the death of his friend Enkidu in the ancient Mesopotamian classic, to the philosophical musings of Leopold Bloom and Stephen Daedelus in James Joyce's 20th century masterpiece, *Ulysses.* In the classroom, teachers need to ascertain in advance whether assigned literature contains existential themes and then provide opportunities for students to reflect on and discuss these ideas in relationship to other course objectives.

Religious Influences in Geography

The constantly shifting pattern on the world atlas of alliances, city-states, empires, confederations, and nations, from the ancient past to the current day, can be far better understood in a context that includes existential themes. To make sense of the changing map of the former Yugoslavia, for example, requires an understanding of the distinctions between Roman Catholicism, Orthodox Christianity, and Islam. Making sense of the division between India, Pakistan, and Bangladesh likewise requires familiarity with differences between Islamic and Hindu thinking. Teachers can help students better comprehend how the landscape has been formed and re-formed by spending time discussing how differences in attitudes on metaphysical issues can dramatically change geographical boundaries.

The Arts and the Quest for Existential Awakening

Howard Gardner has pointed out in his definition of existential intelligence that "total immersion in a work of art" is one way in which individuals can experience and express themselves with respect to ultimate life concerns. A look at the history of music, painting, sculpture, dance, and drama reveals an ongoing concern with the meaning of life, death, suffering, and other existential issues. Seeing Michelangelo's Pieta or attending a performance of Shakespeare's *Merchant of Venice* can cause us to ponder fundamental questions of suffering and mercy. Listening to Beethoven's Fifth Symphony or looking at painter Thomas Cole's series "The Voyage of Life" can engender thoughts about human destiny. In the classroom, teachers can help students appreciate these finer dimensions of the arts and also provide the resources and opportunities for students to express their personal existential concerns by creating their own works of art.

For Further Study

1. Hold a dialogue with members of your learning community (parents, teachers, administrators, students, board members) about integrating the existential intelligence into your school's curriculum. Freely air all points of view, and then develop a constitutionally sound framework that provides opportunities to teach *about* religious issues, raise philosophical themes, and discuss other existential concerns as they relate to various parts of the curriculum.

2. Research the existential dimensions of an academic discipline, such as science, math, history, literature, social studies, economics, psychology, sociology, or anthropology, and consider how existential issues can be more fully incorporated into the regular core curriculum of that subject.

15

MI Theory and Its Critics

Gardner's theory provides a much needed corrective to the shortcomings of traditional psychometric approaches. Instead of probing the bases of bubble-sheet results, Gardner sought to illuminate the mental abilities underlying the actual range of human accomplishment that are found across cultures.

—*Mindy Kornhaber*

Along with the expanding popularity of multiple intelligences, there has been a growing body of writing critical of the theory. In fact, one of the criticisms lodged against MI theory is that there has not been enough acknowledgment of the critical literature on the part of MI advocates. Willingham (2004), for example, observes: "Textbooks [on MI theory] for teachers in training generally offer extensive coverage of the theory, with little or no criticism" (p. 24). Traub (1998) writes: "Few of the teachers and administrators I talked to were familiar with the critiques of multiple intelligences theory; what they knew was that the theory worked for them. They talked about it almost euphorically" (p. 22). In this chapter, I'd like to review some of the major criticisms of MI and attempt to clear up what I believe are some key misconceptions about the theory.

Criticism #1: MI Theory Lacks Empirical Support

Most of those making this complaint about MI theory come from the field of cognitive psychology (Waterhouse, 2006) or from the psychometric, or testing, community (Gottfredson, 2004). Waterhouse writes, "To date there have been no published studies that offer evidence of the validity of the MI." Similarly, Gottfredson argues that the literature on intelligence testing offers virtually no support for the idea of eight autonomous intelligences but over-whelming support for the concept of an overarching single intelligence, frequently attributed to Spearman (1927) and often referred to as "Spearman's g" or simply "the g factor" (see also Brody, 2006). Gottfredson (2004) writes:

> The g factor was discovered by the first mental testers, who found that people who scored well on one type of mental test tended to score well on all of them. Regardless of their contents (words, numbers, pictures, shapes), how they are administered (individually or in groups; orally, in writing, or pantomimed), or what they're intended to measure (vocabulary, mathematical rea-soning, spatial ability), all mental tests measure mostly the same thing. This common factor, g, can be distilled from scores on any broad set of cognitive tests, and it takes the same form among individuals of every age, race, sex, and nation yet studied. In other words, the g factor exists independently of schooling, paper-and-pencil tests, and culture. (p. 35)

Visser, Ashton, and Vernon (2006) put together a battery of 16 tests ostensibly covering the eight intelligences (two tests for each intelligence) and reported the presence of g running through most of the tests. These researchers argued that what Gardner calls intelligences are actually capacities that are secondary or even tertiary to the g factor. In other words, they exist but are subservient to g. J.B. Carroll (1993), who created his own hier-archy of human cognitive abilities with g at the top, compares Word Smart to "fluid intelligence" and Music Smart to "auditory perception" (a mistake on his part, because the multiple intelligences are not dependent upon the senses), while finding no place at all for Body Smart.

Response to Criticism #1

MI theory agrees that the g factor exists. What it disputes is that g is superior to other forms of human cognition. In MI theory, g has its place (primarily in Number/Logic Smart) as an equal alongside the other seven intelligences. It appears that the confusion is a matter of semantics. Most critics in the psychometric community agree that the intelligences in Gardner's model exist and are supported by testing. What they disagree about is whether or not they should be called "intelligences." They want to reserve the word *intelligence* for the g factor, while regarding the other seven intelligences as talents, abilities, capacities, or faculties. Gardner (2003) has written that he intended to be provocative in referring to multiple "intelligences" rather than multiple "talents." He wanted to challenge the sacrosanct nature of intelligence as a singular phenomenon and get people to think more deeply about what it means to be intelligent. The fact that he has stirred up so much controversy from the psychometric community suggests that he has at least partially accomplished his goal, even if he has not fully persuaded them to accept his theory.

The reality is that MI theory is supported empirically by a number of sources. In *Frames of Mind* (1993a), Gardner established eight criteria that needed to be met in order for an intelligence to appear in his theory (see Chapter 1 for a discussion of these). Each of the eight criteria provides a range of empirical data, from studies of brain-damaged individuals and "savant" populations, to evidence from prehistoric humanity and other species, to biographical studies of human development and research on human cultures. Davis, Christodoulou, Seider, and Gardner (2011) point out that many criticisms of MI theory pay scant attention to the criteria, which are supported by hundreds of empirical studies in several fields, including psychology, sociology, neurology, biology, anthropology, and the arts and humanities. Ironically, the fact that the psychometric community has stayed within the narrow confines of numbers and standardized testing actually limits its ability to give broad empirical support to the notion of a pure g-factor intelligence (Gottfredson's argument notwithstanding, g appears to measure "school-like" thinking; see Gardner, 2006b). On the other hand, MI's multiple sources of empirical data considerably expand its validity as a theoretical construct.

Criticism #2: No Solid Research Supports the Effectiveness of Using MI in the Classroom

This criticism parallels the first one in suggesting that MI has no empirical support (or, to put it in a more contemporary context, is not research- or evidence-based). Here we are concerned, however, not with pure theory but, rather, with its practical applications in schools. For example, Collins (1998) writes that "evidence for the specifics of Gardner's theory is weak, and there is no firm research showing that its practical applications have been effective" (p. 95). Willingham (2004) writes:

> [H]ard data are scarce. The most comprehensive study was a three-year examination of 41 schools that claim to use multiple intelligences. It was conducted by Mindy Kornhaber, a longtime Gardner collaborator. The results, unfortunately, are difficult to interpret. They reported that standardized test scores increased in 78 percent of the schools, but they failed to indicate whether the increase in each school was statistically significant. If not, then we would expect scores to increase in half the schools by chance. Moreover, there was no control group, and thus no basis for comparison with other schools in their districts. Furthermore, there is no way of knowing to what extent changes in the school are due to the implementation of ideas of multiple intelligences rather than, for example, the energizing thrill of adopting a new schoolwide program, new statewide standards, or some other unknown factor. (p. 24)

Response to Criticism #2

Perhaps the greatest problem with the argument that MI is not research- or evidence-based is that it is founded upon a very narrow conception of what constitutes authentic research. In the wake of the 2001 No Child Left Behind law, the idea of what constituted valid research began to be limited to highly controlled studies comparing experimental classrooms (implementing a specific educational intervention) to control classrooms, using standardized tests and quantitative tools based on correlation coefficients and levels of statistical significance. More recently, there's been an increased focus on *effect size* (a measure of the magnitude of the difference between an intervention group and a control group expressed in standard deviations) (Slavin, 2013). This has given rise to a list of specific classroom strategies or "influences" that result in positive educational outcomes (see, e.g., Hattie, 2008 for one guide).

There are many problems with using these ostensibly "rigorous" methodologies to validate the success of multiple intelligences in the classroom. First, multiple intelligences do not represent a specific educational intervention such as, for example, Direct Instruction (Marchand-Martella, Slocum, & Martella, 2003), which is implemented uniformly by all trained teachers and frequently receives high marks in rankings of evidence-based teaching methods (see, e.g., Education Consumers Foundation, 2011). MI theory represents a wide range of techniques, attitudes, tools, strategies, and methods, and each teacher is encouraged to develop his own unique approach to implementing them. It is impossible to conduct controlled studies of the kind Willingham demands because multiple intelligences in one classroom could be very different from multiple intelligences in another classroom and because even the control classroom would probably also be using multiple intelligences strategies to some extent. (In other words, how do you find a "pure" MI classroom and a control group that uses absolutely no MI to compare it with?)

Second, to demand a certain level of statistical significance or effect size from a study is to risk rejecting an educational intervention simply for "missing the cut" (e.g., does an effect size of .45 mean an intervention is not as effective as one with an effect size of .52?). While looking very objective, these figures often devolve into subjective impressions after all. Sullivan and Feinn (2012), for example, write: "Cohen classified effect sizes as small ($d = 0.2$), medium ($d = 0.5$), and large ($d \geq 0.8$). According to Cohen, 'a medium effect of .5 is visible to the naked eye of a careful observer. A small effect of .2 is noticeably smaller than medium but not so small as to be trivial.'" We might then dispense with the effect size and simply trust the effectiveness of a study to the "naked eye of a careful observer."

Third, to reduce the success or failure of a study to mere numbers is to reject other valid sources of a program's effectiveness, including individual case studies of children's learning improvement, parent reports of improved attitudes toward school, and documentation of learning progress through projects, problem solving, and portfolios (see Chapter 10 for a discussion of multiple intelligences and assessment methods).

The demand for quantitative precision in education is an unfortunate nod toward positivism—the idea that ultimate truth can be expressed only through numbers or similarly precise scientific formulations (see Comte, 1988). There are many other strands of thought in the Western intellectual tradition that argue for the validity of qualitative forms of research (see, e.g., Dilthey, 1989; Gadamer, 2005; and Polyani, 1974), and methodologies derived from these intellectual movements are especially appropriate to use in guiding educational research (see, e.g., Denzin & Lincoln, 2005).

The fact is that there are many examples of successful implementation of MI theory in educational programs around the world (see Chapter 16). In addition to the study mentioned by Willingham (Kornhaber, Fierros, & Veenema, 2003), which also noted increased levels of parent participation, decreased levels of discipline problems, and increased academic performance for students with learning difficulties, a number of research projects initiated by Harvard Project Zero have won accolades over the years, including Project Spectrum (Gardner, Feldman, & Krechevsky, 1998a, 1998b, 1998c), Practical Intelligences for School (Williams et al., 1996), and Arts Propel (Zessoules & Gardner, 1991), which was called by *Newsweek* magazine one of the two best educational programs in the United States (the other was the graduate school of the California Institute of Technology; Chideya, 1991). To celebrate the 20th anniversary of multiple intelligences theory in 2004, an entire issue of the prestigious *Teachers College Record* at Columbia University was dedicated to the work of multiple intelligences researchers and theoreticians (Shearer, 2004).

Shearer (2009) interviewed key education figures for the 25th anniversary of MI theory, including Noam Chomsky, Linda Darling-Hammond, and Deborah Meier, who viewed the theory of multiple intelligences as an important contribution to American education. In addition, the educational literature is replete with examples of individual schools and teachers who have shared their successes with implementing MI theory (see, e.g., Campbell & Campbell, 2000; Greenhawk, 1997; Hoerr, 2000; and Kunkel, 2007). Finally, many of the specific strategies that are used as part of the implementation of the theory of multiple intelligences are, in fact, evidence-based. Marzano's

(2004) six steps to vocabulary development model, for example, which is viewed as being evidence-based, uses several multiple intelligences strategies. Step 3, for instance—"ask students to construct a picture, pictograph, or symbolic representation of the term"—is a Picture Smart strategy in MI theory. Many of the other strategies covered in this book have been similarly validated by quantitative research. But to expect to quantitatively validate an entire theory of learning consisting of thousands of potential instructional strategies would be a foolish notion, and yet educational researchers who should know better persist in their claim that "MI is not evidence-based."

Criticism #3: MI Theory Dumbs Down the Curriculum to Make All Students Mistakenly Believe They Are Smart

Some critics have accused MI practitioners of using superficial applications of MI theory—strategies of which even Gardner himself would not approve. Willingham (2004), for example, has criticized previous editions of this very book for its "trivial ideas." He cites two spelling strategies—singing spelling words and spelling with leaves and twigs—as examples of trivial applications (note: spelling strategies have been omitted from this revised edition). Collins (1998) criticizes strategies from another multiple intelligences curriculum guide (not by this author) referring to a unit about the oceans in which students build boats and role-play at being sea creatures. He writes of a child using Body Smart to learn U.S. history: "How deeply can a student comprehend a given topic by relying on his strongest intelligence? Using his hands, Dave may be able to learn about the boats of the settlers, but can a kinesthetic approach help him understand central historical issues, like the reasons the Europeans came to America in the first place?" (p. 96). Similarly, critics have suggested that MI theory promulgates an artificial "feel good" attitude where every child is told that he is smart. Barnett, Ceci, and Williams (2006) write: "[M]ere relabeling may not have a permanent curative effect. . . . Focusing on the label rather than on meaningful performances that demonstrate skill may lead children to become further disillusioned once the first blush passes." They indicate that "the focus must be on displaying meaningful skills and competencies, not simply on feeling that one is smart" (p. 101).

Response to Criticism #3

During my 30 years of training teachers in MI, I have all too often seen teachers take the easy way out—believing, for instance, that "rapping math facts" meant they were "doing" multiple intelligences. But I have also seen many wonderfully original ideas related to MI theory created by experienced teachers over the years. Collins (1998) doubts that it is possible to use Body Smart to teach the historical factors that led Europeans to come to America. However, a well-designed role-play that imaginatively puts students at Plymouth Rock on November 11, 1620, and has them improvise reasons why they decided to leave England, gives the highly dramatic Body Smart learner an opportunity to think through the exercise in a more visceral way than can be accomplished by paper-and-pencil activities.

It is also true that it is not enough merely to tell students that they are smart in eight different ways and expect them to blossom. As noted earlier in this book in a discussion of Dweck's (2007) growth mindset, such assurances need to be followed up with solid academic effort leading to tangible improvements in knowledge of history, math, science, reading, and other basic subjects. The argument of MI theory is that textbooks, lectures, and standardized tests are not sufficient to produce this type of understanding, but that something more is required. Students need to investigate ideas in world history, chemistry, ecology, literature, economics, algebra, and other domains by involving their total selves (and whole brains), and this includes using their bodies, imagination, social sensibilities, emotions, and naturalistic inclinations, as well as their verbal and reasoning skills to master new material.

It is interesting to note that most of the criticisms of MI theory have come from academics and journalists—people who are usually far removed from the classroom. Few criticisms actually come from those who have applied the theory in their classrooms and seen the difference it makes in students' lives. This suggests a profound split between those academicians who build their reputations on finding logical holes in accepted ideas (or journalists who can build their journals' circulation) and practitioners who are too busy looking for ways to motivate children and methods to turn their lives around to worry about abstract logical inconsistencies or insufficiencies.

It also bears noting that MI theory was not originally designed by Howard Gardner as an educational model to be applied in the classroom. He initially wanted to convince academic psychologists that there was another, broader way of conceiving of intelligence. Despite arousing controversy, he seems to have failed in this effort among psychometricians. And yet, unexpectedly, he found teachers responding enthusiastically to his model because it filled a need that had not been previously met by educational approaches concerned with standardized testing and lockstep textbook approaches to learning. MI theory succeeded by revealing the positive qualities of all children and providing practical ways for them to experience success in the classroom rather than treating them as colorless denizens of a statistical bell curve. Thus, the most authentic refutation of the critics of MI can be found in the children themselves. Whenever a light goes on in a child's mind in a well-designed MI classroom, the argument supporting MI theory becomes that much stronger and clearer.

For Further Study

1. Read some of the articles critical of multiple intelligences cited in this chapter (e.g., Barnett et al., 2006; Brody, 2006; Collins, 1998; Gottfredson, 2004; Traub, 1998; Visser et al., 2006; Waterhouse, 2006; Willingham, 2004). Which aspects of their criticism do you agree with? Which ideas do you disagree with? Does your attitude toward MI theory change as a result of reading this critical literature? If so, how?

2. Howard Gardner has provided a number of responses to criticisms of MI theory, including to some of the above-mentioned authors (see, e.g., Davis, Christodoulou, Seider, & Gardner, 2011; Gardner, 2006a, 2006b, 2006c; Gardner & Moran, 2006). Read the original critics and then some of his responses, and evaluate the success or failure of his defense of MI theory.

3. In other writing (Armstrong, 2006), I have suggested that today's educational climate is characterized by an overemphasis on academic performance as measured by standardized testing and an underemphasis on the education of the whole child. To what extent has this restrictive educational climate given rise to the criticisms noted in this chapter?

4. Using some of the materials discussed above, organize a debate on MI theory, with one individual or team taking a pro-MI stance and the other individual or team taking an anti-MI stance. Afterward, discuss who did the most effective job of defending their position.

5. Interview veteran colleagues and other school personnel about their attitudes toward MI theory and whether they have changed their opinion about it over the past 10–15 years. If they have a different attitude about it now than previously, ask them to share the reasons for their change in opinion.

16

MI Theory Around the Globe

I have had the opportunity . . . to travel to many other nations. It has been fascinating to discover the ways in which [MI] theory has been interpreted and the activities that it has catalyzed.

—*Howard Gardner*

One of the most exciting developments of the theory of multiple intelligences has been its international influence. MI theory is now a part of the educational scene to one degree or another in most of the nations of the world. In some cases, its effects have been at the governmental level, with MI incorporated into the national education initiatives of some countries. In other cases, effects have been more local, with individual schools and teachers taking the theory and applying it to the unique requirements of their own culture. In this chapter, we'll look at several ways in which MI theory has been applied in cultures around the world.

MI Theory at the Policymaking Level

MI theory has been incorporated at the highest levels of many international policymaking institutions. Gardner (2006a) writes, "I have been amazed to learn of jurisdictions in which the terminology of MI has been incorporated into white papers, recommendations by ministries, and even legislation. . . . I have heard from reliable sources that MI approaches are part of the policy landscape in such diverse lands as Australia, Bangladesh, Canada, China, Denmark, Ireland and the Netherlands" (p. 248). In Bangladesh, for example, with support from UNICEF, the government initiated its Intensive District Approach for All Learners project in the 1990s (Chanda, 2001). As part of this effort, tens of thousands of teachers were trained in MI theory through the initiative Multiple Ways of Teaching and Learning (Ellison & Rothenberger, 1999). India's National Curriculum Framework for School Education required teachers to be familiar with the concepts of multiple intelligences (Sarangapani, 2000). In Geneva, Switzerland, the prestigious International Baccalaureate (IB) Organization, which offers programs to more than 600,000 students in 128 countries, has acknowledged Gardner's role in influencing its own approach to learning: "Howard Gardner has been influential in changing views about learning and the ways we learn. Access and equity within the IB today is much wider than it was previously. It is acknowledged that all students have strengths and weaknesses which must be supported in a strategic way for them to meet their potential" (Reed, 2007).

MI Theory at the Academic Level

Multiple intelligences theory has been the subject of increasing academic research in universities around the world. I have heard personally by e-mail from hundreds of individuals who are pursuing their master's theses and doctoral dissertations on MI theory at institutions such as Middle East Technical University in Ankara, Turkey; the University of Jordan in Amman, Jordan; Mulawaram University in Samarinda, Indonesia; and Ferhat Abbes University in Setif, Algeria. A growing number of internationally oriented academic studies on MI theory have been published in peer-reviewed journals. One topic that has been given much attention is the comparison of people's multiple intelligences profiles compared to estimations of MI profiles of their parents, children, or partners. Journal articles dedicated to this subject have covered populations from Namibia, Zimbabwe, Zambia, and South Africa (Furnham & Akanda, 2004); Malaysia (Swami, Furnham, & Kannan, 2006); China (Furnham & Wu, 2008); and Japan (Furnham & Fukumoto, 2008). Other international studies have looked at MI and information literacy education in Singapore (Mohktar, Majid, & Fu, 2007), Music

Smart aptitude and multiple intelligences among Chinese gifted students in Hong Kong (Chan, 2007), improved academic performance in Kuwaiti middle school reading programs using multiple intelligences (Al-Bahan, 2006), and how children in poor areas of Dar es Salaam, Tanzania, perceive their own multiple intelligences (Dixon, Humble, & Chan, 2016).

MI Theory at the Individual School Level

Thousands of schools around the world have applied MI theory to their curricula. A teacher in Argentina, for example, wrote me about how she taught English as a second language to a group of 1st grade students. Developing a unit on "helpers" (postman, firefighter, doctor, nurse), students visited service-oriented people around town, kept journals, wrote letters, built a model of the community, created a mural, made musical instruments, and reflected orally on their learning while talking into a mirror (Ribot, 2004). In Chile, the Amancay Elementary School of La Florida in Santiago put on MI theme weeks. During the "Week of the Arts," they had a day when children talked with real writers and a day when children painted with painters. They also had a "Scientific Week" that included students' sharing their own inventions and a "Sea Month" focused on Nature Smart (Gundian & Anriquez, 1999). In the Philippines, the MI International High School in Quezon City put MI theory to work in the cause of promoting entrepreneurship among its students, challenging them to develop real-world business plans based on ideas that emerge from MI lessons. For example, a Word Smart group developed Flash Range, a media center that creates books for teens that deal with environmental and personal and emotional growth issues. A Music Smart group created a business called Boom Box Music, which offers musical composition and record production services. A group of People Smart students conceptualized their own family restaurant, Pastuchi, featuring a fusion of Italian and Japanese cuisines. The school has an annual bazaar that sells products made by the various businesses and then donates the profits to a charity that helps the poor (*Manila Times*, 2008).

MI Theory at the Community Level

Beyond formal schooling applications, multiple intelligences theory has also influenced the popular culture in many countries around the world. In China, for example, the Multiple Intelligences Education Society promoted

MI theory through seminars, magazine articles, radio programs, and TV interviews, all coordinated as part of an effort to reform parent education, vocational education, and the formal examination process (Cheung, 2009). In Denmark, the industrial manufacturer Danfoss has created a theme park, Danfoss Universe, that incorporates many strategies and ideas from multiple intelligences. They have essentially created an interactive MI museum, where children and adults participate in more than 50 activities designed to both test their multiple intelligences and to raise awareness about the many different ways of being smart. Activities include turning physical movements into electronic art, negotiating an obstacle course, cooperating with others to move a robot, playing a *theremin* (an electronic musical instrument played without physical contact), unscrambling melodies, being a music producer, putting together tangrams, solving word and visual puzzles, building structures, making predictions about natural phenomena, speaking a foreign language, transmitting images just by thinking, and building a bridge across a lake to an island. Danfoss Universe also contains exhibits for experiencing the primal force of a volcano, a geyser, strong hot winds, and other natural phenomena (Sahl-Madsen & Kyed, 2009)

In the Chinese Special Administrative Region of Macau, multiple intelligences theory appeared in a very unlikely place: the grocery store. Gardner (2006a) writes: "In Macau I received a tour of the island from Mr. U. The next morning he picked me up for my presentation at the Education Ministry. 'Look what my wife picked up at the grocery store,' he said. He showed me a multicolored flyer that depicted each of the intelligences on a separate leaf. The flyer, replete with illustrations, charts, and figures, was an advertisement for Frisogrow processed milk. . . . The consumer was informed, 'If you drink our milk, you will develop each of the different intelligences.' Never before had it occurred to me that the MI in the theory might stand for MIlk!" (p. 245).

What Happens When MI Theory Connects with Another Culture

It's fascinating to study the interaction of MI theory with different cultures around the world. Keep in mind that MI theory itself is a cultural product emanating from contemporary U.S. culture. As such, it embodies many values and ideals that are considered important in the United States, including pluralism, pragmatism, and egalitarianism. What happens when these U.S. values contact the values of another culture is quite instructive. Often it appears that MI theory gains significantly from its contact with another culture.

Here's an example. In Norway, Nature Smart as experienced through outdoor education is given much greater emphasis than it is in the United States. Norwegian education incorporates into its curriculum an important institution called an *utskole*, or outdoor school. It is part of a larger framework in Norwegian culture referred to as *friluftsliv*, which can be roughly translated as outdoor nature life and which encompasses a wide range of physical activities and attitudes regarding nature such as hiking, skiing, ecological awareness, and maritime activities. As part of the utskole, most elementary schools in Norway have a structure called a *gapahuk*, which is often just a hut or lean-to structure set apart from the regular school building and situated in a natural setting. Students engage in a variety of curriculum-related activities in the gapahuk.

In 2005, I had the opportunity to visit a gapahuk while speaking in Norway and saw students learning about Norwegian history by making ancient cooking implements from natural sources such as branches and twigs. Every student in elementary school in Norway has the opportunity to spend one day a week outdoors in the gapahuk. There are also kindergartens in Norway where children spend all day, every day, engaged in an outdoor setting. This contrasts radically with the United States, where outdoor activities, if they occur at all, are usually short and infrequent. The Norwegian experience brings to MI theory a whole new attitude toward Nature Smart (and Body Smart as well), suggesting that these neglected intelligences be honored in a serious way by dedicating a good part of the school week to their robust development in an outdoor setting.

At other times, the theory of multiple intelligences represents a challenge to certain long-established values of a culture. In South Korea, for example, traditional Word Smart and Number/Logic Smart learning is valued so highly that it is often difficult to change parent attitudes to embrace a multiplicity of intelligences. Two South Korean university professors who sought to replicate Harvard Project Zero's Project Spectrum for young children there noted: "In Korea, parents believe that high academic achievement means excellent achievement in linguistic and mathematics. Children who have a weakness in linguistic and mathematics consider themselves as helpless at school" (Jung & Kim, 2005, p. 585). These beliefs have deep cultural origins, according to Jung and Kim: "South Korea is a competitive-oriented society with an examination-oriented culture that continues to influence education today. The state examination is considered to be most difficult; one should prepare for it from birth. By tradition, pencils and cotton threads are displayed at a baby's first birthday, which is the grandest celebration. Family members encourage the baby to grab a pencil, which means the baby will study hard and pass the state examination" (pp. 591–592).

The Project Spectrum assessment tools (described in Chapter 10) were implemented successfully in this South Korean setting and were viewed as a way to help undo some of these deeply entrenched ideas about learning and human development. As Jung and Kim wrote, "The Project Spectrum approach based on MI theory facilitates a child-oriented education by assuming equality and independence among multiple intelligences. . . . Under such an assessment system, children/students will be able to avoid the 'negative self image' too often experienced in the Korean education system and develop into successful and active learners" (p. 591).

Even cultures that have long histories of formal examinations have embraced select aspects of MI theory. In Japan, for example, where students attend "cram schools" before taking university entrance examinations, a range of traditions exist that are harmonious with MI theory. The ancient temple school of Japan, referred to as *terakoya*, taught traditional literacy and numeracy skills to Japanese citizens from all walks of life (Howland, Fujimoto, Ishiwata, & Kamijo, 2009). But Japanese culture also provided many other entry points into the multiple intelligences through calligraphy, haiku, the Kabuki and Noh styles of theater, the traditional tea ceremony, and a wide range of martial arts traditions including sumo wrestling, judo, and jujutsu.

The remarkable thing about multiple intelligences internationally is that it seems to be finding a place for itself in widely diverse cultural contexts, even in cultures that have values that seem to conflict radically with the pluralistic and egalitarian underpinnings of MI theory. The theory of multiple intelligences has found its way into the schools and university systems of Iran and Saudi Arabia; *Multiple Intelligences in the Classroom* has been translated into Farsi, Arabic, and 17 other languages. MI has been taught in the *madrassas* (or holy Islamic schools) of Pakistan (Schmidle, 2007), and according to Gardner, his book *Frames of Mind* was one of only two books in English found in a library in North Korea (the other book was Michael Moore's *Stupid White Men*; Gardner, 2006a).

I think a big reason for the widespread success of MI theory internationally has been its friendliness to cultural diversity. At the core of the model there is the requirement that each intelligence must be culturally valued. Implicit in this requirement is the observation that each of the elements of the multiple intelligences—music, words, logic, pictures, social interaction, physical expression, inner reflection, and nature appreciation—can be found in all cultures. Thus, each country around the world has the opportunity to see its own indigenous traditions honored and celebrated through MI theory.

For Further Study

1. Choose an indigenous culture from any country in the world (including the United States) and describe in detail how the culture celebrates and honors each of the eight intelligences.
2. Make contact with a school using MI theory in another country. Initiate a cultural exchange of ideas regarding specific applications of multiple intelligences.
3. Integrate an MI-oriented practice used in another culture into your own school or classroom (e.g., the utskole, or outdoor school, from Norway for Nature Smart, judo from Japan for Body Smart, or the gamelan musical tradition of Indonesia for Music Smart). Evaluate its effectiveness.
4. To what extent does MI theory reflect the values of 21st century U.S. culture? Examine the ways in which those values either connect or collide with the values of another culture.

Appendix A: Standards-Based MI Lesson Ideas

Level: Grade 1

Subject: Reading: Literature

Standards Platform: Common Core State Standards

Standard: RL.1.2: Retell stories, including key details, and demonstrate understanding of their central message or lesson.

Intelligence	Activity
Word Smart	Read students a story, then ask them to share ideas of what they think the central message or lesson is.
Number/ Logic Smart	Read students a math word problem, ask them to determine the solution, and then discuss whether the answer is the central message or lesson of the "story."
Picture Smart	Have student tell a story by drawing pictures on a storyboard. Then ask them to draw a picture of the central message or lesson on a separate sheet and explain it to the class.
Body Smart	Put on a play based on a story. Then, after the play, ask individual students to act out the central message or lesson.

Intelligence	Activity
Music Smart	Sing a song that tells a story. Then, together as a class, and using the music from the song, add lyrics that tell the central message or lesson.
People Smart	Ask the class to form a circle and then read them a story. Then, select students one at a time to go into the center of the circle and tell what they think is the central message or lesson.
Self Smart	Ask students to make up their own stories based on personal experiences, then have them share the central message or lesson.
Nature Smart	Read an animal fable, then ask students to share the moral (e.g., the central message or lesson).

Level: Grade 3

Subject: Writing

Standards Platform: Common Core State Standards

Standard: W.3.1A–D. Write opinion pieces on topics or texts, supporting a point of view with reasons. (a) Introduce the topic or text they are writing about, state an opinion, and create an organizational structure that lists reasons. (b) Provide reasons that support the opinion. (c) Use linking words and phrases (e.g., *because, therefore, since, for example*) to connect opinion and reasons. (d) Provide a concluding statement or section.

Intelligence	Activity
Word Smart	Read opinion pieces written by published authors, underlining the reasons they give for their opinions, circling any linking words or phrases, and highlight the conclusion.
Number/ Logic Smart	Give students a cognitive organizer that asks them to state their opinion (in a box at the top), give reasons (separate boxes for each reason), and provide linking words and phrases (tiny boxes that separate the "reason" boxes), with a box for a conclusion at the bottom.
Picture Smart	Ask students to write an opinion piece and then color-code it with the opinion in red, the reasons in blue, the linking words and phrases in yellow, and the conclusion in green.
Body Smart	Ask students to write an opinion on a 4 x 6 index card, write supporting reasons on 3 x 5 index cards, write linking words or phrases on 1 x 3 strips of tag board and write a conclusion on a 2 x 6 piece of tag board. Then, ask them to arrange the different components on the floor and have students read the entire composition by walking on, or next to, first the opinion, then the first linking word, then the first supporting reason, then the next linking word or phrase, then the next supporting reason, and so on until they've read and walked on (or next to) the entire piece, including the conclusion.

Continued

Intelligence	Activity
Music Smart	Play a piece of music that shares a strong opinion (e.g., Bob Dylan's "The Times They Are a-Changin'"). Discuss Dylan's primary opinion as expressed in the lyrics while providing supporting reasons for his opinions. (Optional: Reasons can be sung rather than spoken. Also optional: Linking words or phrases may be whispered.) The conclusion should be sung the loudest.
People Smart	Form a group panel discussion or game show called "What's Your Opinion?" where students give their opinion about something and then support it with reasons, linking words or phrases, and a conclusion. The audience can vote on the best reasons and provide others not mentioned while using their own linking words or phrases and conclusions.
Self Smart	Ask students to think of a topic that they have strong feelings about. Ask them to explain the supporting reasons for their strong feelings, including linking words or phrases, and a conclusion.
Nature Smart	Ask students specifically about opinions related to ecological issues such as the disappearance of rain forests, the disintegration of coral reefs, or the growing threats for endangered animals. Then, have them provide supporting reasons for their opinions by writing them down using linking words or phrases and a conclusion.

Level: Grade 5

Subject: Mathematics

Standards Platform: Common Core State Standards

Standard: Geometry: 5MD.4: Measure volumes by counting unit cubes, using cubic cm, cubic in, cubic ft, and improvised units.

Intelligence	Activity
Word Smart	Ask students to write an imaginative story about a man and woman who are building a structure and can't make up their minds about which cubic unit system they'd like to use. Include a narrative about how they resolve the dilemma.
Number/ Logic Smart	Teach students math formulas for converting cubic units into lower and higher measurements (imperial and metric). Ask students to create their own conversion formulas for improvised cubic units.
Picture Smart	Using wire or wood and string, ask students to create visual representations of a cubic unit, cubic inch, cubic foot, and an improvised unit.

Intelligence	Activity
Body Smart	Ask students to work with unit cubes (purchased from a math manipulative supply outlet, or created by the students with carpentry tools or clay) and build cubic meters from cubic centimeters, cubic feet from cubic inches, and cubic volumes from improvised cubic units.
Music Smart	Teach students the musical mnemonic for measuring volume as sung in the video recording "Volume Song For Kids" by Numberrock (available on YouTube at www.youtube.com/watch?v—LZxXUb9iAZc). Then, let them sing the song as they measure and convert volumes on paper.
People Smart	Collaborate as a class to build the largest cubic structure they can out of sugar cubes (or another cheaply available cube source).
Self Smart	Create virtual cities and towns using virtual cubes of different values (cm, in, ft, and units of their own improvisation) via Minecraft.
Nature Smart	Compare the number of cubic inches/feet/cm/m of air breathed on average by human beings per day compared with measurements for other animals with respiratory systems.

Level: Middle School

Subject: Science

Standards Platform: Next Generation Science Standards

Core Idea: ESS3.D: Human activities, such as the release of greenhouse gases from burning fossil fuels, are major factors in the current rise in the earth's mean surface temperature (global warming). Reducing the level of climate change and reducing human vulnerability to whatever climate changes do occur depend on the understanding of climate science, engineering capabilities, and other kinds of knowledge, such as understanding of human behavior and on applying that knowledge wisely in decisions and activities.

Intelligence	Activity
Word Smart	Read widely on the internet from credible sources about major factors contributing to global warming and compare these views with those of climate change skeptics.
Number/ Logic Smart	Study the effects of greenhouse gases on the atmosphere from burning fossil fuels, by learning about both the chemistry of combined elements or molecules and the physics of weather patterns in creating these conditions.
Picture Smart	Create a blueprint of a device or invention designed to mitigate the effects of greenhouse gases from burning fossil fuels.

Continued

Intelligence	Activity
Body Smart	Put on a play that dramatizes the way human activities lead to climate change or how humans can change their behavior to create a healthier climate.
Music Smart	Write a song to inspire people to take personal responsibility in contributing to a healthier climate worldwide.
People Smart	Study the legislative actions needed to counteract global warming and write a class letter to members of Congress, the president of the United States, or other world leaders urging them to pass such legislation and explaining the reasons why.
Self Smart	Examine the effects of climate change on your own life, researching the levels of greenhouse gases in your own community, their effect on your personal health, and the epidemiological figures for respiratory illness in your region.
Nature Smart	Study the impact of climate change on animals, plants, and aquatic life in different areas of the world.

Level: Grade 8

Subject: Mathematics

Standard Platform: Common Core State Standards

Standard: 8.SP.1: Construct and interpret scatter plots for bivariate measurement data to investigate patterns of association between two quantities. Describe patterns such as clustering, outliers, positive or negative association, linear association, and nonlinear association.

Intelligence	Activity
Word Smart	Use data for two literary variables (e.g., number of pages in a novel and readability level as measured on a site such as https://readable.io/text/), plot the data from a variety of novels on a scatter graph, and describe patterns such as clustering, outliers, positive or negative association, linear association, and nonlinear association.
Number/ Logic Smart	Take quantitative data representing two sets of related variables, plot them on a scatter graph, and determine which patterns are represented (e.g., clustering, outliers, positive or negative association, linear association, and nonlinear association).
Picture Smart	Create a work of visual art that uses one or more scatter plots as a design motif while showing patterns such as clustering, outliers, positive or negative association, linear association, and nonlinear association.

Intelligence	Activity
Body Smart	Gather statistics from a given population (e.g., members of the classroom) with regard to two variables relating to physical attributes (e.g., height and weight) or skill (e.g., distance throwing and running speed) and plot the data on a scatter graph indicating patterns such as clustering, outliers, positive or negative association, linear association, and nonlinear association.
Music Smart	Collect data from the Billboard Top 100 of the past 10 years, compare two variables (e.g., length of song and highest ranking on the charts), plot the data on a scatter graph, and look for patterns such as clustering, outliers, positive or negative association, linear association, and nonlinear association.
People Smart	Conduct an opinion poll of members of the class (or entire school) on who they supported in a recent political campaign (e.g., presidential election) and where they stand with respect to a particular social issue (e.g., abortion) and plot the two sets of data on a scatter graph, looking for the above patterns.
Self Smart	Take data from two variables that are directly related to your personal life (e.g., the time you get up in the morning and the level of tiredness during the first period of school on a scale of 1 to 10) and plot them on a scatter graph, looking for the above patterns.
Nature Smart	Collect data from a natural phenomenon (such as duration of a geyser's eruption and the intervals between its eruptions) and plot on a scatter graph, looking for above patterns.

Level: High School Accomplished

Subject: Visual Arts

Standards Platform: National Art Standards

Standard: VA: Re.7.2.IIa: Evaluate the effectiveness of an image or images to influence ideas, feelings, and behaviors of specific audiences.

Intelligence	Activity
Word Smart	Select a famous work of art (e.g., Andy Warhol's painting of Campbell Soup cans) and research what has been written about it both in nonfiction and fiction, with a view to assessing its effectiveness in influencing ideas, feelings, and behaviors of specific audiences.
Number/Logic Smart	Pick an image that has mathematical qualities (e.g., fractals, infinity sign), and examine the ways in which the image has been used, both in math and in other fields (e.g., history, science, literature).

Continued

Intelligence	Activity
Picture Smart	Choose a generic visual image (e.g., circle, triangle, cube, line, cross, swastika) and discuss the effect that the image has had throughout history on different populations.
Body Smart	Study a particular work of sculpture (e.g., Rodin's *The Thinker*) and examine the effect of this image on popular notions of what it means to "think" or be "rational."
Music Smart	Research instances where a work of visual art has influenced the creation of a musical composition (e.g., the song ''Mona Lisa'' as sung by Nat King Cole) and evaluate the effectiveness of the song in expressing qualities of that work of art.
People Smart	Study a painting with social significance such as *Guernica* by Pablo Picasso and research its effect on political, social, and artistic sensibilities in different populations.
Self Smart	Create a work of visual art and show it to your family, friends, and classmates, keeping notes on their personal reactions, thoughts, and ideas in relation to it.
Nature Smart	Study the nature art of Hudson River School painter Thomas Cole and research its effects on American attitudes toward the United States' expansive frontier and diminishing natural resources.

Appendix B:
Books About the Theory
of Multiple Intelligences and
Its Application to Education

Armstrong, T. (1999). *7 kinds of smart. Discovering and identifying your multiple intelligences—Revised and updated with information on two new kinds of smart.* New York: Plume.

Armstrong, T. (2000). *In their own way: Discovering and encouraging your child's multiple intelligences.* New York: Tarcher/Putnam.

Armstrong, T. (2003). *The multiple intelligences of reading and writing: Making the words come alive.* Alexandria, VA: ASCD.

Armstrong, T. (2014). *You're smarter than you think: A kid's guide to multiple intelligences.* Minneapolis, MN: Free Spirit Publishing.

Arnold, E. (2007). *The MI strategy bank: 800+ multiple intelligence ideas for the elementary classroom.* Chicago: Chicago Review Press.

Barkman, R. (1999). *Science through multiple intelligences: Patterns that inspire inquiry.* Chicago: Chicago Review Press.

Baum, S., Viens, J., & Slatin, B. (2005). *Multiple intelligences in the elementary classroom: A teacher's toolkit.* New York: Teachers College Press.

Bellanca, J. (2008). *200+ active learning strategies and projects for engaging students' multiple intelligences* (2nd ed.). Thousand Oaks, CA: Corwin.

Berman, M. (2001). *A multiple intelligences road to an ELT classroom.* Carmarthen, UK: Crown House Publishing.

Campbell, B. (2007). *Handbook of differentiated instruction using the multiple intelligences: Lesson plans and more.* New York: Pearson.

Campbell, B., & Campbell, L. (1999). *Multiple intelligences and student achievement: Success stories from six schools.* Alexandria, VA: ASCD.

Campbell, L., Campbell, B., & Dickinson, D. (2003). *Teaching and learning through multiple intelligences* (3rd ed.). Upper Saddle River, NJ: Allyn & Bacon.

Chen, J. Q., Moran, S., & Gardner, H. (Eds.). (2009). *Multiple intelligences around the world.* San Francisco: Jossey-Bass.

Christison, M. A. (2005). *Multiple intelligences and language learning: A guidebook of theory, activities, inventories, and resources.* Palm Springs, CA: Alta Book Center Publishers.

DeAmicis, B. (2003). *Multiple intelligences made easy: Strategies for your curriculum.* Chicago: Chicago Review Press.

Faculty of New City School. (1994). *Celebrating multiple intelligences.* St. Louis, MO: Author.

Faculty of New City School. (1996). *Succeeding with multiple intelligences: Teaching through the personal intelligences.* St. Louis, MO: Author.

Gardner, H. (2000). *Intelligence reframed: Multiple intelligences for the 21st century.* New York: Basic Books.

Gardner, H. (2006). *Multiple intelligences: New horizons in theory and practice.* New York: Basic Books.

Gardner, H. (2011). *Creating minds: An anatomy of creativity seen through the lives of Freud, Einstein, Picasso, Stravinsky, Eliot, Graham, and Gandhi.* New York: Basic Books.

Gardner, H. (2011). *Frames of mind: The theory of multiple intelligences.* New York: Basic Books.

Gardner, H., Feldman, D. H., & Krechevsky, M. (Eds.). (1998). *Project Zero frameworks for early childhood education, Vol. 1: Building on children's strengths: The experience of Project Spectrum.* New York: Teachers College Press.

Gardner, H., Feldman, D. H., & Krechevsky, M. (Eds.). (1998). *Project Zero frameworks for early childhood education, Vol. 2: Project Spectrum: Early learning activities.* New York: Teachers College Press.

Gardner, H., Feldman, D. H., & Krechevsky, M. (Eds.). (1998). *Project Zero frameworks for early childhood education, Vol. 3: Project Spectrum: Preschool assessment handbook.* New York: Teachers College Press.

Hirsh, R. A. (2004). *Early childhood curriculum: Incorporating multiple intelligences, developmentally appropriate practices, and play.* New York: Pearson.

Hoerr, T. R. (2000). *Becoming a multiple intelligences school.* Alexandria, VA: ASCD.

Hoerr, T. R., Boggeman, S., & Wallach, C. (2010). *Celebrating every learner: Activities and strategies for creating a multiple intelligences classroom* (2nd ed). San Francisco: Jossey-Bass.

Kagan, S. (1998). *Multiple intelligences: The complete MI book.* San Clemente, CA: Kagan Cooperative Learning.

Koch, K. (2016). *8 great smarts: Discover and nurture your child's intelligences.* Chicago: Moody Publishers.

Kornhaber, M., Fierros, E., & Veenema, S. (2003). *Multiple intelligences: Best ideas from research and practice.* Upper Saddle River, NJ: Pearson/Allyn & Bacon.

Lazear, D. (1998). *The rubrics way: Using multiple intelligences to assess understanding.* Chicago: Chicago Review Press.

Lazear, D. (1999). *Eight ways of knowing: Teaching for multiple intelligences* (3rd ed.). Thousand Oaks, CA: Corwin.

Lazear, D. (1999). *Multiple intelligence approaches to assessment: Solving the assessment conundrum* (Rev. ed.). Chicago: Chicago Review Press.

Lazear, D. (2003). *Eight ways of teaching: The artistry of teaching with multiple intelligences.* Thousand Oaks, CA: Corwin.

Lilienstein, J. (2012). *101 learning activities to stretch & strengthen your child's multiple intelligences.* Summerland, CA: Frontsiders.

Massie, M. R. (2016). *Ellie Rae discovers eight ways to be SMART: A book about Howard Gardner's theory of multiple intelligences.* CreateSpace Independent Publishing Platform.

McKenzie, W. (2005). *Multiple intelligences and instructional technology* (2nd ed.). Washington, DC: International Society for Technology in Education.

Nicholson-Nelson, K. (1999). *Developing students' multiple intelligences (Grades K–8).* New York: Scholastic.

Puchta, H., & Rinvolocri, M. (2007). *Multiple intelligences in EFL: Exercises for secondary and adult students.* Cambridge, UK: Cambridge University Press.

Schaler, J.A. (2006). *Howard Gardner under fire: The rebel psychologist faces his critics.* Chicago: Open Court.

Schiller, P., & Phipps, P. (2006). *Starting with stories: Engaging multiple intelligences through children's books.* Lewisville, NC: Gryphon House.

Schiller, P., & Phipps, P. (2011). *The complete daily curriculum for early childhood: Over 1200 easy activities to support multiple intelligences and learning styles.* Silver Spring, MD: Gryphon House.

Shearer, B. (1996). *The MIDAS: A professional manual.* Kent, OH: MI Research and Consulting.

Shearer, B. (2009). (Ed.). *MI at 25: Assessing the impact and future of multiple intelligences for teaching and learning.* New York: Teachers College Press.

Shearer, B. (2013). *Multiple intelligences inspired! A Common Core toolkit* (2nd ed.). Kent, OH: MI Research and Consulting.

Shearer, B., & Fleetham, M. (2008). *Creating extra-ordinary teachers: Multiple intelligences in the classroom and beyond.* New York: Network Continuum.

Silver, H. F., Strong, R. W., & Perini, M. J. (2000). *So each may learn: Integrating learning styles and multiple intelligences.* Alexandria, VA: ASCD.

Stefanakis, E. H. (2002). *Multiple intelligences and portfolios: A window into the learner's mind.* Portsmouth, NH: Heinemann.

Sudarsana, M. (2013). *Multiple intelligences for designing environments: Designing preschool environments.* Amazon Digital Services.

Teele, S. (2004). *Overcoming barricades to reading: A multiple intelligences approach.* Thousand Oaks, CA: Corwin.

Teele, S. (2015). *Rainbows of intelligence: Exploring how students learn.* New York: Skyhorse Publishing.

Viens, J., & Kallenbach, S. (2004). *Multiple intelligences and adult literacy: A sourcebook for practitioners.* New York: Teachers College Press.

Zwiers, J. (2004). *Developing academic thinking skills in grades 6–12: A handbook of multiple intelligences activities.* Newark, DE: International Reading Association.

References

Adria, M., & Mao, Y. (2017). *Handbook of research on citizen engagement and public partici-pation in the era of new media*. Hershey, PA: IGI Global.

Al-Bahan, E. M. (2006, Spring). Multiple intelligences styles in relation to improved aca-demic performance in Kuwaiti middle school reading. *Digest of Middle East Studies, 18–34.*

Archer, D. (2015). *The ADHD advantage: What you thought was a diagnosis may be your greatest strength*. New York: Avery.

Armstrong, T. (1987a). Describing strengths in children identified as "learning disabled" using Howard Gardner's theory of multiple intelligences as an organizing frame-work. *Dissertation Abstracts International, 48*, 8A. (University Microfilms No. 8725-844)

Armstrong, T. (1987b). *In their own way: Discovering and encouraging your child's personal learning style*. New York: Tarcher/Putnam.

Armstrong, T. (1999). *7 kinds of smart: Discovering and identifying your multiple intelli-gences—Revised and updated with information on two new kinds of smart*. New York: Plume.

Armstrong, T. (2000). *In their own way: Discovering and encouraging your child's multiple intelligences* (Revised and updated). New York: Tarcher/Putnam.

Armstrong, T. (2006). *The best schools: How human development research should inform educational practice*. Alexandria, VA: ASCD.

Armstrong, T. (2012). *Neurodiversity in the classroom: Strength-based strategies to help stu-dents with special needs succeed in school and life*. Alexandria VA: ASCD.

Armstrong, T. (2014). *You're smarter than you think: A kid's guide to multiple intelligences.* Minneapolis, MN: Free Spirit Publishing.

Armstrong, T. (2016). *The power of the adolescent brain: Strategies for teaching middle and high school students.* Alexandria, VA: ASCD.

Barnett, S. M., Ceci, S. J., & Williams, W. M. (2006). Is the ability to make a bacon sandwich a mark of intelligence? and other issues: Some reflections on Gardner's theory of multiple intelligences. In J. A. Schaler (Ed.), *Howard Gardner Under Fire: The Rebel Psychologist Faces His Critics* (pp. 95–114). Chicago: Open Court.

Baron-Cohen, S. (1998). Superiority on the embedded figures task in autism and in normal males: Evidence of an "innate talent"? *Behavioral and Brain Sciences, 21*(1), 408–409.

Baron-Cohen, S. (2003). *The essential difference: The truth about the male and female brain.* New York: Basic Books.

Berger, R. (2013). Deeper learning: Highlighting student work. *Edutopia.* Retrieved from https://www.edutopia.org/blog/deeper-learning-student-work-ron-berger

Blume, H. (1998, September 30). Neurodiversity. *Atlantic.* Retrieved from http://www.theatlantic.c./doc/199809u/Neurodiversity

Bonny, H., & Savary, L. (1990). *Music and your mind.* Barrytown, NY: Station Hill Press.

Brody, N. (2006). Geocentric theory: A valid alternative to Gardner's theory of intelligence. In J. A. Schaler (Ed.), *Howard Gardner Under Fire: The Rebel Psychologist Faces His Critics* (pp. 73–94). Chicago: Open Court.

Campbell, L., & Campbell, B. (2000). *Multiple intelligences and student achievement: Success stories from six schools.* Alexandria, VA: ASCD.

Carini, P. (1977). *The art of seeing and the visibility of the person.* Grand Forks, ND: Center for Teaching and Learning, University of North Dakota.

Carroll, J. B. (1993). *Human cognitive abilities: A survey of factor-analytic studies.* Cambridge, UK: Cambridge University Press.

Chan, D. (2007). Music Smart aptitude and multiple intelligences among Chinese gifted students in Hong Kong: Do self-perceptions predict abilities? *Personality and Individual Differences, 43*(6), 1604–1615.

Chanda, S. (2001, March). Multiple ways of teaching and learning in Bangladesh. *Teachers Forum.* Available: http://www.unicef.org/teachers/forum/0301.htm

Chen, J. Q., Moran, S., & Gardner, H. (Eds.) (2009). *Multiple intelligences theory around the world.* San Francisco: Jossey-Bass.

Cheung, H. H. P. (2009). Multiple intelligences in China. In J. Q. Chen, S. Moran, & H. Gardner, (Eds.), *Multiple intelligences theory around the world* (pp. 43–54). San Francisco: Jossey-Bass.

Chideya, A. (1991, December 2). Surely for the spirit, but also for the mind. *Newsweek,* 61.

Collins, J. (1998, October 19). Seven kinds of smart. *Time,* 94–96.

Comte, A. (1988). *Introduction to positive philosophy.* Indianapolis, IN: Hackett.

Connor, J. O., & Pope, D. C. (2013, September). Not just robo-students: Why full engagement matters and how schools can promote it. *Journal of Youth and Adolescence, 42*(9), 1426–1442.

Cooperrider, D. L. (2001) Why appreciative inquiry? In C. Royal & S. A. Hammond (Eds.), *Lessons from the field: Applying appreciative inquiry*, p. 12. Bend, OR: Thin Book Publishing.

Davis, K., Christodoulou, J., Seider, S., & Gardner, H. (2011). The theory of multiple intelligences. In R. J. Sternberg & S. B. Kaufman, (Eds.), *The Cambridge handbook of intelligence* (pp. 485–503). Cambridge, UK; New York: Cambridge University Press.

Denzin, N., & Lincoln, Y. (Eds.). (2005). *The Sage book of qualitative research* (3rd ed.). Thousand Oaks, CA: Sage.

Dewey, J. (1997). *Experience and education.* New York: Free Press.

Diehl, J. J. et al. (2014, November 1). Neural correlates of language and non-language visuospatial processing in adolescents with reading disability. *Neuroimage, 101*, 653–666.

Dilthey, W. (1989). *Introduction to the human sciences: An attempt to lay a foundation for the study of society and history.* Detroit, MI: Wayne State University Press.

Dixon, P., Humble, S., & Chan, D. W. (2016). How children living in poor areas of Dar Es Salaam, Tanzania perceive their own multiple intelligences. *Oxford Review of Education, 42*(2), 230–248.

Donkin, W. (2001). *The wayfarers: Meher Baba with the God-intoxicated.* Myrtle Beach, SC: The Sheriar Foundation.

Dreikurs, R. (1993). *Logical consequences: The new approach to discipline.* New York: Plume.

Dweck, C. (2007). *Mindset: The new psychology of success.* New York: Ballantine.

Dykens, E. M. (2006). Toward a positive psychology of mental retardation. *American Journal of Orthopsychiatry, 76*(2), 185–193.

Education Consumers Foundation (2011, November 28). *Direct instruction: What the research says.* Arlington, VA. Retrieved from http://education-consumers.org/pdf/DI_Research.pdf

Edwards, B. (2012). *Drawing on the right side of the brain* (4th ed). Los Angeles: Tarcher/Perigee.

Edwards, C., Gandini, L., & Foreman, G. (2011). *The hundred languages of children: The Reggio Emilia experience in transformation* (3rd ed.). Santa Barbara, CA: Praeger.

Ellison, L., & Rothenberger, B. (1999). In Bangladesh: The multiple ways of teaching and learning. *Educational Leadership, 57*(1), 54–57.

Faculty of New City School. (1994). *Celebrating multiple intelligences: Teaching for success.* St. Louis, MO: New City School.

Faculty of New City School. (1996). *Succeeding with multiple intelligences: Teaching through the personal intelligences.* St. Louis, MO: New City School.

Feldman, D. H. (1980). *Beyond universals in cognitive development.* Norwood, NJ: Ablex.

Feynman, R. (2005). *The pleasure of finding things out: The best short works of Richard P. Feynman.* New York: Basic Books.

Fisher, D., & Frey, N. (2014). *Checking for understanding: Formative assessment techniques for your classroom* (2nd ed.). Alexandria, VA: ASCD.

Foote, A. (1991). *Arts PROPEL: A handbook for visual arts.* Cambridge, MA: Harvard Project Zero.

Froebel, F. (2005). *The education of man.* Mineola, NY: Dover Publications.

Furnham, A., & Akanda, A. (2004). African parents' estimation of their own and their children's multiple intelligences. *Current Psychology, 22*(4), 281–294.

Furnham, A., & Fukumoto, S. (2008). Japanese parents' estimates of their own and their children's multiple intelligences: Cultural modesty and moderate differentiation. *Japanese Psychological Research, 50*(2), 63–76.

Furnham, A., & Wu, J. (2008). Gender differences in estimates of one's own and parental intelligence in China. *Individual Differences Research, 6*(1), 1–12.

Gadamer, H. G. (2005). *Truth and method.* New York: Continuum.

Gallup Youth Development Specialists. (2007). *Strengths Explorer for ages 10 to 14.* Washington, DC: Gallup Press.

Gardner, H. (1979). The child is father to the metaphor. *Psychology Today, 12*(10), 81–91.

Gardner, H. (1983). *Frames of mind: The theory of multiple intelligences.* New York: Basic Books.

Gardner, H. (1993a). *Frames of mind: The theory of multiple intelligences* (10th anniversary ed.). New York: Basic Books.

Gardner, H. (1993b). *Multiple intelligences: The theory in practice.* New York: Basic Books.

Gardner, H. (1995). Reflections on multiple intelligences: Myths and messages. *Phi Delta Kappan, 77*(3), 200–208.

Gardner, H. (1999). *Intelligence reframed: Multiple intelligences for the 21st century.* New York: Basic Books.

Gardner H. (2003, April 21). Multiple intelligences after twenty years. Paper presented at the annual meeting of the American Educational Research Association, Chicago.

Gardner, H. (2004). Audiences for the theory of multiple intelligences. *Teachers College Record, 106*(1), 212.

Gardner, H. (2006a). *Multiple intelligences: New horizons in theory and practice.* New York: Basic Books.

Gardner, H. (2006b). On failing to grasp the core of MI theory: A response to Visser et al. *Intelligence, 34*(5), 503–505.

Gardner, H. (2006c). Replies to my critics. In J. A. Schaler (Ed.), *Howard Gardner under fire: The rebel psychologist faces his critics* (pp. 277–307). Chicago: Open Court.

Gardner, H. (2011). *Frames of mind: The theory of multiple intelligences.* New York: Basics Books.

Gardner, H., Feldman, D. H., & Krechevsky, M. (Eds.). (1998a). *Project Zero frameworks for early childhood education, Vol. 1: Building on children's strengths: The experience of Project Spectrum.* New York: Teachers College Press.

Gardner, H., Feldman, D. H., & Krechevsky, M. (Eds.). (1998b). *Project Zero frameworks for early childhood education, Vol. 2: Project Spectrum: Early learning activities.* New York: Teachers College Press.

Gardner, H., Feldman, D. H., & Krechevsky, M. (Eds.). (1998c). *Project Zero frameworks for early childhood education, Vol. 3: Project Spectrum: Preschool assessment handbook.* New York: Teachers College Press.

Gardner, H., & Moran, S. (2006). The science of multiple intelligences theory: A response to Lynn Waterhouse. *Educational Psychologist, 4*(4), 227–232.

Gentile, J. R. (1988). *Instructional improvement: Summary and analysis of Madeline Hunter's essential elements of instruction and supervision.* Oxford, OH: National Staff Development Council.

Goleman, D. (2006). *Emotional intelligence: Why it can matter more than IQ.* New York: Bantam.

Goodlad, J. I. (2004). *A place called school* (20th anniversary edition). New York: McGraw-Hill.

Goodman, J., & Weinstein, M. (1980). *Playfair: Everybody's guide to noncompetitive play.* San Luis Obispo, CA: Impact.

Gottfredson, L. S. (2004). Schools and the "g" factor. *Wilson Quarterly, 28*(3), 35–45.

Grandin, T., & Johnson, C. (2006). *Animals in translation: Using the mysteries of autism to decode animal behavior.* New York: Simon & Schuster.

Greenhawk, J. (1997). Multiple intelligences meet standards. *Educational Leadership, 5*(1), 62–64.

Gundian, X., & Anríquez, C. (1999, September). An innovative project for Chilean education: Colegio Amancay de La Florida. *New Horizons for Learning.* Available: http://www.newhorizon.org/trans/international/gundian.htm

Haft, S., Witt, P. J., Thomas, T. (Producers), & Weir, P. (Director). (1989). *Dead Poets Society.* Burbank, CA: Touchstone Pictures.

Hart, L. (1981). Don't teach them; help them learn. *Learning, 9*(8), 39–40.

Hartmann, T. (1997). *ADD: A different perception.* Nevada City, CA: Underwood Books.

Hattie, J. (2008). *Visible learning: A synthesis of over 800 meta-analyses related to achievement.* New York: Routledge.

Hawkins, T. (2012, December 28). Will less art and music in the classroom really help students soar academically? *The Washington Post.* Retrieved from: http://wapo.st/2rt3AV6

Hess, K. K. (2013). *A guide for using Webb's depth of knowledge with Common Core State Standards.* Common Core Institute.

Hoerr, T. R. (2000). *Becoming a multiple intelligences school.* Alexandria, VA: ASCD.

Howland, D., Fujimoto, T., Ishiwata, K., & Kamijo, M. (2009). Multiple intelligences perspectives from Japan. In J. Q. Chen, S. Moran, & H. Gardner, (Eds), *Multiple intelligences theory around the world* (pp. 76–94). San Francisco: Jossey-Bass.

Johnson, R. S., Mims-Cox, S., & Doyle-Nichols, A. R. (2006). *Developing portfolios in education: A guide to reflection, inquiry, and assessment.* Thousand Oaks, CA: Sage.

Jung, T., & Kim, M-H. (2005). The application of multiple intelligences theory in South Korea: The Project Spectrum approach for young children. *School Psychology International, 26*(5), 581–594.

Kallick, B. & Zmuda, A. (2017, March). Orchestrating the move to student-driven learning. *Educational Leadership, 74*(6), 53–57.

Karolyi, C. von, Winner, E., Gray, W., & Sherman, G. F. (2003, June). Dyslexia linked to talent: Global visual-spatial ability. *Brain and Language, 85*(3), 427–31.

Kluth, P. (2008). *Just give him the whale! 20 ways to use fascinations, areas of expertise, and strengths to support students with autism.* Baltimore: Brookes Publishing Co.

Kornhaber, M., Fierros, E., & Veenema, S. (2003). *Multiple intelligences: Best ideas from research and practice.* Upper Saddle River, NJ: Allyn & Bacon.

Kovalik, S. (1993). *ITI: The model—Integrated Thematic Instruction* (2nd ed.). Black Diamond, WA: Books for Educators.

Kovalik, S. (2001). *Exceeding expectations: A user's guide to implementing brain research in the classroom.* Black Diamond, WA: Books for Educators.

Kozik, P. L. (2008, June). Examining the effects of appreciative inquiry on IEP meetings and transition planning. Doctoral dissertation, Syracuse University. Retrieved from http://appreciativeinquiry.case.edu/uploads/PL%20Kozik%20Dissertation%208-08.pdf

Kunkel, C. (2007). The power of Key: Celebrating 20 years of innovation at the Key Learning Community. *Phi Delta Kappan, 89*(3), 204–209.

Kuo, F. E., & Taylor, A. F. (2004, September). A potential natural treatment for attention deficit/hyperactivity disorder. *American Journal of Public Health, 94*(9), 1580–1586.

Lenhoff, H. M., Wang, P. P., Greenberg, F., & Bellugi, U. (1997, December). Williams syndrome and the brain. *Scientific American, 277*(6), 68–73.

Louv, R. (2008). *Last child in the woods: Saving our children from nature-deficit disorder.* Chapel Hill, NC: Algonquin Books.

Manila Times. (2008, June 15). *Multiple Intelligence High School: A school for future responsible entrepreneurs.* Available: http://www.manilatimes.net/national/2008/june/15/yehey/weekend/20080615week3.html

Marchand-Martella, N. E., Slocum, T. A., & Martella, R. E. (2003). *An introduction to direct instruction.* Upper Saddle River, NJ: Allyn & Bacon.

Marzano, R. (2004). *Building background knowledge for academic achievement: Research on what works in schools.* Alexandria, VA: ASCD.

Marzano, R. (2017). *The new art and science of teaching.* Bloomington, IN: Solution Tree; and Alexandria, VA: ASCD.

Marzano, R. J., Brandt, R. S., Hughes, C. S., Jones, B. F., Presseisen, B. Z., & Rankin, S. C. (1988). *Dimensions of thinking: A framework for curriculum and instruction.* Alexandria, VA: ASCD.

Matthews, G. B. (1996). *The philosophy of childhood.* Cambridge, MA: Harvard University Press.

McCloskey, D. N., & Ziliak, S. (2008). *The cult of statistical significance: How standard error costs us jobs, justice, and lives.* Ann Arbor, MI: University of Michigan Press.

MI in the Classrooms, St. Louis, MO: New City School, [website] 2013–2017. Retrieved from: http://www.newcityschool.org/academics/multiple-intelligences/mi-in-the-classrooms.

Miller, A. (1996). *The drama of the gifted child* (Rev. ed.). New York: Basic Books.

Mohktar, I. A., Majid, S., & Fu, S. (2007). Information literacy education through mediated learning and multiple intelligences. *Reference Services Review, 35*(3), 463–486.

Montagu, A. (1988). *Growing young* (2nd ed.). Westport, CT: Bergin and Garvey.

Montessori, M. (1972). *The secret of childhood.* New York: Ballantine.

Morehead, J. (2012, June 19). Stanford University's Carol Dweck on the growth mindset and education. *OneDublin.org.* Available: https://onedublin.org/2012/06/19/stanford-universitys-carol-dweck-on-the-growth-mindset-and-education/

Morrison, P., & Morrison, P. (1994). *Powers of ten.* New York: W. H. Freeman.

Moss, C. M., & Brookhart, S. M. (2009). *Advancing formative assessment in every classroom: A guide for instructional leaders.* Alexandria, VA: ASCD.

Mottron, L. (2011). Changing perceptions: The power of autism. *Nature, 479*(7371), 33–35.

Musca, T. (Producer), & Menéndez, R. (Director). (1987). *Stand and deliver.* Burbank, CA: Warner Bros.

Nelsen, J. (1999). *Positive time-out and over 50 ways to avoid power struggles in the home and the classroom.* New York: Prima.

Nord, W. A., & Haynes, C. C. (1998). *Taking religion seriously across the curriculum.* Alexandria, VA: ASCD.

Paugh, P., & Dudley-Marling, C. (2011, September). Speaking deficit into (or out of) existence: How language constrains classroom teachers' knowledge about instructing diverse learners. *International Journal of Inclusive Education, 15*(8), 819–833.

Paul, R. (1992). *Critical thinking: What every person needs to survive in a rapidly changing world.* Santa Rosa, CA: Foundation for Critical Thinking.

Pestalozzi, J. H. (2013). *How Gertrude teaches her own children: An attempt to help mothers teach their own children.* Amazon Digital Services.

Plato. (1952). *The dialogues of Plato* (B. Jowett, Trans.). In R. M. Hutchins (Ed.), *Great Books of the Western World* (Vol. 7). Chicago: Encyclopedia Britannica.

Polya, G. (2014). *How to solve it: A new aspect of mathematical method.* Princeton, NJ: Princeton University Press.

Polyani, K. (1974). *Personal knowledge: Toward a post-critical philosophy.* Chicago: University of Chicago Press.

Popham, J. (2008). *Transformative assessment.* Alexandria, VA: ASCD.

Postman, N., & Weingartner, C. (1971). *Teaching as a subversive activity.* New York: Delta.

Price-Mitchell, M. (2015, April 7). Metacognition: Nurturing self-awareness in the classroom. *Edutopia.* Retrieved from https://www.edutopia.org/blog/8-pathways-metacognition-in-classroom-marilyn-price-mitchell

Ravitch, D. (2016). *The death and life of the great American school system: How testing and choice are undermining education* (3rd ed.). New York: Basic Books.

Recer, P. (2002, April 30). Study: Science literacy poor in U.S. Associated Press.

Reed, J. (2007, September). Learning with IB. *IB World.* Available: http://www.ibo.org/ibworld/sept07/

Ribot, N. (2004, March). My experience using the multiple intelligences. *New Horizons of Learning.* Available: http://www.newhorizons.org/trans/international/ribot.htm

Rose, C. (1987). *Accelerated learning.* New York: Dell.

Rosenthal, R., & Jacobson, L. (2004). *Pygmalion in the classroom: Teacher expectation and pupils' intellectual development.* New York: Crown House Publishing.

Rousseau, J. J. (1979). *Emile: Or on education* (A. Bloom, Trans.). New York: Basic Books.

Rundle, L.B. (2016, May 1). Jane Goodall in conversation. *Reader's Digest Asia/Pacific.* Retrieved from https://www.pressreader.com/australia/readers-digest-asia-pacific/20160501/282600262033981

Sacks, O. (1985). *The man who mistook his wife for a hat.* New York: HarperCollins.

Sacks, O. (1995). *An anthropologist on Mars.* New York: Vintage.

Sacks, O. (2007). *Musicophilia: Tales of music and the brain* (Rev. and expanded ed.). New York: Vintage.

Sahl-Madsen, C., & Kyed, P. (2009). The explorama: Multiple intelligences in the science park, Danfoss Universe. In J. Q. Chen, S. Moran, & H. Gardner, (Eds.), *Multiple intelligences theory around the world* (pp. 169–183). San Francisco: Jossey-Bass.

Sarangapani, P. M. (2000). The great Indian tradition. Available: http://www.india-seminar.com/2000/493/493%20padma%20m%20sarangapani.htm

Schmidle, N. (2007, January 22). Reforming Pakistan's "dens of terror." *TruthDig.* Available: http://www.truthdig.com/report/item/20070122_nicholas_schmidle_reforming_pakistans_dens_of_terror/

Schneps M. H., Brockmole, J. R., Sonnert, G., & Pomplun, M. (2012, April 27). History of reading struggles linked to enhanced learning in low spatial frequency scenes. *PLOS.* Available: http://journals.plos.org/plosone/article?id=10.1371/journal.pone.0035724

Scripp, L. (1990). *Transforming teaching through Arts PROPEL portfolios: A case study of assessing individual student work in the high school ensemble.* Cambridge, MA: Harvard Graduate School of Education.

Shaw, P., et al. (2007, December 4). Attention deficit/hyperactivity disorder is characterized by a delay in cortical maturation. *Proceedings of the National Academy of Sciences, 104*(49), 19649–19654.

Shearer, B. (1994). *Multiple Intelligence Developmental Assessment Scales (MIDAS).* Kent, OH: Multiple Intelligences Research and Consulting.

Shearer, B. (2004). Multiple intelligences after 20 years. *Teachers College Record, 106*(1), 2–16.

Shearer, B. (2009). *MI at 25: Assessing the impact and future of multiple intelligences for teaching and learning.* New York: Teachers College Press.

Shearer, B. (2013). *The MIDAS Handbook: Common miracles in your school.* Kent, OH: Multiple Intelligences Research and Consulting.

Silver, H., Strong, R., & Perini, M. (1997). Integrating learning styles and multiple intelligences. *Educational Leadership, 55*(1), 22–29.

Singer, J. (1999). Why can't you be normal for once in your life? In M. Corker & S. French (Eds.), *Disability discourse* (pp. 59–67). Buckingham, UK: Open University Press.

Slavin, R. (2013, January 9). Effect size matters in educational research. *Education Week,* Retrieved from http://blogs.edweek.org/edweek/sputnik/2013/01/effect_size_matters_in_educational_research.html

Spearman, C. (1927). *The abilities of man: Their nature and measurement.* London: Macmillan.

Spencer, J. (2017, March). The genius of design. *Educational Leadership, 74*(6), 16–21.

Spolin, V. (1986). *Theater games for the classroom.* Evanston, IL: Northwestern University Press.

Strauss, V. (2014, January 18). Everything you need to know about the Common Core: Ravitch. *The Washington Post.* Retrieved from https://www.washingtonpost.com/news/answer-sheet/wp/2014/01/18/everything-you-need-to-know-about-common-core-ravitch/?utm_term=.7502bd0b147a

Sullivan, G. M., & Feinn, R. (2012, September). Using effect size—or why the P value is not enough. *Journal of Graduate Medical Education, 4*(3): 279–282. Retrieved from https://www.ncbi.nlm.nih.gov/pmc/articles/PMC3444174/

Swami, V., Furnham, A., & Kannan, K. (2006). Estimating self, parental, and partner intelligences: A replication in Malaysia. *Journal of Social Psychology, 146*(6), 645–655.

Tammet, D. (2007). *Born on a blue day: Inside the extraordinary mind of an autistic savant.* New York: Free Press.

Tomlinson, C. A. (2014). *The differentiated classroom: Responding to the needs of all learners* (2nd ed.). Alexandria, VA: ASCD.

Traphagen, K., & Zorich, T. (2013, Spring). *Time for deeper learning: Lessons from five high schools.* Boston: National Center on Time & Learning.

Traub, J. (1998, October 26). Multiple intelligence disorder. *The New Republic, 219*(17), 20–23.

Visser, B., Ashton, M., & Vernon, P. (2006). Beyond G: Putting multiple intelligences to the test. *Intelligence, 34*(5), 487–502.

Wallis, C. (2008, June 8). No Child Left Behind: Doomed to fail? *Time.* Available: http://www.time.com/time/nation/article/0,8599,1812758,00.html

Walters, J., & Gardner, H. (1986, March 30). The crystallizing experience: Discovery of an intellectual gift. (ERIC Document Reproduction Service No. ED 254 544)

Wang, S. S. (2014, March 27). How autism can help you land a job. *Wall Street Journal.* Available: https://www.wsj.com/articles/SB10001424052702304418404579465561364868556

Warren, C. (2008, July 1). Coudl this be teh sercet to sussecc? *American Way.* Available: http://dyslexia.yale.edu/DYS_secretsuccess.html

Waterhouse, L. (2006). Multiple intelligences, the Mozart effect, and emotional intelligence: A critical review. *Educational Psychologist, 4*(4), 207–225. Retrieved from http://ocw.metu.edu.tr/pluginfile.php/9276/mod_resource/content/1/s15326985ep4104_1.pdf

Webb, N. (1997). *Criteria for alignment of expectations and assessments on mathematics and science education.* Washington, DC: CCSSO.

Weinreich-Haste, H. (1985). The varieties of intelligence: An interview with Howard Gardner. *New Ideas in Psychology, 3*(4), 47–65.

White, H. A., & Shaw, P. (2011, April). Creative style and achievement in adults with attention deficit/hyperactivity disorder. *Journal of Personality and Individual Differences, 5*(5), 673–677.

Wiggins, G., & McTighe, J. (2005). *Understanding by design.* Alexandria, VA: ASCD.

Williams, W., Blythe, T., White, N., Li, J., Sternberg, R., & Gardner, H. (1996). *Practical intelligence for school.* New York: HarperCollins College Publishers.

Willingham, D. (2004). Reframing the mind. *Education Next, 4*(3), 19–24.

Yeager, D. S., & Dweck, C. S. (2012). Mindsets that promote resilience: When students believe that personal characteristics can be developed. *Educational Psychologist, 47*(4), 302–314.

Zessoules, R., & Gardner, H. (1991). Authentic assessment: Beyond the buzzword and into the classroom. In V. Perrone (Ed.), *Assessment in Schools* (pp. 47–71). Washington, DC: ASCD.

Index

The letter *f* following a page number denotes a figure.

About the Author

Thomas Armstrong is the executive director of the American Institute for Learning and Human Development and the author of six other books published by ASCD, including *The Power of the Adolescent Brain: Strategies for Teaching Middle and High School Students* (2016), *Neurodiversity in the Classroom: Strength-Based Strategies to Help Students with Special Needs Succeed in School and Life* (2014), *The Best Schools: How Human Development Research Should Inform Educational Practice* (2006), *The Multiple Intelligences of Reading and Writing* (2003), *Awakening Genius in the Classroom* (1998), and *ADD/ADHD Alternatives in the Classroom* (1999). He has also written several trade books, including *The Myth of the ADHD Child: 101 Ways to Improve Your Child's Behavior and Attention Span Without Drugs, Labels, or Coercion* (Tarcher/Perigee, 2017), *The Power of Neurodiversity: Unleashing the Advantages of Your Differently Wired Brain* (DaCapo, 2011), *The Human Odyssey: Navigating the Twelve Stages of Life* (Sterling, 2007), *In Their Own Way: Discovering and Encouraging Your Child's Multiple Intelligences* (Tarcher, 2000), and *7 Kinds of Smart: Identifying and*

Developing Your Multiple Intelligences (Plume, 1999). His books have been translated into 27 languages.

Armstrong has given more than 1000 presentations in 44 states and 29 countries over the past 30 years. For further information about his work, or to schedule a keynote or workshop, e-mail thomas@institute4learning. com; visit his website and blog at www.institute4learning.com; connect with him on Twitter @Dr_Armstrong; write: P.O. Box 548, Cloverdale, CA 95425; phone: 707-894-4646; or fax: 707-894-4474.

Acknowledgments

I have many people to thank for helping me write the four editions of *Multiple Intelligences in the Classroom*. First, I must thank the founder of MI theory, Howard Gardner, for his support of my own fledgling efforts to apply his model to the classroom. If he had been Maria Montessori, I would have had to study at his feet for years before being able to go out and teach his theory. But his philosophy of "letting a hundred MI applications bloom" and his generosity toward me—he provided feedback on the initial manuscript of this book as well as a preface for the first edition—was optimal for my independent Self Smart inclinations. I owe a huge debt of gratitude to him for all he has done to support me in my career.

I also want to thank Ron Brandt for seeing the possibilities of MI theory back in 1993. Many thanks also to Genny Ostertag, the director of content acquisitions at ASCD, for the many wonderful suggestions she made for expanding the material in this 4th edition. I also want to thank several others at ASCD who have supported me in the writing of the four editions of this book: Nancy Modrak, Marge Scherer, Scott Willis, Carolyn Pool, Julie Houtz, Liz Wegner, and the publisher at ASCD, Stefani Roth.

I want to acknowledge my debt to Mert Hanley, the one-time director of the Teacher's Center at West Irondequoit School District in upstate New

York, who made it possible for me to conduct MI workshops in several Rochester-area school districts—work that helped build the foundation for what eventually became *Multiple Intelligences in the Classroom*. Others who have supported my work with multiple intelligences over the years include DeLee Lanz, Sue Teele, David Thornburg, Branton Shearer, Tom Hoerr, Dee Dickinson, and my ex-wife, Barbara Turner. I also want to thank my literary agent, Joëlle Delbourgo, who has championed my literary efforts now for over 10 years, and I hope for many more years to come. Finally, I want to thank the thousands of teachers I've worked with over the years who've taken the ideas in this book and translated them into learning activities that have put a sparkle in countless students' eyes.

Related ASCD Resources

At the time of publication, the following resources were available (ASCD stock numbers in parentheses).

Print Products

The Differentiated Classroom: Responding to the Needs of All Learners, 2nd Edition by Carol Ann Tomlinson (#108029)

The Formative Five: Fostering Grit, Empathy, and Other Success Skills Every Student Needs by Thomas R. Hoerr (#116043)

Neurodiversity in the Classroom: Strength-Based Strategies to Help Students with Special Needs Succeed in School and Life by Thomas Armstrong (#113017)

The Power of the Adolescent Brain: Strategies for Teaching Middle and High School Students by Thomas Armstrong (#116017)

Understanding How Young Children Learn: Bringing the Science of Child Development to the Classroom by Wendy L. Ostroff (#112003)

For up-to-date information about ASCD resources, go to www.ascd.org. You can search the complete archives of *Educational Leadership* at www.ascd.org/el.

ASCD EDge® Group

Exchange ideas and connect with other educators interested in multiple intelligences on the social networking site ASCD EDge at http://ascdedge.ascd.org/

ASCD myTeachSource®

Download resources from a professional learning platform with hundreds of research-based best practices and tools for your classroom at http://myteachsource.ascd.org/

For more information, send an e-mail to member@ascd.org; call 1-800-933-2723 or 703-578-9600; send a fax to 703-575-5400; or write to Information Services, ASCD, 1703 N. Beauregard St., Alexandria, VA 22311-1714 USA.